PELHAM GRENVILLE WODEHOUSE (his brothers were Ernest Armine, Philip Peverel and Richard Lancelot, so he got off fairly lightly) was born in England in 1881 while his mother was on a visit from Hong Kong, to which she shortly returned with the infant Plum. Like many youths of the time, quite a number of whom became writers, he was sent back to England for schooling and raised by aunts, shadows of whom haunt much of his later work.

At his public school, Dulwich, he developed a lifelong passion for cricket and discovered that he could get paid for writing. Two years of working for a London bank persuaded him and the world of finance that they were irreconcilably incompatible, and he never worked again, except to write 130 books and hundreds of short stories, articles and song lyrics, and to people the literary universe with such immortals as Jeeves, Bertie Wooster, the Hon. Galahad Threepwood, Lord Emsworth, Mr. Mulliner, Aunt Agatha and Roberta (Bobbie) Wickham.

Because British copyright law protects work for a period of 50 years after the author's death, Wodehouse's first book, *The Pothunters*, published in 1902, will be in copyright for a total 123 years, which must be a record or close to it.

A resident of the United States since 1947, Wodehouse became a citizen in 1955, but all the same was knighted by the Queen a few weeks before his death in 1975. As on most days, Wodehouse's last day began with work on his next book.

—D. R. Bensen

P.G. WODEHOUSE
available in IPL editions:

IF I WERE YOU
FULL MOON
PLUM'S PEACHES
SERVICE WITH A SMILE
TALES FROM THE DRONES CLUB
THE UNCOLLECTED WODEHOUSE
WODEHOUSE ON CRIME

and
WHO'S WHO IN WODEHOUSE
edited by Daniel Garrison

THE UNCOLLECTED
WODEHOUSE

EDITED AND INTRODUCED BY DAVID A. JASEN
FOREWORD BY MALCOLM MUGGERIDGE

INTERNATIONAL POLYGONICS, LTD.
New York City

Library of Congress Card Catalog # 92-70285
ISBN 1-55882-119-8

Printed and manufactured in the United States of America.
First IPL printing April 1992.
10 9 8 7 6 5 4 3 2 1

To my brother PETER O. JASEN

Dear Peter,

It is customary, and indeed, clichéd to say things like "... without whose invaluable help, this book would not have been possible." So, I will not say it, but we know that it's true.

CONTENTS

FOREWORD

A substantial cache of uncollected Wodehouse such as David Jasen has got together might seem surprising in view of Wodehouse's long and famous career as a writer and the many published volumes of his stories and occasional pieces. Yet here it is—juvenilia, early contributions to *Punch*, school stories, lyrics, romances in his inimitable vein—all the familiar Wodehousean offerings. And what is more, all up to scratch. An astonishing thing about Wodehouse is the very high professional standard he maintained up to the very end, covering a span of some seven decades during which he kept going a steady flow of wordage irrespective of his circumstances; as steadily in a prison camp, or in the maternity home in which he was briefly incarcerated by the French, or in a hotel room, as in his own workroom and in front of his own typewriter.

This professionalism was not unconnected with one of Wodehouse's most estimable qualities—his humility, which made him just no trouble whatever as a contributor. The copy would always arrive on time, exactly the right length, on exactly the right theme and treated in exactly the right way. I recall his telling me once, when he was among the best known and highest paid writers in the world, how helpful he had found the suggestions of an American magazine editor for improving a short story Wodehouse had recently submitted to him. He was totally lacking in the sort of self-importance, not to say pomposity, which successful writers are liable to generate, and loved to recount how, when Hilaire Belloc had pronounced him the age's most accomplished writer of English prose, Hugh Walpole, a now largely forgotten but in his day bestselling novelist who took very seriously his position as a contemporary man-of-letters, asked Wodehouse in a voice of incredulity: "Now, whatever can Belloc have meant by that?"

Wodehouse was not given to generalizing about his *oeuvre*, or to drawing attention to intimations of development in his fiction or characterizations. Jeeves, Bertie Wooster, Aunt Agatha and the rest of his bright creations were as they were from the beginning, and any suggestion that they or their circumstances might change with the years—for instance, I once put it to him that Jeeves might be given a life peerage by a Labour Government—failed to register. If anything, he had a preference for his earlier over his later works, and I can readily imagine the satisfaction the present volume would have given him precisely because it consists largely of leftovers from long ago. Once I did ask him which of his books he liked best, and after some rumination he said that *Mike* had a special place in his esteem because it conveyed so well the scene and atmosphere of a cricket match. It was one of his very first novels to be published, and appeared serially in the *Captain*, a superior version of the *Boys' Own Paper*. Both magazines were going strong in my schooldays.

I confess the nomination of *Mike* as his favourite work rather surprised me, as I should have expected him to see it as a charming early effort preparing the way for his world-famous Jeeves books. Yet on consideration I realised that it fitted in with his character and romantic disposition. The world of the twentieth century as it developed in his lifetime was little to his taste, and he sought a sanctuary from it in the fantasy of a schoolboy world such as is portrayed in *Mike* and other such stories—one or two in THE UNCOLLECTED WODEHOUSE—in which games are the chief pursuit, to excel at them is the mark of a hero, and the playing-fields of Eton (in Wodehouse's case, Dulwich) are truly the dry-run for Battles of Waterloo to come. His immense popularity, especially among a readership largely drawn from a frightened bourgeoisie on the run, was partly at any rate due to the fact that there were many others likewise seeking a sanctuary. George Orwell for one. His abiding admiration for Wodehouse went strangely with his ardent left-wing views, and when I told him of Wodehouse's choice of *Mike* as his best book, rather by way of illustrating how faulty an author's judgement was liable to be of his own works, Orwell was vehemently insistent that Wodehouse was perfectly right, *Mike* was his best book. Another ardent Wodehouse fan was Evelyn Waugh, who might have had himself in mind when, in an elegant tribute to Wodehouse on the occasion of his eightieth birthday, he wrote:

> For Mr Wodehouse there has been no fall of Man; no aboriginal calamity. His characters have never tasted the forbidden fruit. They are still in Eden. The gardens of Blandings Castle are that original garden from which we are all exiled. The chef Anatole prepares the ambrosia for the im-

mortals of high Olympus. Mr Wodehouse's idyllic world can never stale.

All the same, it would be the greatest possible mistake to regard Wodehouse as merely a purveyor of escapist literature to a dying class. Beneath the cheerful comedy and the prevailing good humour there is a sharp, clear, but possibly unconscious, satirical intent. When I once put this to Wodehouse he denied the imputation as hilariously as if I had detected Freudian or Marxist intimations in his work. The fact remains, however, that Wodehouse's picture of the English upper classes in a decomposing society, despite its whimsicality, is far more convincing than, say, Galsworthy's in his *Forsyte Saga*. People tend to believe that only what is serious is true, whereas in practice almost the exact converse is the case. Shakespeare's Sir John Falstaff is, I am sure, far more like the average Elizabethan knight than anything to be found in Spenser's *Faerie Queene*, as Cervante's Don Quixote is a more authentic expression of the spirit of chivalry and knight-errantry than Tennyson's Sir Galahad.

In this connection it is interesting that in the 1939-45 war the German Intelligence—the *Abwehr*—used Wodehouse's novels as source material in equipping and briefing agents destined to be dropped by parachute in England. Their instinct here was sound enough, but as so often happened with them, the execution was faulty, and an unfortunate agent was actually launched on an under-cover mission in Cambridgeshire wearing spats, which, of course, led to his almost immediate apprehension. It was as though we had dropped in Bavaria an agent arrayed in leather shorts, decorated braces and smoking an enormous meerschaum pipe.

The fact is that clowns—and Wodehouse was a clown of the very highest quality, with the fleeting melancholy of a clown lurking in his ever cheerful countenance—are more acutely observant than sociologists, and far more given to speaking the truth. Laughter, indeed, is a great equalizer between the impulse to adulate and a propensity to scorn those, as the Book of Common Prayer has it, set in authority over us—which is why, incidentally, laughter is so abhorrent to all authoritarians whatever their ideology. So a social historian interested in our time—assuming, of course, that there are any such—will be wise to look to Wodehouse to steer him between the ravings of a Karl Marx, the moral vacuities of a Woodrow Wilson

or Franklin Roosevelt, and the empty rhetoric of a Winston Church-
ill. In a lunatic age he was a voice of sanity.

Personally speaking, the most touching item in David Jasen's collection was Wodehouse's first *Punch* contribution, "An Unfinished
Collection." It recalled to me so very vividly the moment when I
found myself, out of the blue as it were, sitting in the editorial chair
in the old *Punch* office in Bouverie Street and wondering helplessly
what the magazine was about. I confess I never really found out, but
in so far as I did begin to get a glimmering, it involved shaping up to
a certain brand of English humour, doggedly held onto by the natives, of which Wodehouse's piece was a near-perfect example. In
essence, it is a sort of mystique of failure—in "An Unfinished Collection" the narrator is a failed writer who collects rejection slips—
whereby a whole variety of misfortunes, like having manuscripts
returned, or being overdrawn at the bank, or having to help with the
washing up, are luxuriated in to the point of being funny. The
nearest American practitioner is, of course, Thurber, but not even
he reaches the heights of masochism of the English variety. The
whole edifice of Wodehouse's humour is founded on this glorifica-
tion of failure and inadequacy, though naturally, with the passing of
the years, it grew more sophisticated; Mike turns into Bertie Wooster and the precocious Psmith into Jeeves.

It is a pleasant memory to me now to think that almost the first
thing I did when I was editor of *Punch* was to get Wodehouse back as
a contributor. That was in the early fifties, and he was still under a
cloud as a result of his wartime broadcasts to America from Berlin.
In England everything is forgiven to those who live a long time; with
longevity even Queen Victoria became popular, and I feel quite sure
that if Oscar Wilde had managed to live on into his nineties he would
have been knighted, and perhaps been made an honorary Scout
Commissioner to boot. Happily, Wodehouse comfortably exceeded
his allotted three score years and ten, and duly received his honour
to the plaudits of all who only a decade or so before had so resolutely
put him in the dog-house. By that time he did not need my support,
and I rejoiced from afar. The publication of THE UNCOLLECTED
WODEHOUSE is an occasion for a different sort of celebration by all
vendors of words—to use St. Augustine's apt expression—in honour
of the greatest vendor of us all.

MALCOLM MUGGERIDGE

The Uncollected
WODEHOUSE

Introduction

It wasn't much of a Spring this year. True, there were all the signs, the papers said the swallows came back, and the green buds appeared as usual, but for the first time in thirty years, there was no new Wodehouse to read.

The great master, Pelham Grenville Wodehouse, died on February 14, 1975, at his Long Island home, at the age of 93. He was a man who loved to write. Once he got started, at the turn of this century, he kept it up every day until and including the day of his death. He wrote in virtually every literary form: articles, short stories, novels, verse, lyrics, plays and musical comedies. *The Cat Nappers*, a Bertie and Jeeves story, was his last, and 96th, book. Only six weeks before his death, the world's most popular and prodigious humorist, now an American citizen, was made a Knight Commander of the British Empire by Queen Elizabeth II.

While doing research for my biography of Wodehouse (*P. G. Wodehouse: A Portrait of a Master*, published in 1974), I came upon many early examples of his diverse writings, mostly published in England, and all too good to be forgotten. A few selections had been preserved in book form in England, but none of them had been collected in the United States.

I brought these gems to Plum and proposed to him that they should be collected and published in book form. He entered delightedly into this plan, making suggestions of pieces to be included in this volume, and promised to write a foreword for it. Unfortunately, he died before this book was put together.

I present here a few of these treasures, not only for those thousands of inconsolable Wodehouse fans, but for those new generations who continue to discover with delight Bertie Wooster and Jeeves . . . . Mr. Mulliner . . . . Lord Emsworth . . . . the Empress of Blandings . . . . the Oldest Member . . . . Psmith . . . . Ukridge . . . .

The special world of Blandings Castle and the Drones Club, that best of all possible worlds, is timeless and there it is always Spring. Enter.

D. A. J.

Part One
EARLY NEWSPAPER
AND
MAGAZINE ARTICLES

1900–1909

P. (for Pelham—his wife and good friends called him "Plum") G. (for Grenville) Wodehouse (pronounced Wood-house) was born on October 15, 1881, the third of four boys, in Guildford, a hamlet just outside London. Shortly thereafter, his mother returned to Hong Kong where his father, Henry Ernest, was a magistrate. Plum Wodehouse spent his childhood in England, being looked after by a governess and relatives. He attended Dulwich College, a private school for boys of upper-middle-class families where he soon established himself athletically and intellectually, receiving his colors for his play on the first-string rugby, football, and cricket teams, and editing the school magazine.

The first article in this anthology, "Some Aspects of Game Captaincy," was the first for which he was paid. During his last year at Dulwich, he entered a competition sponsored by The Public School Magazine, a periodical devoted to the adolescent, and won the first prize. The article appeared in the February, 1900 issue.

Since his father did not approve of his writing, Mr. Wodehouse went to work at the London branch of the Hong Kong and Shanghai Bank. He toiled dutifully for two years only to discover that he had made more money from his contributions to magazines than from his work at the bank. He resigned and obtained a position on the century-old evening newspaper, The Globe. For seven years he wrote a daily humor column called "By the Way."

About the same time he started work on The Globe, he began submitting articles and poems to Punch, even then the most famous humor magazine in the world. This section also includes "An Unfinished Collection," his first Punch article, which appeared in the issue of September 17, 1902.

SOME ASPECTS OF
GAME-CAPTAINCY

To the Game-Captain (of the football variety) the world is peopled by three classes, firstly the keen and regular player, next the partial slacker, thirdly, and lastly, the entire, abject and absolute slacker.

Of the first class, the keen and regular player, little need be said. A keen player is a gem of purest rays serene, and when to his keenness he adds regularity and punctuality, life ceases to become the mere hollow blank that it would otherwise become, and joy reigns supreme.

The absolute slacker (to take the worst at once, and have done with it) needs the pen of a Swift before adequate justice can be done to his enormities. He is a blot, an excrescence. All those moments which are not spent in avoiding games (by means of that leave which is unanimously considered the peculiar property of the French nation) he uses in concocting ingenious excuses. Armed with these, he faces with calmness the disgusting curiosity of the Game-Captain, who officiously desires to know the reason of his non-appearance on the preceding day. These excuses are of the "had-to-go-and-see-a-man-about-a-dog" type, and rarely meet with that success for which their author hopes. In the end he discovers that his chest is weak, or his heart is subject to palpitations, and he forthwith produces a document to this effect, signed by a doctor. This has the desirable result of muzzling the tyrannical Game-Captain, whose sole solace is a look of intense and withering scorn. But this is seldom fatal, and generally, we rejoice to say, ineffectual.

The next type is the partial slacker. He differs from the absolute slacker in that at rare intervals he actually turns up, changed withal into the garb of the game, and thirsting for the fray. At this point begins the time of trouble for the Game-Captain. To begin with, he is forced by stress of ignorance to ask the newcomer his name. This is, of course, an insult of the worst kind. "A being who does not know my name," argues the partial slacker, "must be something not far from a criminal lunatic." The name is, however, extracted, and the partial slacker strides to the arena. Now arises insult No. 2. He is wearing his cap. A hint as to the advisability of removing this pièce de résistance not being taken, he is ordered to assume a capless state, and by these means a coolness springs up between him and the G. C. Of this the Game-Captain is made aware when the game commences. The partial slacker, scorning to insert his head in the scrum, assumes a commanding position outside and from this point criticises the Game-Captain's decisions with severity and pith. The last end of the partial slacker is generally a sad one. Stung by some pungent home-thrust, the Game-Captain is fain to try chastisement, and by these means silences the enemy's battery.

Sometimes the classes overlap. As for instance, a keen and regular player may, by some more than usually gross bit of bungling on the part of the G.-C., be moved to a fervour and eloquence worthy of Juvenal. Or, again, even the absolute slacker may for a time emulate the keen player, provided an opponent plant a shrewd kick on a tender spot. But, broadly speaking, there are only three classes.

AN UNFINISHED COLLECTION

A silence had fallen upon the smoking room. The warrior just back from the front had enquired after George Vanderpoop, and we, who knew that George's gentle spirit had, to use a metaphor after his own heart, long since been withdrawn from circulation, were feeling uncomfortable and wondering how to break the news.

Smithson is our specialist in tact, and we looked to him to be spokesman.

"George," said Smithson at last, "the late George Vanderpoop—"

"Late!" exclaimed the warrior; "is he dead?"

"As a doornail," replied Smithson sadly. "Perhaps you would care to hear the story. It is sad, but interesting. You may recollect that, when you sailed, he was starting his journalistic career. For a young writer he had done remarkably well. The *Daily Telephone* had printed two of his contributions to their correspondence column, and a bright pen picture of his, describing how Lee's Lozenges for the Liver had snatched him from almost certain death, had quite a vogue. Lee, I believe, actually commissioned him to do a series on the subject."

"Well?" said the warrior.

"Well, he was, as I say, prospering very fairly, when in an unlucky moment he began to make a collection of editorial rejection forms. He had always been a somewhat easy prey to scourges of that description. But when he had passed safely through a sharp attack of Philatelism and a rather nasty bout of Autographomania, everyone hoped and believed that he had turned the corner. The progress of his last illness was very rapid. Within a year he wanted but one specimen to make the complete set. This was the one published from the offices of the *Scrutinizer*. All the rest he had obtained with the greatest ease. I remember his telling me that a single short story of his, called "The Vengeance of Vera Dalrymple," had been instrumental in securing no less than thirty perfect specimens. Poor George! I was with him when he made his first attempt on the *Scrutinizer*. He had baited his hook with an essay on Evolution. He read me one or two passages from it. I stopped him at the third paragraph, and congratulated him in advance, little thinking that it was sympathy rather than congratulations that he needed. When I saw him a week afterwards he was looking haggard. I questioned him, and by slow degrees drew out the story. The article on Evolution had been printed.

" 'Never say die, George,' I said. 'Send them "Vera Dalrymple." No paper can take that.'

"He sent it. The *Scrutinizer*, which had been running for nearly a century without publishing a line of fiction, took it and asked for more. It was as if there were an editorial conspiracy against him."

"Well?" said the man of war.

"Then," said Smithson, "George pulled himself together. He wrote a parody of 'The Minstrel Boy.' I have seen a good many parodies, but never such a parody as that. By return of post came a long envelope bearing the crest of the *Scrutinizer*. 'At last,' he said, as he tore it open.

" 'George, old man,' I said, 'your hand.'

"He looked at me a full minute. Then with a horrible, mirthless laugh he fell to the ground, and expired almost instantly. You will readily guess what killed him. The poem had been returned, *but without a rejection form!*"

DAMON AND PYTHIAS
A Romance

SINCE Earth was first created,
  Since Time began to fly,
No friends were e'er so mated,
  So firm as JONES and I.
Since primal Man was fashioned
  To people ice and stones,
No pair, I ween, had ever been
  Such chums as I and JONES.

In fair and foulest weather,
  Beginning when but boys,
We faced our woes together,
  We shared each other's joys.
Together, sad or merry,
  We acted hand in glove,
Until—'twas careless, very—
  I chanced to fall in love.

The lady's points to touch on,
  Her name was JULIA WHITE,
Her lineage high, her scutcheon
  Untarnished; manners, bright;
Complexion, soft and creamy;
  Her hair, of golden hue;
Her eyes, in aspect, dreamy,
  In colour, greyish blue.

For her I sighed, I panted;
  I saw her in my dreams;
I vowed, protested, ranted;
  I sent her chocolate creams.
Until methought one morning
  I seemed to hear a voice,
A still, small voice of warning.
  "Does JONES approve your choice?"

To JONES of my affection
  I spoke that very night.
If he had no objection,
  I said I'd wed Miss WHITE.
I asked him for his blessing,
  But, turning rather blue,
He said: "It's most distressing,
  But *I* adore her, too."

"Then, JONES," I answered, sobbing,
  "My wooing's at an end,
I couldn't think of robbing
  My best, my only friend.
The notion makes me furious—
  I'd much prefer to die."
"Perhaps you'll think it curious,"
  Said JONES, "but so should I."

Nor he nor I would falter
  In our resolve one jot.
I bade him seek the altar,
  He vowed that he would not.
"She's yours, old fellow. Make her
  As happy as you can."
"Not so," said I, "you take her—
  You are the lucky man."

At length—the situation
  Had lasted now a year—
I had an inspiration,
  Which seemed to make things clear.
"Supposing," I suggested,
  "We ask Miss WHITE to choose?
I should be interested
  To hear her private views.

"Perhaps she has a preference—
  I own it sounds absurd—
But I submit, with deference,
  That she might well be heard.
In clear, commercial diction
  The case in point we'll state,
Disclose the cause of friction,
  And leave the rest to Fate."

We did, and on the morrow
    The postman brought us news.
Miss WHITE expressed her sorrow
    At having to refuse.
Of all her many reasons
    This seemed to me the pith:
Six months before (or rather more)
    She'd married Mr. SMITH.

THE HAUNTED TRAM

Ghosts of The Towers, The Grange, The Court,
    Ghosts of the Castle Keep.
Ghosts of the finicking, "high-life" sort
    Are growing a trifle cheap.
But here is a spook of another stamp,
    No thin, theatrical sham,
But a spectre who fears not dirt nor damp:
    He rides on a London tram.

By the curious glance of a mortal eye
    He is not seen. He's heard.
His steps go a-creeping, creeping by,
    He speaks but a single word.
You may hear his feet: you may hear them plain,
    For—it's odd in a ghost—they crunch.
You may hear the whirr of his rattling chain,
    And the ting of his ringing punch.

The gathering shadows of night fall fast;
    The lamps in the street are lit;
To the roof have the eerie footsteps passed,
    Where the outside passengers sit.
To the passenger's side has the spectre paced;
    For a moment he halts, they say,
Then a ring from the punch at the unseen waist,
    And the footsteps pass away.

That is the tale of the haunted car;
    And if on that car you ride
You won't, believe me, have journeyed far
    Ere the spectre seeks your side.
Ay, all unseen by your seat he'll stand,
    And (unless it's a wig) your hair
Will rise at the touch of his icy hand,
    And the sound of his whispered "Fare!"

At the end of the trip, when you're getting down
    (And you'll probably simply fly!)
Just give the conductor half-a-crown,
    Ask who is the ghost and why.
And the man will explain with bated breath
    (And point you a moral) thus:
" 'E's a pore young bloke wot wos crushed to death
        By people as fought
        As they didn't ought
For seats on a crowded bus."

THE NEW ADVERTISING

"In Denmark," said the man of ideas, coming into the smoking room, "I see that they have original ideas on the subject of advertising. According to the usually well-informed *Daily Lyre*, all 'bombastic' advertising is punished with a fine. The advertiser is expected to describe his wares in restrained, modest language. In case this idea should be introduced into England, I have drawn up a few specimen advertisements which, in my opinion, combine attractiveness with a shrinking modesty at which no censor could cavil."

And in spite of our protests, he began to read us his first effort, descriptive of a patent medicine.

"It runs like this," he said:

Timson's Tonic for Distracted Deadbeats
Has been known to cure

* * *

We Hate to Seem to Boast,
but
Many Who have Tried It Are Still
Alive

* * *

Take a Dose or Two in Your Spare Time
It's Not Bad Scuff

* * *

Read what an outside stockbroker says:
"Sir—After three months' steady absorption of your Tonic
I was no worse."

* * *

We do not wish to thrust ourselves forward in any way. If
you prefer other medicines, by all means take them. Only we
just thought we'd mention it—casually, as it were—that TIM-
SON'S is PRETTY GOOD.

"How's that?" inquired the man of ideas. "Attractive, I fancy,
without being bombastic. Now, one about a new novel. Ready?

MR. LUCIEN LOGROLLER'S LATEST
The Dyspepsia of the Soul
The Dyspepsia of the Soul
The Dyspepsia of the Soul
Don't buy it if you don't want to, but just listen to a few of
the criticisms.
THE DYSPEPSIA OF THE SOUL
"Rather . . . rubbish."—*Spectator*
"We advise all insomniacs to read Mr. Logroller's soporific
pages."—*Outlook*
"Rot."—*Pelican*
THE DYSPEPSIA OF THE SOUL
Already in its first edition.

"What do you think of that?" asked the man of ideas.
We told him.

1914–1919

In 1909, Mr. Wodehouse took his annual five-week vacation and came to
New York City to try to sell his short stories. His first sale was to Cosmo-
politan, which paid him $300 for "The Good Angel." When a second story
was sold the same day, he promptly forwarded his resignation to The
Globe. From that moment he would earn his living exclusively from his
free-lance writing. While in Great Britain, he had gained a literary reputation upon which he quickly enlarged by virtue of his successes in America,
where he eventually asked for and got as much as $6,000 for a short story
in a magazine.

From 1915 to 1918, Mr. Wodehouse was the drama critic for Frank
Crowninshield's magazine "devoted to society and the arts," Vanity Fair.
During this period, he wrote a good portion of the magazine under various
pen-names. In "My Life as A Drama Critic" he gives us a glimpse of his
job.

His proficiency in the theatre was so great that, in addition to his many
short stories and novels, he turned out eighteen plays and wrote singly or
collaborated on thirty-two musical comedies. As a lyricist, he created over
200 songs, his most famous lyric being "Bill," from Show Boat. 1917 was
his banner year in musical comedy. He had five shows running simultaneously on Broadway, a feat still to be equalled. Indeed, with Guy Bolton
and Jerome Kern, P. G. Wodehouse formulated the American musical
comedy as we know it today. And we can get an idea of his contributions
from such articles as "The Agonies of Writing a Musical Comedy" and "On
the Writing of Lyrics."

He was not always the impartial reviewer that professional critics are
supposed to be. In "The Past Theatrical Season," the fearless reporter gives
his forthright pronouncements as to the best performances given by unstarred
actors.

THE SECRET PLEASURES
OF REGINALD

I found Reggie in the club one Saturday afternoon. He was reclining in a long chair, motionless, his eyes fixed glassily on the ceiling. He frowned a little when I spoke. "You don't seem to be doing anything," I said.

"It's not what I'm doing, it's what I am *not* doing that matters."

It sounded like an epigram, but epigrams are so little associated with Reggie that I ventured to ask what he meant.

He sighed. "Ah well," he said. "I suppose the sooner I tell you, the sooner you'll go. Do you know Bodfish?"

I shuddered. "Wilkinson Bodfish? I do."

"Have you ever spent a weekend at Bodfish's place in the country?"

I shuddered again. "I have."

"Well, I'm *not* spending the weekend at Bodfish's place in the country."

"I see you're not. But—"

"You don't understand. I do not mean that I am simply absent from Bodfish's place in the country. I mean that I am *deliberately* not spending the weekend there. When you interrupted me just now, I was not strolling down to Bodfish's garage, listening to his prattle about his new car."

I glanced around uneasily.

"Reggie, old man, you're—you're not—This hot weather—"

"I am perfectly well, and in possession of all my faculties. Now tell me. Can you imagine anything more awful than to spend a weekend with Bodfish?"

On the spur of the moment I could not.

"Can you imagine anything more delightful, then, than *not* spending a weekend with Bodfish? Well, that's what I'm doing now. Soon, when you have gone—if you have any other engagements, please don't let me keep you—I shall not go into the house and not listen to Mrs. Bodfish on the subject of young Willie Bodfish's premature intelligence."

I got his true meaning. "I see. You mean that you will be thanking your stars that you aren't with Bodfish."

"That is it, put crudely. But I go further. I don't indulge in a mere momentary self-congratulation, I do the thing thoroughly. If I were weekending at Bodfish's, I should have arrived there just half an hour ago. I therefore selected that moment for beginning not to weekend with Bodfish. I settled myself in this chair and I did not have my back slapped at the station. A few minutes later I was not whirling along the country roads, trying to balance the car with my legs and an elbow. Time passed, and I was not shaking hands with Mrs. Bodfish. I have just had the most corking half-hour, and shortly—when you have remembered an appointment— I shall go on having it. What I am really looking forward to is the happy time after dinner. I shall pass it in not playing bridge with Bodfish, Mrs. Bodfish, and a neighbor. Sunday morning is the best part of the whole weekend, though. That is when I shall most enjoy myself. Do you know a man named Pringle? Next Saturday I am not going to stay with Pringle. I forget who is not to be my host the Saturday after that. I have so many engagements of this kind that I lose track of them."

"But, Reggie, this is genius. You have hit on the greatest idea of the age. You might extend this system of yours."

"I do. Some of the jolliest evenings I have spent have been not at the theatre."

"I have often wondered what it was that made you look so fit and happy."

"Yes. These little non-visits of mine pick me up and put life into me for the coming week. I get up on Monday morning feeling like a lion. The reason I selected Bodfish this week, though I was practically engaged to a man named Stevenson who lives out in Connecticut, was that I felt rundown and needed a real rest. I shall be all right on Monday."

"And so shall I," I said, sinking into the chair beside him.

"You're not going to the country?" he asked regretfully.

"I am not. I, too, need a tonic. I shall join you at Bodfish's. I really feel a lot better already."

I closed my eyes, and relaxed, and a great peace settled upon me.

MY BATTLE WITH DRINK

I could tell my story in two words—the two words "I drank." But I was not always a drinker. This is the story of my downfall—and of my rise—for through the influence of a good woman, I have, thank Heaven, risen from the depths.

The thing stole upon me gradually, as it does upon so many young men. As a boy, I remember taking a glass of root beer, but it did not grip me then. I can recall that I even disliked the taste. I was a young man before temptation really came upon me. My downfall began when I joined the Yonkers Shorthand and Typewriting College.

It was then that I first made acquaintance with the awful power of ridicule. They were a hard-living set at college—reckless youths. They frequented movie palaces. They thought nothing of winding up an evening with a couple of egg-phosphates and a chocolate fudge. They laughed at me when I refused to join them. I was only twenty. My character was undeveloped. I could not endure their scorn. The next time I was offered a drink I accepted. They were pleased, I remember. They called me "Good old Plum!" and a good sport and other complimentary names. I was intoxicated with sudden popularity.

How vividly I can recall that day! The shining counter, the placards advertising strange mixtures with ice cream as their basis, the busy men behind the counter, the half-cynical, half-pitying eyes of the girl in the cage where you bought the soda checks. She had seen so many happy, healthy boys through that little hole in the wire netting, so many thoughtless boys all eager for their first soda, clamoring to set their foot on the primrose path that leads to destruction.

It was an apple marshmallow sundae, I recollect. I dug my spoon into it with an assumption of gaiety which I was far from feeling. The first mouthful almost nauseated me. It was like cold hair-oil. But I stuck to it. I could not break down now. I could not bear to forfeit the newly-won esteem of my comrades. They were gulping their sundaes down with the speed and enjoyment of old hands. I set my teeth, and persevered, and by degrees a strange exhilaration began to steal over me. I felt that I had burnt my boats and bridges; that I had crossed the Rubicon. I was reckless. I ordered another round. I was the life and soul of that party.

The next morning brought remorse. I did not feel well. I had pains, physical and mental. But I could not go back now. I was too weak to dispense with my popularity. I was only a boy, and on the previous evening the captain of the Checkers Club, to whom I looked up with an almost worshipping reverence, had slapped me on the back and told me that I was a corker. I felt that nothing could be excessive payment for such an honor. That night I gave a party at which orange phosphate flowed like water. It was the turning point.

I had got the habit!

I will pass briefly over the next few years. I continued to sink deeper and deeper into the slough. I knew all the drugstore clerks in New York by their first names, and they called me by mine. I no longer even had to specify the abomination I desired. I simply handed the man my ten cent check and said: "The usual, Jimmy," and he understood.

At first, considerations of health did not trouble me. I was young and strong, and my constitution quickly threw off the effects of my dissipation. Then, gradually, I began to feel worse. I was losing my grip. I found a difficulty in concentrating my attention on my work. I had dizzy spells. I became nervous and distrait. Eventually I went to a doctor. He examined me thoroughly, and shook his head.

"If I am to do you any good," he said, "you must tell me all. You must hold no secrets from me."

"Doctor," I said, covering my face with my hands, "I am a confirmed soda-fiend."

He gave me a long lecture and a longer list of instructions. I must take air and exercise and I must become a total abstainer from sundaes of all descriptions. I must avoid limeade like the plague, and if anybody offered me a Bulgarzoon I was to knock him down and shout for the nearest policeman.

I learned then for the first time what a bitterly hard thing it is for a man in a large and wicked city to keep from soda when once he has got the habit. Everything was against me. The old convivial circle began to shun me. I could not join in their revels and they began to look on me as a grouch. In the end, I fell, and in one wild orgy undid all the good of a month's abstinence. I was desperate then. I felt that nothing could save me, and I might as well give up the struggle. I drank two pin-ap-o-lades, three grapefruit-olas and an egg-zoolak, before pausing to take breath.

And then, the next day, I met May, the girl who effected my reformation. She was a clergyman's daughter who, to support her widowed mother, had accepted a non-speaking part in a musical comedy production entitled "Oh Joy! Oh Pep!" Our acquaintance ripened, and one night I asked her out to supper.

I look on that moment as the happiest of my life. I met her at the stage door, and conducted her to the nearest soda-fountain. We were inside and I was buying the checks before she realized where she was, and I shall never forget her look of mingled pain and horror.

"And I thought you were a live one!" she murmured.

It seemed that she had been looking forward to a little lobster and champagne. The idea was absolutely new to me. She quickly convinced me, however, that such was the only refreshment which she would consider, and she recoiled with unconcealed aversion from my suggestion of a Mocha Malted and an Eva Tanguay. That night I tasted wine for the first time, and my reformation began.

It was hard at first, desperately hard. Something inside me was trying to pull me back to the sundaes for which I craved, but I resisted the impulse. Always with her divinely sympathetic encouragement, I gradually acquired a taste for alcohol. And suddenly, one evening, like a flash it came upon me that I had shaken off the cursed yoke that held me down: that I never wanted to see the inside of a drugstore again. Cocktails, at first repellent, have at last become palatable to me. I drink highballs for breakfast. I am saved.

IN DEFENSE OF ASTIGMATISM

This is peculiarly an age where novelists pride themselves on the breadth of their outlook and the courage with which they refuse to ignore the realities of life; and never before have authors had such scope in the matter of the selection of heroes. In the days of the old-fashioned novel, when the hero was automatically Lord Blank or Sir Ralph Asterisk, there were, of course, certain rules that had to be observed, but today—why, you can hardly hear yourself think for the uproar of earnest young novelists proclaiming how free and unfettered they are. And yet, no writer has had the pluck to make his hero wear glasses.

In the old days, as I say, this was all very well. The hero was a young lordling, sprung from a line of ancestors who had never done anything with their eyes except wear a piercing glance before which lesser men quailed. But now novelists go into every class of society for their heroes, and surely, at least an occasional one of them must have been astigmatic. Kipps undoubtedly wore glasses; so did Bunker Bean; so did Mr. Polly, Clayhanger, Bibbs, Sheridan, and a score of others. Then why not say so?

Novelists are moving with the times in every other direction. Why not in this?

It is futile to advance the argument that glasses are unromantic. They are not. I know, because I wear them myself, and I am a singularly romantic figure, whether in my rimless, my Oxford gold-bordered, or the plain gent's spectacles which I wear in the privacy of my study.

Besides, everybody wears glasses nowadays. That is the point I wish to make. For commercial reasons, if for no others, authors ought to think seriously of this matter of goggling their heroes. It is an admitted fact that the reader of a novel likes to put himself in the hero's place—to imagine, while reading, that he is the hero. What an audience the writer of the first romance to star a spectacled hero will have. All over the country thousands of short-sighted men will polish their glasses and plunge into his pages. It is absurd to go on writing in these days for a normal-sighted public. The growing tenseness of life, with its small print, its newspapers read by artificial light, and its flickering motion pictures, is whittling down the section of the populace which has perfect sight to a mere handful.

I seem to see that romance. In fact, I think I shall write it myself. " 'Evadne,' murmured Clarence, removing his pince-nez and polishing them tenderly. . . .' " " 'See,' cried Clarence, 'how clearly every leaf of yonder tree is mirrored in the still water of the lake. I can't see myself, unfortunately, for I have left my glasses on the parlor piano, but don't worry about me: go ahead and see!". . . . "Clarence adjusted his tortoiseshell-rimmed spectacles with a careless gesture, and faced the assassins without a tremor." Hot stuff? Got the punch? I should say so. Do you imagine that there will be a single man in this country with the price of the book in his pocket and a pair of pince-nez on his face who will not scream and kick like an angry child if you withhold my novel from him?

And just pause for a moment to think of the serial and dramatic rights of the story. All editors wear glasses, so do all theatrical managers. My appeal will be irresistible. All I shall have to do will be to see that the check is for the right figure and to supervise the placing of the electric sign

SPECTACLES OF FATE

BY P. G. WODEHOUSE

over the doors of whichever theatre I happen to select for the production of the play.

Have you ever considered the latent possibilities for dramatic situations in short sight? You know how your glasses cloud over when you come into a warm room out of the cold? Well, imagine your hero in such a position. He has been waiting outside the murderer's den preparatory to dashing in and saving the heroine. He dashes in. "Hands up, you scoundrels," he cries. And then his glasses get all misty, and there he is, temporarily blind, with a full-size desperado backing away and measuring the distance in order to hand him one with a pickaxe.

Or would you prefer something less sensational, something more in the romantic line? Very well. Hero, on his way to the Dowager Duchess's ball, slips on a banana-peel and smashes his only pair of spectacles. He dare not fail to attend the ball, for the dear Duchess would never forgive him; so he goes in and proposes to a girl he particularly dislikes because she is dressed in pink, and the heroine told him that she was going to wear pink. But the heroine's pink dress was late in coming home from the modiste's and she had to turn up in blue. The heroine comes in just as the other girl is accepting him, and there you have a nice, live, peppy, kick-off for your tale of passion and human interest.

But I have said enough to show that the time has come when novelists, if they do not wish to be left behind in the race, must adapt themselves to modern conditions. One does not wish to threaten, but, as I say, we astigmatics are in a large minority and can, if we get together, make our presence felt. Roused by this article to a sense of the injustice of their treatment, the great army of glass-wearing citizens could very easily make novelists see reason. A boycott of non-spectacled heroes would soon achieve the necessary reform. Perhaps there will be no need to let matters go as far as that. I hope not. But, if this warning should be neglected, if we have any more of these novels about men with keen gray eyes or snapping black eyes or cheerful blue eyes—any sort of eyes, in fact, lacking some muscular affliction, we shall know what to do.

PHOTOGRAPHERS AND ME

I look in my glass, dear reader, and what do I see? Nothing so frightfully hot, believe me. The face is slablike, the ears are large and fastened on at right-angles. Above the eyebrows comes a stagnant sea of bald forehead, stretching away into the distance with nothing to relieve it but a few wisps of lonely hair. The nose is blobby, the eyes dull, like those of a fish not in the best of health. A face, in short, taking it for all in all, which should be reserved for the gaze of my nearest and dearest who, through long habit, have got used to it and can see through to the pure white soul beneath. At any rate, a face not to be scattered about at random and come upon suddenly by nervous people and invalids.

And yet, just because I am an author, I have to keep on being photographed. It is the fault of publishers and editors, of course, really, but it is the photographer who comes in for the author's hate.

Something has got to be done about this practice of publishing authors' photographs. We have to submit to it, because editors and publishers insist. They have an extraordinary superstition that it helps an author's sales. The idea is that the public sees the photograph, pauses spell-bound for an instant, and then with a cry of ecstasy rushes off to the book-shop and buys copy after copy of the gargoyle's latest novel.

Of course, in practice, it works out just the other way. People read a review of an author's book and are told that it throbs with a passion so intense as almost to be painful, and are on the point of digging seven-and-sixpence out of their child's money-box to secure a copy, when their eyes fall on the man's photograph at the side of the review, and they find that he has a face like a rabbit and wears spectacles and a low collar. And this man is the man who is said to have laid bare the soul of a woman as with a scalpel.

Naturally their faith is shaken. They feel that a man like that cannot possibly know anything about Woman or any other subject except where to go for a vegetarian lunch, and the next moment they have put down the hair-pin and the child is seven-and-six in hand and the author his ten per cent., or whatever it is, to the bad. And all because of a photograph.

For the ordinary man, the recent introduction of high-art methods into photography has done much to diminish the unpleasantness of the operation. In the old days of crude and direct posing, there was no escape for the sitter. He had to stand up, backed by a rustic stile and a flabby canvas sheet covered with exotic trees, glaring straight into the camera. To prevent any eleventh-hour retreat, a sort of spiky thing was shoved firmly into the back of his head leaving him with the choice of being taken as he stood or having an inch of steel jabbed into his skull. Modern methods have changed all that.

There are no photographs nowadays. Only "camera portraits" and "lens impressions." The full face has been abolished. The ideal of the present-day photographer is to eliminate the sitter as far as possible and concentrate on a general cloudy effect. I have in my possession two studies of my Uncle Theodore—one taken in the early 'nineties, the other in the present year. The first shows him, evidently in pain, staring before him with a fixed expression. In his right hand he grasps a scroll. His left rests on a moss-covered wall. Two sea-gulls are flying against a stormy sky.

As a likeness, it is almost brutally exact. My uncle stands forever condemned as the wearer of a made-up tie.

The second is different in every respect. Not only has the sitter been taken in the popular modern "one-twentieth face," showing only the back of the head, the left ear and what is either a pimple or a flaw in the print, but the whole thing is plunged in the deepest shadow. It is as if my uncle had been surprised by the camera while chasing a black cat in his coal-cellar on a moonlight night. There is no question as to which of the two makes the more attractive picture. My family resemble me in that respect. The less you see of us, the better we look.

A PLEA FOR INDOOR GOLF

Indoor golf is that which is played in the home. Whether you live in a palace or a hovel, an indoor golf-course, be it only of nine holes, is well within your reach. A house offers greater facilities than an apartment, and I have found my game greatly improved since I went to live in the country. I can, perhaps, scarcely do better than give a brief description of the sporting nine-hole course which I have recently laid out in my present residence.

All authorities agree that the first hole on every links should be moderately easy, in order to give the nervous player a temporary and fictitious confidence.

At Wodehouse Manor, therefore, we drive off from the front door—in order to get the benefit of the door-mat—down an entry fairway, carpeted with rugs and without traps. The hole—a loving-cup—is just under the stairs; and a good player ought to have no difficulty in doing it in two.

The second hole, a short and simple one, takes you into the telephone booth. Trouble begins with the third, a long dog-leg hole through the kitchen into the dining-room. This hole is well trapped with table-legs, kitchen utensils, and a moving hazard in the person of Clarence the cat, who is generally wandering about the fairway. The hole is under the glass-and-china cupboard, where you are liable to be bunkered if you loft your approach-shot excessively.

The fourth and fifth holes call for no comment. They are without traps, the only danger being that you may lose a stroke through hitting the maid if she happens to be coming down the back stairs while you are taking a mashie-shot. This is a penalty under the local rule.

The sixth is the indispensable water-hole. It is short, but tricky. Teeing off from just outside the bathroom door, you have to loft the ball over the side of the bath, holing out in the little vent pipe, at the end where the water runs out.

The seventh is the longest hole on the course. Starting at the entrance of the best bedroom, a full drive takes you to the head of the stairs, whence you will need at least two more strokes to put you dead on the pin in the drawing-room. In the drawing-room the fairway is trapped with photograph frames—with glass, complete

—these serving as casual water: and anyone who can hole out on the piano in five or under is a player of class. Bogey is six, and I have known even such a capable exponent of the game as my Uncle Reginald, who is plus two on his home links on Park Avenue, to take twenty-seven at the hole. But on that occasion he had the misfortune to be bunkered in a photograph of my Aunt Clara and took no fewer than eleven strokes with his niblick to extricate himself from it.

The eighth and ninth holes are straightforward, and can be done in two and three respectively, provided you swing easily and avoid the canary's cage. Once trapped there, it is better to give up the hole without further effort. It is almost impossible to get out in less than fifty-six, and after you have taken about thirty the bird gets visibly annoyed.

THE ALARMING SPREAD
OF POETRY

To the thinking man there are few things more disturbing than the realization that we are becoming a nation of minor poets. In the good old days poets were for the most part confined to garrets, which they left only for the purpose of being ejected from the offices of magazines and papers to which they attempted to sell their wares. Nobody ever thought of reading a book of poems unless accompanied by a guarantee from the publisher that the author had been dead at least a hundred years. Poetry, like wine, certain brands of cheese, and public buildings, was rightly considered to improve with age; and no connoisseur could have dreamed of filling himself with raw, indigestible verse, warm from the maker.

Today, however, editors are paying real money for poetry; publishers are making a profit on books of verse; and many a young man who, had he been born earlier, would have sustained life on a crust of bread, is now sending for the manager to find out how the restaurant dares try to sell a fellow champagne like this as genuine Pommery Brut. Naturally this is having a marked effect on the life of the community. Our children grow to adolescence with the feeling that they can become poets instead of working. Many an embryo bill clerk has been ruined by the heady knowledge that poems are paid for at the rate of a dollar a line. All over the country promising young plasterers and rising young motormen are throwing up steady jobs in order to devote themselves to the new profession. On a sunny afternoon down in Washington Square one's progress is positively impeded by the swarms of young poets brought out by the warm weather. It is a horrible sight to see those unfortunate youths, who ought to be sitting happily at desks writing "Dear Sir, Your favor of the tenth inst. duly received and contents noted. In reply we beg to state. . . ." wandering about with their fingers in their hair and their features distorted with the agony of composition, as they try to find rhymes to "cosmic" and "symbolism."

And, as if matters were not bad enough already, along comes Mr. Edgar Lee Masters and invents *vers libre*. It is too early yet to judge the full effects of this man's horrid discovery, but there is no doubt that he has taken the lid off and unleashed forces over which none can have any control. All those decent restrictions which used to check poets have vanished, and who shall say what will be the outcome?

Until Mr. Masters came on the scene there was just one thing which, like a salient fortress in the midst of an enemy's advancing army, acted as a barrier to the youth of the country. When one's son came to one and said, "Father, I shall not be able to fulfill your dearest wish and start work in the fertilizer department. I have decided to become a poet," although one could no longer frighten him from his purpose by talking of garrets and starvation, there was still one weapon left. "What about the rhymes, Willie?" you replied, and the eager light died out of the boy's face, as he perceived the catch in what he had taken for a good thing. You pressed your advantage. "Think of having to spend your life making one line rhyme with another! Think of the bleak future, when you have used up 'moon' and 'June,' 'love' and 'dove,' 'May' and 'gay'! Think of the moment when you have ended the last line but one of your poem with 'windows' or 'warmth' and have to buckle to, trying to make the thing couple up in accordance with the rules! What then, Willie?"

Next day a new hand had signed on in the fertilizer department.

But now all that has changed. Not only are rhymes no longer

necessary, but editors positively prefer them left out. If Longfellow had been writing today he would have had to revise "The Village Blacksmith" if he wanted to pull in that dollar a line. No editor would print stuff like:

> Under the spreading chestnut tree
> The village smithy stands.
> The smith a brawny man is he
> With large and sinewy hands.

If Longfellow were living in these hyphenated, free and versy days, he would find himself compelled to take his pen in hand and dictate as follows:

> In life I was the village smith,
> I worked all day
> But
> I retained the delicacy of my complexion
> Because
> I worked in the shade of the chestnut tree
> Instead of in the sun
> Like Nicholas Blodgett, the expressman.
> I was large and strong
> Because
> I went in for physical culture
> And deep breathing
> And all those stunts.
> I had the biggest biceps in Spoon River.

Who can say where this thing will end? *Vers libre* is within the reach of all. A sleeping nation has wakened to the realization that there is money to be made out of chopping its prose into bits. Something must be done shortly if the nation is to be saved from this menace. But what? It is no good shooting Edgar Lee Masters, for the mischief has been done, and even making an example of him could not undo it. Probably the only hope lies in the fact that poets never buy other poets' stuff. When once we have all become poets, the sale of verse will cease or be limited to the few copies which individual poets will buy to give to their friends.

MY LIFE AS A DRAMATIC CRITIC

I had always wanted to be a dramatic critic. A taste for sitting back and watching other people work, so essential to the make-up of this sub-species of humanity, has always been one of the leading traits in my character.

I have seldom missed a first night. No sooner has one periodical got rid of me than another has had the misfortune to engage me, with the result that I am now the foremost critic of the day, read assiduously by millions, fawned upon by managers, courted by stagehands. My lightest word can make or mar a new production. If I say a piece is bad, it dies. It may not die instantly. Generally it takes forty weeks in New York and a couple of seasons on the road to do it, but it cannot escape its fate. Sooner or later it perishes. That is the sort of man I am.

Whatever else may be charged against me, I have never deviated from the standard which I set myself at the beginning of my career. If I am called upon to review a play produced by a manager who is considering one of my own works, I do not hesitate. I praise that play.

If an actor has given me a lunch, I refuse to bite the hand that has fed me. I praise that actor's performance. I can only recall one instance of my departing from my principles. That was when the champagne was corked, and the man refused to buy me another bottle.

As is only natural, I have met many interesting people since I embarked on my career. I remember once lunching with rare Ben Jonson at the Mermaid Tavern—this would be back in Queen Elizabeth's time, when I was beginning to be known in the theatrical world—and seeing a young man with a nobby forehead and about three inches of beard doing himself well at a neighboring table at the expense of Burbage the manager.

"Ben," I asked my companion, "who is that youth?" He told me that the fellow was one Bacon, a new dramatist who had learned his technique by holding horses' heads in the Strand, and who, for some reason or other, wrote under the name of Shakespeare. "You must see his *Hamlet*," said Ben enthusiastically. "He read me the script last night. They start rehearsals at the Globe next week. It's a pippin. In the last act every blamed character in the cast who isn't already dead jumps on everyone else's neck and slays him. It's a skit, you know, on these foolish tragedies which every manager is putting on just now. Personally, I think it's the best thing since *The Prune-Hater's Daughter*."

I was skeptical at the moment, but time proved the correctness of my old friend's judgment; and, having been present after the opening performance at a little supper given by Burbage at which sack ran like water, and anybody who wanted another malvoisie and seltzer simply had to beckon to the waiter, I was able to conscientiously praise it in the highest terms.

I still treasure the faded newspaper clipping which contains the advertisement of the play, with the legend, "Shakespeare has put one over. A scream from start to finish."—Wodehouse, in *The Weekly Bear-Baiter* (with which is incorporated *The Scurvy Knaves' Gazette*).

The lot of a dramatic critic is, in many respects, an enviable one. Lately, there has been the growing practice among critics of roasting a play on the morning after production, and then having another go at it in the Sunday edition under the title of "Second Swats" or "The Past Week in the Theatre," which has made it pretty rocky going for dramatists who thus get it twice in the same place, and experience the complex emotions of the commuter who, coming home in the dark, trips over the baby's cart and bumps his head against the hat stand.

There is also no purer pleasure than that of getting into a theatre on what the poet Milton used to call "the nod." I remember Brigham Young saying to me once with not unnatural chagrin, "You're a lucky man, Wodehouse. It doesn't cost you a nickel to go to a theatre. When I want to take in a show with the wife, I have to buy up the whole of the orchestra floor. And even then it's a tight fit."

My fellow critics and I escape this financial trouble, and it gives us a good deal of pleasure, when the male star is counting the house over the heroine's head (during their big love scene) to see him frown as he catches sight of us and hastily revise his original estimate.

THE AGONIES OF WRITING A MUSICAL COMEDY
Which Shows Why Librettists Pick at the Coverlet

The trouble about musical comedy, and the reason why a great many otherwise kindly and broadminded persons lie in wait round the corner with sudden scowls, their whole being intent on beating it with a brick the moment it shows its head, is that, from outside, it looks too easy.

You come into the crowded theatre and consider that each occupant of an orchestra chair is contributing three or four cents to the upkeep of a fellow who did nothing but dash off the stuff that keeps the numbers apart, and your blood boils. A glow of honest resentment fills you at the thought of anyone having such an absolute snap. You little know what the poor bird has suffered, and how inadequate a reward are his few yens per week for what he has been through. Musical comedy is not dashed off. It grows—slowly and painfully, and each step in its growth either bleaches another tuft of the author's hair or removes it from the parent skull altogether.

The average musical comedy comes into being because somebody—not the public, but a manager—wants one. We will say that Mr. and Mrs. Whoosis, the eminent ballroom dancers, have decided that they require a different sphere for the exhibition of their talents. They do not demand a drama. They commission somebody to write them a musical comedy. Some poor, misguided creature is wheedled into signing a contract: and, from that moment, his troubles begin.

An inspiration gives him a pleasing and ingenious plot. Full of optimism, he starts to write it. By the time he has finished an excellent first act, he is informed that Mr. and Mrs. Whoosis propose to sing three solos and two duets in the first act and five in the second, and will he kindly build his script accordingly? This baffles the author a little. He is aware that both artistes, though extremely gifted northward as far as the ankle-bone, go all to pieces above that level, with the result that by the time you reach the zone where the brains and voice are located, there is nothing stirring whatever. And he had allowed for this in his original conception of the play, by making Mrs. Whoosis a deaf-mute and Mr. Whoosis a Trappist monk under the perpetual vow of silence. The unfolding of the plot he had left to the other characters, with a few ingenious gaps where the two stars could come on and dance.

He takes a stiff bracer, ties a vinegar-soaked handkerchief round his forehead, and sets to work to remodel his piece. He is a trifle discouraged, but he perseveres. With almost superhuman toil he contrives the only possible story which will fit the necessities of the case. He has wrapped up the script and is about to stroll round the corner to mail it, when he learns from the manager who is acting as intermediary between the parties concerned in the production that there is a slight hitch. Instead of having fifty thousand dollars deposited in the bank to back the play, it seems that the artistes merely said in their conversation that it would be awfully jolly if they *did* have that sum, or words to that effect.

By this time our author has got the thing into his system: or, rather, he has worked so hard that he feels he cannot abandon the venture now. He hunts for another manager who wants something musical, and at length finds one. The only proviso is that this manager does not need a piece built around two stars, but one suited to the needs of Jasper Cutup, the well-known comedian, whom he has under contract. The personality of Jasper is familiar to the author, so he works for a month or two and remoulds the play to fit him. With the script under his arm he staggers to the manager's office. The manager reads the script—smiles—chuckles—thoroughly enjoys it. Then a cloud passes athwart his brow. "There's only one thing the matter with this piece," he says. "You seem to have written it to star a comedian." "But you said you wanted it for Jasper Cutup," gasps the author, supporting himself against the water-cooler. "Well, yes, that is so," replies the manager. "I remember I did want a piece for him then, but he's gone and signed up with K. and Lee. What I wish you would do is to take this script and twist it to be a vehicle for Pansy Glucose."

"Pansy Glucose?" moans the author. "The ingenue?" "Yes," says the manager. "It won't take long. Just turn your Milwaukee pickle manufacturer into a debutante, and the thing is done. Get to work as soon as you can. I want this rushed."

All this is but a portion of the musical comedy author's troubles. We will assume that he eventually finds a manager who really does put the piece into rehearsal. We will even assume that he encounters none of the trials to which I have alluded. We will even go further and assume that he is commissioned to write a musical comedy without any definite stellar personality in mind, and that when he has finished it the manager will do his share by providing a suitable cast. Is he in soft? No, dear reader, he is not in soft. You have forgotten the "Gurls." Critics are inclined to reproach, deride, blame and generally hammer the author of a musical comedy be- cause his plot is not so consecutive and unbroken as the plot of a farce or a comedy. They do not realize the conditions under which he is working. It is one of the immutable laws governing musical plays that at certain intervals during the evening the audience de- mand to see the chorus. They may not be aware that they so demand, but it is nevertheless a fact that, unless the chorus come on at these fixed intervals, the audience's interest sags. The raciest farce-scenes cannot hold them, nor the most tender love passages. They want the gurls, the whole gurls, and nothing but the gurls.

Thus it comes about that the author, having at last finished his first act, is roused from his dream of content by a horrid fear. He turns to the script, and discovers that his panic was well grounded. He has carelessly allowed fully twenty pages to pass without once bringing on the chorus.

This is where he begins to clutch his forehead and to grow gray at the temples. He cannot possibly shift musical number four, which is a chorus number, into the spot now occupied by musical number three, which is a duet, because three is a "situation" num- ber, rooted to its place by the exigencies of the story. The only thing to do is to pull the act to pieces and start afresh. And when you consider that this sort of thing happens not once but a dozen times between the start of a musical comedy book and its comple- tion, can you wonder that this branch of writing is included among the dangerous trades and that librettists always end by picking at the coverlet?

Then there is the question of cast. The author builds his hero in such a manner that he requires an actor who can sing, dance, be funny, and carry a love interest. When the time comes to cast the piece, he finds that the only possible man in sight wants fifteen hundred a week and, anyway, is signed up for the next five years with the rival syndicate. He is then faced with the alternative of revising his play to suit either: a) Jones, who can sing and dance, but is not funny; b) Smith, who is funny, but cannot sing and dance; c) Brown, who is funny and can sing and dance, but who cannot carry a love-interest and, through working in revue, has developed a habit of wandering down to the footlights and chatting with the audience. Whichever actor is given the job, it means more rewriting.

Overcome this difficulty, and another arises. Certain scenes are constructed so that A gets a laugh at the expense of B; but B is a five-hundred-a-week comedian and A is a two-hundred-a-week juvenile, and B refuses to "play straight" even for an instant for a social inferior. The original line is such that it cannot be simply switched from one to the other. The scene has to be entirely reconstructed and further laugh lines thought of. Multiply this by a hundred, and you will begin to understand why, when you see a librettist, he is generally lying on his back on the sidewalk with a crowd standing round, saying, "Give him air."

So, do not grudge the librettist his thousand a week or whatever it is. Remember what he has suffered and consider his emotions on the morning after the production when he sees lines which he invented at the cost of permanently straining his brain, attributed by the critics to the impromptu invention of the leading comedian. Of all the saddest words of tongue or pen, the saddest—to a musical comedy author—are these in the morning paper: "The bulk of the humor was sustained by Walter Wiffle, who gagged his way merrily through the piece."

ON THE WRITING OF LYRICS

The musical comedy lyric is an interesting survival of the days, long since departed, when poets worked. As everyone knows, the only real obstacle in the way of turning out poetry by the mile was the fact that you had to make the darned stuff rhyme.

Many lyricists rhyme as they pronounce, and their pronunciation is simply horrible. They can make "home" rhyme with "alone," and "saw" with "more," and go right off and look their innocent children in the eye without a touch of shame.

But let us not blame the erring lyricist too much. It isn't his fault that he does these things. It is the fault of the English language. Whoever invented the English language must have been a prose-writer, not a versifier; for he has made meagre provision for the poets. Indeed, the word "you" is almost the only decent chance he has given them. You can do something with a word like "you." It rhymes with "sue," "eyes of blue," "woo," and all sorts of succulent things, easily fitted into the fabric of a lyric. And it has the enormous advantage that it can be repeated thrice at the end of a refrain when the composer has given you those three long notes, which is about all a composer ever thinks of. When a composer hands a lyricist a "dummy" for a song, ending thus,

> Tiddley-tum, tiddley-tum,
>   Pom-pom-pom, pom-pom-pom,
>   Tum, tum, tum,

the lyricist just shoves down "You, you, you" for the last line, and then sets to work to fit the rest of the words to it. I have dwelled on this, for it is noteworthy as the only bright spot in a lyricist's life, the only real cinch the poor man has.

But take the word "love."

When the board of directors, or whoever it was, was arranging the language, you would have thought that, if they had had a spark of pity in their systems, they would have tacked on to that emotion of thoughts of which the young man's fancy lightly turns in spring, some word ending in an open vowel. They must have known that lyricists would want to use whatever word they selected as a label for the above-mentioned emotion far more frequently than any other word in the language. It wasn't much to ask of them to choose a word capable of numerous rhymes. But no, they went and made it "love," causing vast misery to millions.

"Love" rhymes with "dove," "glove," "above," and "shove." It is true that poets who print their stuff instead of having it sung take a mean advantage by ringing in words like "prove" and "move"; but the lyricist is not allowed to do that. This is the wretched unfairness of the lyricist's lot. The language gets him both ways. It won't let him rhyme "love" with "move," and it won't let him rhyme "maternal" with "colonel." If he tries the first course, he is told that the rhyme, though all right for the eye, is wrong for the ear. If he tries the second course, they say that the rhyme, though more or less ninety-nine percent pure for the ear, falls short when tested by the eye. And, when he is driven back on one of the regular, guaranteed rhymes, he is taunted with triteness of phrase.

No lyricist wants to keep linking "love" with "skies above" and "turtle dove," but what can he do? You can't do a thing with "shove"; and "glove" is one of those aloof words which are not good mixers. And—mark the brutality of the thing—there is no word you can substitute for "love." It is just as if they did it on purpose.

"Home" is another example. It is the lyricist's staff of life. But all he can do is to roam across the foam, if he wants to use it. He can put in "Nome," of course, as a pinch-hitter in special crises, but very seldom; with the result that his poetic soul, straining at its bonds, goes and uses "alone," "bone," "tone," and "thrown," exciting hoots of derision.

But it is not only the paucity of rhymes that sours the lyricist's life. He is restricted in his use of material, as well. If every audience to which a musical comedy is destined to play were a metropolitan audience, all might be well; but there is the "road" to consider. And even a metropolitan audience likes its lyrics as much as possible in the language of everyday. That is one of the thousand reasons why new Gilberts do not arise. Gilbert had the advantage of being a genius, but he had the additional advantage of writing for a public which permitted him to use his full vocabulary, and even to drop into foreign languages, even Latin and a little Greek when he felt like it. (I allude to that song in "The Grand Duke.")

And yet the modern lyricist, to look on the bright side, has advantages that Gilbert never had. Gilbert never realised the possibilities of Hawaii, with its admirably named beaches, shores, and musical instruments. Hawaii—capable as it is of being rhymed with "higher"—has done much to sweeten the lot—and increase the annual income of an industrious and highly respectable but down-trodden class of the community.

THE PAST THEATRICAL SEASON
And the Six Best Performances
by Unstarred Actors

What lessons do we draw from the past theatrical season?

In the first place, the success of *The Wanderer* proves that the day of the small and intimate production is over and that what the public wants is the large spectacle. In the second place, the success of *Oh, Boy!**—(I hate to refer to it, as I am one of the trio who perpetrated it; but, honestly, we're simply turning them away in droves, and Rockefeller has to touch Morgan for a bit if he wants to buy a ticket from the speculators)—proves that the day of the large spectacle is over and that what the public wants is the small and intimate production.

Then, the capacity business done by *The Thirteenth Chair* shows clearly that what the proletariat demands nowadays, is the plotty piece and that the sun of the bright-dialogue comedy has set; while the capacity business done by *A Successful Calamity* shows clearly that the number of the plotty piece is up.

You will all feel better and more able to enjoy yourselves now that a trained critical mind has put you right on this subtle point.

No review of a theatrical season would be complete without a tabulated list—or even an untabulated one—of the six best performances by unstarred actors during the past season.

---

* Editor's Note: Anna Wheaton, Marie Carroll, Edna May Oliver, Tom Powers, Hal Forde, and Stephen Maley appeared in Comstock and Elliott's production of *Oh, Boy!*, the successor to *Very Good, Eddie*, at the Princess Theatre, located on the south side of 39th Street.

The present past season—that is to say, the past season which at present is the last season—has been peculiarly rich in hot efforts by all sorts of performers. My own choice would be: 1. Anna Wheaton, in *Oh, Boy!* 2. Marie Carroll, in the piece at the Princess Theatre. 3. Edna May Oliver, in Comstock and Elliott's new musical comedy. 4. Tom Powers, in the show on the south side of 39th Street. 5. Hal Forde, in the successor to *Very Good, Eddie.* 6. Stephen Maley, in *Oh, Boy!*

You would hardly credit the agony it gives me to allude, even in passing, to the above musical mélange, but one must be honest to one's public. In case there may be any who dissent from my opinion, I append a supplementary list of those entitled to honorable mention: 1. The third sheep from the O. P. side in *The Wanderer.* 2. The trick lamp in *Magic.* 3. The pink pajamas in *You're in Love.* 4. The knife in *The Thirteenth Chair.* 5. The Confused Noise Without in *The Great Divide.* 6. Jack Merritt's hair in *Oh, Boy!*

There were few discoveries among the dramatists. Of the older playwrights, Barrie produced a new one and an ancient one, but the Shakespeare boom, so strong last year, petered out. There seems no doubt that the man, in spite of a flashy start, had not the stuff. I understand that some of his things are doing fairly well on the road. Clare Kummer, whose "Dearie" I have so frequently sung in my bath, to the annoyance of all, suddenly turned right round, dropped song-writing, and ripped a couple of hot ones right over the plate. Mr. Somerset Maugham succeeded in shocking Broadway so that the sidewalks were filled with blushing ticket-speculators.

Most of the critics have done good work during this season. As for myself, I have guided the public mind in this magazine soundly and with few errors. If it were not for the fact that nearly all the plays I praised died before my review appeared, while the ones I said would not run a week are still packing them in, I could look back to a flawless season.

As you can see, I have had a very pleasant theatrical season. The weather was uniformly fine on the nights when I went to the theatre. I was particularly fortunate in having neighbors at most of the plays who were not afflicted with coughs or a desire to explain the plot to their wives. I have shaken hands with A. L. Erlanger and been nodded to on the street by Lee Shubert. I have broadened my mind by travel on the road with a theatrical company, with the result that, if you want to get me out of New York, you will have to use dynamite.

Take it for all in all, a most satisfactory season, full of pregnant possibilities—and all that sort of thing.

Part Two
UNCOLLECTED
SHORT
STORIES

Wodehouse wrote extensively for the magazines. At first, he concentrated on what he knew best—stories for and about adolescent boys involved with sports. First published in The Public School Magazine, *and then in the prestigious* Captain, *he soon enjoyed an enormous success. This gave him the confidence to write for adults, and his reputation was enhanced by appearances in such popular magazines as the* Strand *in England and the* Saturday Evening Post *in the United States.*

For these magazines, he wrote humorous stories about romantically-entangled couples. Then he created specific characters and placed them in comedy situations. He evolved eight different series characters, with separate and distinct casts, who occasionally met in other series. The first of these was Reggie Pepper, who would eventually be transformed into the more famous Bertie Wooster. Another memorable "first" presented in this collection is the appearance of Wodehouse's first butler, Keggs, who was the prototype for his most famous creation, the magnificent Jeeves. It is proof that even in the beginning, Plum had the matter firmly in hand.

These stories represent works from the different phases in the development of his unique style. Some have been chosen for their historical value, others for their introduction of familiar characters. And some because they do not normally "fit" with the greater part of his writings, and yet they cannot be ignored. But the outstanding characteristics of the Wodehouse humor are present in all these stories.

WHEN PAPA SWORE IN
HINDUSTANI

In America, I Like You, *Mr. Wodehouse wrote about his literary beginnings: "There were so many evening papers and weekly papers and monthly magazines that you were practically sure of landing your whimsical piece somewhere or other after about say thirty-five shots."* Answers, *one of the many weekly papers available at the turn of the century, printed "When Papa Swore in Hindustani," the first of 271 short stories published by P. G. Wodehouse.*

"Sylvia!"

"Yes, papa."

"That infernal dog of yours—"

"Oh, papa!"

"Yes, that infernal dog of yours has been at my carnations again!"

Colonel Reynolds, V.C., glared sternly across the table at Miss Sylvia Reynolds, and Miss Sylvia Reynolds looked in a deprecatory manner back at Colonel Reynolds, V.C.; while the dog in question—a foppish pug—happening to meet the colonel's eye in transit, crawled unostentatiously under the sideboard, and began to wrestle with a bad conscience.

"Oh, naughty Tommy!" said Miss Reynolds mildly, in the direction of the sideboard.

"Yes, my dear," assented the colonel; "and if you could convey to him the information that if he does it once more—yes, just once more!—I shall shoot him on the spot you would be doing him a kindness." And the colonel bit a large crescent out of his toast, with all the energy and conviction of a man who has thoroughly made up his mind. "At six o'clock this morning," continued he, in a voice of gentle melancholy, "I happened to look out of my bedroom window, and saw him. He had then destroyed two of my best plants, and was commencing on a third, with every appear-

First Appearance: England—*Answers*, August 24, 1901

ance of self-satisfaction. I threw two large brushes and a boot at him."

"Oh, papa! They didn't hit him?"

"No, my dear, they did not. The brushes missed him by several yards, and the boot smashed a fourth carnation. However, I was so fortunate as to attract his attention, and he left off."

"I can't think what makes him do it. I suppose it's bones. He's got bones buried all over the garden."

"Well, if he does it again, you'll find that there will be a few more bones buried in the garden!" said the colonel grimly; and he subsided into his paper.

Sylvia loved the dog partly for its own sake, but principally for that of the giver, one Reginald Dallas, whom it had struck at an early period of their acquaintance that he and Miss Sylvia Reynolds were made for one another. On communicating this discovery to Sylvia herself he had found that her views upon the subject were identical with his own; and all would have gone well had it not been for a melancholy accident.

One day while out shooting with the colonel, with whom he was doing his best to ingratiate himself, with a view to obtaining his consent to the match, he had allowed his sporting instincts to carry him away to such a degree that, in sporting parlance, he wiped his eye badly. Now, the colonel prided himself with justice on his powers as a shot; but on this particular day he had a touch of liver, which resulted in his shooting over the birds, and under the birds, and on each side of the birds, but very rarely at the birds. Dallas being in especially good form, it was found, when the bag came to be counted, that, while he had shot seventy brace, the colonel had only managed to secure five and a half!

His bad marksmanship destroyed the last remnant of his temper. He swore for half an hour in Hindustani, and for another half-hour in English. After that he felt better. And when, at the end of dinner, Sylvia came to him with the absurd request that she might marry Mr. Reginald Dallas he did not have a fit, but merely signified in fairly moderate terms his entire and absolute refusal to think of such a thing.

This had happened a month before, and the pug, which had changed hands in the earlier days of the friendship, still remained, at the imminent risk of its life, to soothe Sylvia and madden her father.

It was generally felt that the way to find favour in the eyes of Sylvia—which were a charming blue, and well worth finding favour in—was to show an intelligent and affectionate interest in her dog. This was so up to a certain point; but no farther, for the mournful recollection of Mr. Dallas prevented her from meeting their advances in quite the spirit they could have wished.

However, they persevered, and scarcely a week went by in which Thomas was not rescued from an artfully arranged horrible fate by somebody.

But all their energy was in reality wasted, for Sylvia remembered her faithful Reggie, who corresponded vigorously every day, and refused to be put off with worthless imitations. The lovesick swains, however, could not be expected to know of this, and the rescuing of Tommy proceeded briskly, now one, now another, playing the rôle of hero.

The very day after the conversation above recorded had taken place a terrible tragedy occurred.

The colonel, returning from a poor day's shooting, observed through the mist that was beginning to rise a small form busily engaged in excavating in the precious carnation-bed. Slipping in a cartridge, he fired; and the skill which had deserted him during the day came back to him. There was a yelp; then silence. And Sylvia, rushing out from the house, found the luckless Thomas breathing his last on a heap of uprooted carnations.

The news was not long in spreading. The cook told the postman, and the postman thoughtfully handed it on to the servants at the rest of the houses on his round. By noon it was public property; and in the afternoon, at various times from two to five, nineteen young men were struck, quite independently of one another, with a brilliant idea.

The results of this idea were apparent on the following day.

"Is this all?" asked the colonel of the servant, as she brought in a couple of letters at breakfast-time.

"There's a hamper for Miss Sylvia, sir."

"A hamper, is there? Well, bring it in."

"If you please, sir, there's several of them."

"What? Several? How many are there?"

"Nineteen, sir," said Mary, restraining with some difficulty an inclination to giggle.

"Eh? What? Nineteen? Nonsense! Where are they?"

"We've put them in the coachhouse for the present, sir. And if you please, sir, cook says she thinks there's something alive in them."

"Something alive?"

"Yes, sir. And John says he thinks it's dogs, sir!"

The colonel uttered a sound that was almost a bark, and, followed by Sylvia, rushed to the coachhouse. There, sure enough, as far as the eye could reach, were the hampers; and, as they looked, a sound proceeded from one of them that was unmistakably the plaintive note of a dog that has been shut up, and is getting tired of it.

Instantly the other eighteen hampers joined in, until the whole coachhouse rang with the noise.

The colonel subsided against a wall, and began to express himself softly in Hindustani.

"Poor dears!" said Sylvia. "How stuffy they must be feeling!"

She ran to the house, and returned with a basin of water.

"Poor dears!" she said again. "You'll soon have something to drink."

She knelt down by the nearest hamper, and cut the cord that fastened it. A pug jumped out like a jack-in-the-box, and rushed to the water. Sylvia continued her work of mercy, and by the time the colonel had recovered sufficiently to be able to express his views in English, eighteen more pugs had joined their companion.

"Get out, you brute!" shouted the colonel, as a dog insinuated itself between his legs. "Sylvia, put them back again this minute! You had no business to let them out. Put them back!"

"But I can't, papa. I can't catch them."

She looked helplessly from him to the seething mass of dogs, and back again.

"Where's my gun?" began the colonel.

"Papa, don't! You couldn't be so cruel! They aren't doing any harm, poor things!"

"If I knew who sent them—"

"Perhaps there's something to show. Yes; here's a visiting-card in this hamper."

"Whose is it?" bellowed the colonel through the din.

"J. D'Arcy Henderson, The Firs," read Sylvia, at the top of her voice.

"Young blackguard!" bawled the colonel.

"I expect there's one in each of the hampers. Yes; here's another. W. K. Ross, The Elms."

The colonel came across, and began to examine the hampers with his own hand. Each hamper contained a visiting-card, and each card bore the name of a neighbour. The colonel returned to the breakfast-room, and laid the nineteen cards out in a row on the table.

"H'm!" he said, at last. "Mr. Reginald Dallas does not seem to be represented."

Sylvia said nothing.

"No; he seems not to be represented. I did not give him credit for so much sense." Then he dropped the subject, and breakfast proceeded in silence.

A young gentleman met the colonel on his walk that morning.

"Morning, colonel!" said he.

"Good-morning!" said the colonel grimly.

"Er—colonel, I—er—suppose Miss Reynolds got that dog all right?"

"To which dog do you refer?"

"It was a pug, you know. It ought to have arrived by this time."

"Yes. I am inclined to think it has. Had it any special characteristics?"

"No, I don't think so. Just an ordinary pug."

"Well, young man, if you will go to my coachhouse, you will find nineteen ordinary pugs; and if you would kindly select your beast, and shoot it, I should be much obliged."

"Nineteen?" said the other, in astonishment. "Why, are you setting up as a dog-fancier in your old age, colonel?"

This was too much for the colonel. He exploded.

"Old age! Confound your impudence! Dog-fancier! No, sir! I have not become a dog-fancier in what you are pleased to call my old age! But while there is no law to prevent a lot of dashed young puppies like yourself, sir—like yourself—sending your confounded pug-dogs to my daughter, who ought to have known better than to have let them out of their dashed hampers, I have no defence.

"Dog-fancier! Gad! Unless those dogs are removed by this time to-morrow, sir, they will go straight to the Battersea Home, where I devoutly trust they will poison them. Here are the cards of the other gentlemen who were kind enough to think that I might wish to set up for a dog-fancier in my old age. Perhaps you will kindly return them to their owners, and tell them what I have just said." And he strode off, leaving the young man in a species of trance.

"Sylvia!" said the colonel, on arriving home.

"Yes, papa."

"Do you still want to marry that Dallas fellow? Now, for Heaven's sake, don't start crying! Goodness knows I've been worried enough this morning without that. Please answer a plain question in a fairly sane manner. Do you, or do you not?"

"Of course I do, papa."

"Then you may. He's the furthest from being a fool of any of the young puppies who live about here, and he knows one end of a gun from the other. I'll write to him now."

"Dear Dallas" (wrote the colonel),—"I find, on consideration, that you are the only sensible person in the neighbourhood. I hope you will come to lunch to-day. And if you still want to marry my daughter, you may."

To which Dallas replied by return of messenger:

"Thanks for both invitations. I will."

An hour later he arrived in person, and the course of true love pulled itself together, and began to run smooth again.

A CORNER IN LINES

Mr. Wodehouse began to build his reputation by writing superb stories for the school boy. His early short stories appeared in such magazines as The Public School Magazine, The Captain, *and* Pearson's. *The three stories that follow are representative of this period in his writing life.*

Of all the useless and irritating things in this world, lines are probably the most useless and the most irritating. In fact, I only

First Appearance: England—*Pearson's*, January 1905

know of two people who ever got any good out of them. Dunstable, of Day's, was one, Linton, of Seymour's, the other. For a portion of one winter term they flourished on lines. The more there were set, the better they liked it. They would have been disappointed if masters had given up the habit of doling them out.

Dunstable was a youth of ideas. He saw far more possibilities in the routine of life at Locksley than did the majority of his contemporaries, and every now and then he made use of these possibilities in a way that caused a considerable sensation in the school.

In the ordinary way of school work, however, he was not particularly brilliant, and suffered in consequence. His chief foe was his form-master, Mr. Langridge. The feud between them had begun on Dunstable's arrival in the form two terms before, and had continued ever since. The balance of points lay with the master. The staff has ways of scoring which the school has not. This story really begins with the last day but one of the summer term. It happened that Dunstable's people were going to make their annual migration to Scotland on that day, and the Headmaster, approached on the subject both by letter and in person, saw no reason why—the examinations being over—Dunstable should not leave Locksley a day before the end of term.

He called Dunstable to his study one night after preparation.

"Your father has written to me, Dunstable," he said, "to ask that you may be allowed to go home on Wednesday instead of Thursday. I think that, under the special circumstances, there will be no objection to this. You had better see that the matron packs your boxes."

"Yes, sir," said Dunstable. "Good business," he added to himself, as he left the room.

When he got back to his own den, he began to ponder over the matter, to see if something could not be made out of it. That was Dunstable's way. He never let anything drop until he had made certain that he had exhausted all its possibilities.

Just before he went to bed he had evolved a neat little scheme for scoring off Mr. Langridge. The knowledge of his plans was confined to himself and the Headmaster. His dorm-master would imagine that he was going to stay on till the last day of term. Therefore, if he misbehaved himself in form, Mr. Langridge would set him lines in blissful ignorance of the fact that he would not be there next day to show them up. At the beginning of the following term, moreover, he would not be in Mr. Langridge's form, for he was certain of his move up.

He acted accordingly.

He spent the earlier part of Wednesday morning in breaches of the peace. Mr. Langridge, instead of pulling him up, put him on to translate; Dunstable went on to translate. As he had not prepared the lesson and was not an adept at construing unseen, his performance was poor.

After a minute and a half, the form-master wearied.

"Have you looked at this, Dunstable?" he asked.

There was a time-honoured answer to this question.

"Yes, sir," he said.

Public-school ethics do not demand that you should reply truthfully to the spirit of a question. The letter of it is all that requires attention. Dunstable had *looked* at the lesson. He was looking at it then. Masters should practise exactness of speech. A certain form at Harrow were in the habit of walking across a copy of a Latin author before morning-school. They could then say with truth that they "had been over it." This is not an isolated case.

"Go on," said Mr. Langridge.

Dunstable smiled as he did so.

Mr. Langridge was annoyed.

"What are you laughing at? What do you mean by it? Stand up. You will write out the lesson in Latin and English, and show it up to me by four this afternoon. I know what you are thinking. You imagine that because this is the end of the term you can do as you please, but you will find yourself mistaken. Mind—by four o'clock."

At four o'clock Dunstable was enjoying an excellent tea in Green Street, Park Lane, and telling his mother that he had had a most enjoyable term, marred by no unpleasantness whatever. His holidays were sweetened by the thought of Mr. Langridge's baffled wrath on discovering the true inwardness of the recent episode.

When he returned to Locksley at the beginning of the winter term, he was at once made aware that that episode was not to be considered closed. On the first evening, Mr. Day, his housemaster, sent for him.

"Well, Dunstable," he said, "where is that imposition?"
Dunstable affected ignorance.

"Please, sir, you set me no imposition."

"No, Dunstable, no." Mr. Day peered at him gravely through
his spectacles. "*I* set you no imposition; but Mr. Langridge did."

Dunstable imitated that eminent tactician, Br'er Rabbit. He "lay
low and said nuffin."

"Surely," continued Mr. Day, in tones of mild reproach, "you
did not think that you could take Mr. Langridge in?"

Dunstable rather thought he *had* taken Mr. Langridge in; but he
made no reply.

"Well," said Mr. Day. "I must set you some punishment. I shall
give the butler instructions to hand you a note from me at three
o'clock to-morrow." (The next day was a half-holiday.) "In that
note you will find indicated what I wish you to write out."

Why this comic-opera secret-society business, Dunstable wondered. Then it dawned upon him. Mr. Day wished to break up his
half-holiday thoroughly.

That afternoon Dunstable retired in disgust to his study to brood
over his wrongs; to him entered Charles, his friend, one C. J.
Linton, to wit, of Seymour's, a very hearty sportsman.

"Good," said Linton. "Didn't think I should find you in.
Thought you might have gone off somewhere as it's such a ripping
day. Tell you what we'll do. Scull a mile or two up the river and
have tea somewhere."

"I should like to awfully," said Dunstable, "but I'm afraid I
can't."

And he explained Mr. Day's ingenious scheme for preventing
him from straying that afternoon.

"Rot, isn't it," he said.

"Beastly. Wouldn't have thought old Day had it in him. But I'll
tell you what," he said. "Do the impot now, and then you'll be able
to start at three sharp, and we shall get in a good time on the river.
Day always sets the same thing. I've known scores of chaps get
impots from him, and they all had to do the Greek numerals. He's
mad on the Greek numerals. Never does anything else. You'll be as
safe as anything if you do them. Buck up, I'll help."

They accordingly sat down there and then. By three o'clock an
imposing array of sheets of foolscap covered with badly-written
Greek lay on the study table.

"That ought to be enough," said Linton, laying down his pen. "He can't set you more than we've done, I should think."

"Rummy how alike our writing looks," said Dunstable, collecting the sheets and examining them. "You can hardly tell which is which even when you know. Well, there goes three. My watch is slow, as it always is. I'll go and get that note."

Two minutes later he returned, full of abusive references to Mr. Day. The crafty pedagogue appeared to have foreseen Dunstable's attempt to circumvent him by doing the Greek numerals on the chance of his setting them. The imposition he had set in his note was ten pages of irregular verbs, and they were to be shown up in his study before five o'clock. Linton's programme for the afternoon was out of the question now. But he loyally gave up any other plans which he might have formed in order to help Dunstable with his irregular verbs. Dunstable was too disgusted with fate to be properly grateful.

"And the worst of it is," he said, as they adjourned for tea at half-past four, having deposited the verbs on Mr. Day's table, "that all those numerals will be wasted now."

"I should keep them, though," said Linton. "They may come in useful. You never know."

Towards the end of the second week of term Fate, by way of compensation, allowed Dunstable a distinct stroke of luck. Mr. Forman, the master of his new form, set him a hundred lines of Virgil, and told him to show them up next day. To Dunstable's delight, the next day passed without mention of them; and when the day after that went by, and still nothing was said, he came to the conclusion that Mr. Forman had forgotten all about them.

Which was indeed the case. Mr. Forman was engaged in editing a new edition of the "Bacchae," and was apt to be absent-minded in consequence. So Dunstable, with a glad smile, hove the lines into a cupboard in his study to keep company with the Greek numerals which he had done for Mr. Day, and went out to play fives with Linton.

Linton, curiously enough, had also had a stroke of luck in a rather similar way. He told Dunstable about it as they strolled back to the houses after their game.

"Bit of luck this afternoon," he said. "You remember Appleby setting me a hundred-and-fifty the day before yesterday? Well, I showed them up to-day, and he looked through them and chucked them into the waste-paper basket under his desk. I thought at the time I hadn't seen him muck them up at all with his pencil, which is his usual game, so after he had gone at the end of school I nipped to the basket and fished them out. They were as good as new, so I saved them up in case I get any more."

Dunstable hastened to tell of his own good fortune. Linton was impressed by the coincidence.

"I tell you what," he said, "we score either way. Because if we never get any more lines—"

Dunstable laughed.

"Yes, I know," Linton went on, "we're bound to. But even supposing we don't, what we've got in stock needn't be wasted."

"I don't see that," said Dunstable. "Going to have 'em bound in cloth and published? Or were you thinking of framing them?"

"Why, don't you see? Sell them, of course. There are dozens of chaps in the school who would be glad of a few hundred lines cheap."

"It wouldn't work. They'd be spotted."

"Rot. It's been done before, and nobody said anything. A chap in Seymour's who left last Easter sold all his stock lines by auction on the last day of term. They were Virgil mostly and Greek numerals. They sold like hot cakes. There were about five hundred of them altogether. And I happen to know that every word of them has been given up and passed all right."

"Well, I shall keep mine," said Dunstable. "I am sure to want all the lines in stock that I can get. I used to think Langridge was fairly bad in the way of impots, but Forman takes the biscuit easily. It seems to be a sort of hobby of his. You can't stop him."

But it was not until the middle of preparation that the great idea flashed upon Dunstable's mind.

It was the simplicity of the thing that took his breath away. That and its possibilities. This was the idea. Why not start a Lines Trust in the school? An agency for supplying lines at moderate rates to all who desired them? There did not seem to be a single flaw in the scheme. He and Linton between them could turn out enough material in a week to give the Trust a good working capital. And as for the risk of detection when customers came to show up the goods supplied to them, that was very slight. As has been pointed out before, there was practically one handwriting common to the whole school when it came to writing lines. It resembled the movements of a fly that had fallen into an ink-pot, and subsequently taken a little brisk exercise on a sheet of foolscap by way of restoring the circulation. Then, again, the attitude of the master to whom the lines were shown was not likely to be critical. So that everything seemed in favour of Dunstable's scheme.

Linton, to whom he confided it, was inclined to scoff at first, but when he had had the beauties of the idea explained to him at length, became an enthusiastic supporter of the scheme.

"But," he objected, "it'll take up all our time. Is it worth it? We can't spend every afternoon sweating away at impots for other people."

"It's all right," said Dunstable, "I've thought of that. We shall need to pitch in pretty hard for about a week or ten days. That will give us a good big stock, and after that if we turn out a hundred each every day it will be all right. A hundred's not much fag if you spread them over a day."

Linton admitted that this was sound, and the Locksley Lines Supplying Trust, Ltd., set to work in earnest.

It must not be supposed that the Agency left a great deal to chance. The writing of lines in advance may seem a very speculative business; but both Dunstable and Linton had had a wide experience of Locksley masters, and the methods of the same when roused, and they were thus enabled to reduce the element of chance to a minimum. They knew, for example, that Mr. Day's favourite imposition was the Greek numerals, and that in nine cases out of ten that would be what the youth who had dealings with him would need to ask for from the Lines Trust. Mr. Appleby, on the other hand, invariably set Virgil. The oldest inhabitant had never known him to depart from this custom. For the French masters extracts from the works of Victor Hugo would probably pass muster.

A week from the date of the above conversation, everyone in the school, with the exception of the prefects and the sixth form, found in his desk on arriving at his form-room a printed slip of paper. (Spiking, the stationer in the High Street, had printed it.) It was nothing less than the prospectus of the new Trust. It set forth in glowing terms the advantages offered by the agency. Dunstable had written it—he had a certain amount of skill with his pen—and Linton had suggested subtle and captivating additions. The whole presented rather a striking appearance.

The document was headed with the name of the Trust in large letters. Under this came a number of "scare headlines" such as:

SEE WHAT YOU SAVE!

NO MORE WORRY!

PEACE, PERFECT PEACE!

WHY DO LINES WHEN WE DO THEM
FOR YOU?

Then came the real prospectus:

The Locksley Lines Supplying Trust, Ltd. has been instituted to meet the growing demand for lines and other impositions. While there are masters at our public schools there will always be lines. At Locksley the crop of masters has always flourished—and still flourishes—very rankly, and the demand for lines has greatly taxed the powers of those to whom has been assigned the task of supplying them.

It is for the purpose of affording relief to these that the Lines Trust has been formed. It is proposed that all orders for lines shall be supplied out of our vast stock. Our charges are moderate, and vary between threepence and sixpence per hundred lines. The higher charge is made for Greek impositions, which, for obvious reasons, entail a greater degree of labour on our large and efficient staff of writers.

All orders, which will be promptly executed, should be forwarded to Mr. P. A Dunstable, 6 College Grounds, Locksley, or to Mr. C. J. Linton, 10 College Grounds, Locksley. *Payment must be inclosed with order, or the latter will not be executed.* Under no conditions will notes of hand or cheques be accepted as legal tender. There is no trust about us except the name.

Come in your thousands. We have lines for all. If the Trust's stock of lines were to be placed end to end it would reach part of the way to London. You pay the threepence. We do the rest."

Then a blank space, after which came a few "unsolicited testimonials":

"Lower Fifth" writes: "I was set two hundred lines of Virgil on Saturday last at one o'clock. Having laid in a supply from your agency I was enabled to show them up at five minutes past one. The master who gave me the commission was unable to restrain his admiration at the rapidity and neatness of my work. You may make what use of this you please."

"Dexter's House" writes: "Please send me one hundred (100) lines from Aeneid, Book Two. Mr. Dexter was so delighted with the last I showed him that he has asked me to do some more."

"Enthusiast" writes: "Thank you for your Greek numerals. Day took them without blinking. So beautifully were they executed that I can hardly believe even now that I did not write them myself."

* * *

There could be no doubt about the popularity of the Trust. It caught on instantly.

Nothing else was discussed in the form-rooms at the quarter to eleven interval, and in the houses after lunch it was the sole topic of conversation. Dunstable and Linton were bombarded with questions and witticisms of the near personal sort. To the latter they replied with directness, to the former evasively.

"What's it all *about?*" someone would ask, fluttering the leaflet before Dunstable's unmoved face.

"You should read it carefully," Dunstable would reply. "It's all there."

"But what are you playing at?"

"We tried to make it clear to the meanest intelligence. Sorry you can't understand it."

While at the same time Linton, in his form-room, would be explaining to excited inquirers that he was sorry, but it was impossible to reply to their query as to who was running the Trust. He was not at liberty to reveal business secrets. Suffice it that there the lines were, waiting to be bought, and he was there to sell them. So that if anybody cared to lay in a stock, large or small, according to taste, would he kindly walk up and deposit the necessary coin?

But here the public showed an unaccountable disinclination to deal. It was gratifying to have acquaintances coming up and saying admiringly: "You *are* an *ass*, you know," as if they were paying the highest of compliments—as, indeed, they probably imagined that they were. All this was magnificent, but it was not business. Dunstable and Linton felt that the whole attitude of the public towards the new enterprise was wrong. Locksley seemed to regard the Trust as a huge joke, and its prospectus as a literary *jeu d'esprit*.

In fact, it looked very much as if—from a purely commercial point of view—the great Lines Supplying Trust was going to be what is known in theatrical circles as a frost.

For two whole days the public refused to bite, and Dunstable and Linton, turning over the stacks of lines in their studies, thought gloomily that this world is no place for original enterprise.

Then things began to move.

It was quite an accident that started them. Jackson, of Dexter's, was teaing with Linton, and, as was his habit, was giving him a condensed history of his life since he last saw him. In the course of this he touched on a small encounter with M. Gaudinois which had occurred that afternoon.

"So I got two pages of 'Quatre-Vingt Treize' to write," he concluded, "for doing practically nothing."

All Jackson's impositions, according to him, were given him for doing practically nothing. Now and then he got them for doing literally nothing—when he ought to have been doing form-work.

"Done 'em?" asked Linton.

"Not yet; no," replied Jackson. "More tea, please."

"What you want to do, then," said Linton, "is to apply to the Locksley Lines Supplying Trust. That's what you must do."

"You needn't rot a chap on a painful subject," protested Jackson. "I wasn't rotting," said Linton. "Why don't you apply to the Lines Trust?"

"Then do you mean to say that there really is such a thing?" Jackson said incredulously. "Why I thought it was all a rag."

"I know you did. It's the rotten sort of thing you would think. Rag, by Jove! Look at this. Now do you understand that this is a genuine concern?

He got up and went to the cupboard which filled the space between the stove and the bookshelf. From this resting-place he extracted a great pile of manuscript and dumped it down on the table with a bang which caused a good deal of Jackson's tea to spring from its native cup on to its owner's trousers.

"When you've finished," protested Jackson, mopping himself with a handkerchief that had seen better days.

"Sorry. But look at these. What did you say your impot was? Oh, I remember. Here you are. Two pages of 'Quatre-Vingt Treize.' I don't know which two pages, but I suppose any will do."

Jackson was amazed.

"Great Scott! what a wad of stuff! When did you do it all?"

"Oh, at odd times. Dunstable's got just as much over at Day's. So you see the Trust is a jolly big show. Here are your two pages. That looks just like your scrawl, doesn't it? These would be fourpence in the ordinary way, but you can have 'em for nothing this time."

"Oh, I say," said Jackson gratefully, "that's awfully good of you."

After that the Locksley Lines Supplying Trust, Ltd. went ahead with a rush. The brilliant success which attended its first specimen —M. Gaudinois took Jackson's imposition without a murmur—promoted confidence in the public, and they rushed to buy. Orders poured in from all the houses, and by the middle of the term the organisers of the scheme were able to divide a substantial sum.

"How are you getting on round your way?" asked Linton of Dunstable at the end of the sixth week of term.

"Ripping. Selling like hot cakes."

"So are mine," said Linton. "I've almost come to the end of my stock. I ought to have written some more, but I've been a bit slack lately."

"Yes, buck up. We must keep a lot in hand."

"I say, did you hear that about Merrett in our house?" asked Linton.

"What about him?"

"Why, he tried to start a rival show. Wrote a prospectus and everything. But it didn't catch on a bit. The only chap who bought any of his lines was young Shoeblossom. He wanted a couple of hundred for Appleby. Appleby was on to them like bricks. Spotted Shoeblossom hadn't written them, and asked who had. He wouldn't say, so he got them doubled. Everyone in the house is jolly sick with Merrett. They think he ought to have owned up."

"Did that smash up Merrett's show? Is he going to turn out any more?"

"Rather not. Who'd buy 'em?"

It would have been better for the Lines Supplying Trust if Merrett had not received this crushing blow and had been allowed to carry on a rival business on legitimate lines. Locksley was conservative in its habits, and would probably have continued to support the old firm.

As it was, the baffled Merrett, a youth of vindictive nature, brooded over his defeat, and presently hit upon a scheme whereby things might be levelled up.

One afternoon, shortly before lock-up, Dunstable was surprised by the advent of Linton to his study in a bruised and dishevelled condition. One of his expressive eyes was closed and blackened. He also wore what is known in ring circles as a thick ear.

"What on earth's up?" inquired Dunstable, amazed at these phenomena. "Have you been scrapping?"

"Yes—Merrett—I won. What are you up to—writing lines? You may as well save yourself the trouble. They won't be any good."

Dunstable stared.

"The Trust's bust," said Linton.

He never wasted words in moments of emotion.

"What!"

" 'Bust' was what I said. That beast Merrett gave the show away."

"What did he do? Surely he didn't tell a master?"

"Well, he did the next thing to it. He hauled out that prospectus, and started reading it in form. I watched him do it. He kept it under the desk and made a foul row, laughing over it. Appleby couldn't help spotting him. Of course, he told him to bring him what he was reading. Up went Merrett with the prospectus."

"Was Appleby sick?"

"I don't believe he was, really. At least, he laughed when he read the thing. But he hauled me up after school and gave me a long jaw, and made me take all the lines I'd got to his house. He burnt them. I had it out with Merrett just now. He swears he didn't mean to get the thing spotted, but I knew he did."

"Where did you scrag him!"

"In the dormitory. He chucked it after the third round."

There was a knock at the door.

"Come in," shouted Dunstable.

Buxton appeared, a member of Appleby's house.

"Oh, Dunstable, Appleby wants to see you."

"All right," said Dunstable wearily.

Mr. Appleby was in facetious mood. He chaffed Dunstable genially about his prospectus, and admitted that it had amused him. Dunstable smiled without enjoyment. It was a good thing, perhaps, that Mr. Appleby saw the humorous rather than the lawless side of the Trust; but all the quips in the world could not save that institution from ruin.

Presently Mr. Appleby's manner changed. "I am a funny dog, I know," he seemed to say; "but duty is duty, and must be done."

"How many lines have you at your house, Dunstable?" he asked.

"About eight hundred, sir."

"Then you had better write me eight hundred lines, and show them up to me in this room at—shall we say at ten minutes to five? It is now a quarter to, so that you will have plenty of time."

Dunstable went, and returned five minutes later, bearing an armful of manuscript.

"I don't think I shall need to count them," said Mr. Appleby. "Kindly take them in batches of ten sheets, and tear them in half, Dunstable."

"Yes, sir."

The last sheet fluttered in two sections into the surfeited waste-paper basket.

"It's an awful waste, sir," said Dunstable regretfully.

Mr. Appleby beamed.

"We must, however," he said, "always endeavour to look on the bright side, Dunstable. The writing of these eight hundred lines will have given you a fine grip of the rhythm of Virgil, the splendid prose of Victor Hugo, and the unstudied majesty of the Greek Numerals. Good-night, Dunstable."

"Good-night, sir," said the President of the Locksley Lines Supplying Trust, Ltd.

THE AUTOGRAPH HUNTERS

Dunstable had his reasons for wishing to obtain Mr. Montagu Watson's autograph, but admiration for that gentleman's novels was not one of them.

It was nothing to him that critics considered Mr. Watson one of the most remarkable figures in English literature since Scott. If you had told him of this, he would merely have wondered in his coarse, material way how much Mr. Watson gave the critics for saying so. To the reviewer of the *Weekly Booklover* the great man's latest effort, "The Soul of Anthony Carrington" (Popgood and Grooly: 6s.) seemed "a work that speaks eloquently in every line of a genius that time cannot wither nor custom stale." To Dunstable, who got it out of the school library, where it had been placed at the request of a literary prefect, and read the first eleven pages, it seemed rot, and he said as much to the librarian on returning it.

Yet he was very anxious to get the novelist's autograph. The fact was that Mr. Day, his house-master, a man whose private life was in other ways unstained by vicious habits, collected autographs. Also Mr. Day had behaved in a square manner towards Dunstable on several occasions in the past, and Dunstable, always ready to punish bad behaviour in a master, was equally anxious to reward and foster any good trait which he might exhibit.

On the occasion of the announcement that Mr. Watson had taken the big white house near Chesterton, a couple of miles from the school, Mr. Day had expressed in Dunstable's hearing a wish

First Appearance: England—*Pearson's*, February 1905

that he could add that celebrity's signature to his collection. Dunstable had instantly determined to play the part of a benevolent Providence. He would get the autograph and present it to the house-master, as who should say, "see what comes of being good." It would be pleasant to observe the innocent joy of the recipient, his child-like triumph, and his amazement at the donor's ingenuity in securing the treasure. A touching scene—well worth the trouble involved in the quest.

And there would be trouble. For Mr. Montagu Watson was notoriously a foe to the autograph-hunter. His curt, type-written replies (signed by a secretary) had damped the ardour of scores of brave men and—more or less—fair women. A genuine Montagu Watson was a prize in the autograph market.

Dunstable was a man of action. When Mark, the boot-boy at Day's, carried his burden of letters to the post that evening there nestled among them one addressed to M. Watson, Esq., The White House, Chesterton. Looking at it casually, few of his friends would have recognised Dunstable's handwriting. For it had seemed good to that man of guile to adopt for the occasion the rôle of a backward youth of twelve years old. He thought tender years might touch Mr. Watson's heart.

This was the letter:

Dear Sir,—I am only a littel boy, but I think your books ripping. I often wonder how you think of it all. Will you please send me your ortograf? I like your books very much. I have named my white rabit Montagu after you. I punched Jones II in the eye to-day becos he didn't like your books. I have spent the only penny I have on the stampe for this letter which I might have spent on tuck. I want to be like Maltby in "The Soul of Anthony Carrington" when I grow up.

> *Your sincere reader,*
> P. A. Dunstable,

It was a little unfortunate, perhaps, that he selected Maltby as his ideal character. That gentleman was considered by critics a masterly portrait of the cynical *roué*. But it was the only name he remembered.

"Hot stuff!" said Dunstable to himself, as he closed the envelope.

"Little beast!" said Mr. Watson to himself as he opened it. It arrived by the morning post, and he never felt really himself till after breakfast.

"Here, Morrison," he said to his secretary, later in the morning: "just answer this, will you? The usual thing—thanks and most deeply grateful, y'know."

Next day the following was included in Dunstable's correspondence:

> Mr. Montagu Watson presents his compliments to Mr. P. A. Dunstable, and begs to thank him for all the kind things he says about his work in his letter of the 18th inst., for which he is deeply grateful.

"Foiled!" said Dunstable, and went off to Seymour's to see his friend Linton.

"Got any notepaper?" he asked.

"Heaps," said Linton. "Why? Want some?"

"Then get out a piece. I want to dictate a letter."

Linton stared.

"What's up? Hurt your hand?"

Dunstable explained.

"Day collects autographs, you know, and he wants Montagu Watson's badly. Pining away, and all that sort of thing. Won't smile until he gets it. I had a shot at it yesterday, and got this."

Linton inspected the document.

"So I can't send up another myself, you see."

"Why worry?"

"Oh, I'd like to put Day one up. He's not been bad this term. Come on."

"All right. Let her rip."

Dunstable let her rip.

> Dear Sir,—I cannot refrain from writing to tell you what an inestimable comfort your novels have been to me during years of sore tribulation and distress—

"Look here," interrupted Linton with decision at this point. "If you think I'm going to shove my name at the end of this rot, you're making the mistake of a lifetime."

"Of course not. You're a widow who has lost two sons in South Africa. We'll think of a good name afterwards. Ready?

"Ever since my darling Charles Herbert and Percy Lionel were taken from me in that dreadful war, I have turned for consolation to the pages of 'The Soul of Anthony Carrington' and—"

"What, another?" asked Linton.

"There's one called 'Pancakes.'"

"Sure? Sounds rummy."

"That's all right. You have to get a queer title nowadays if you want to sell a book."

"Go on, then. Jam it down."

"—and 'Pancakes.' I hate to bother you, but if you could send me your autograph I should be more grateful than words can say. Yours admiringly."

"What's a good name? How would Dorothy Maynard do?"

"You want something more aristocratic. What price Hilda Foulke-Ponsonby?"

Dunstable made no objection, and Linton signed the letter with a flourish.

They installed Mrs. Foulke-Ponsonby at Spiking's in the High Street. It was not a very likely address for a lady whose blood was presumably of the bluest, but they could think of none except that obliging stationer who would take in letters for them.

There was a letter for Mrs. Foulke-Ponsonby next day. Whatever his other defects as a correspondent, Mr. Watson was at least prompt with his responses.

Mr. Montagu Watson presented his compliments, and was deeply grateful for all the kind things Mrs. Foulke-Ponsonby had said about his work in her letter of the 19th inst. He was, however, afraid that he scarcely deserved them. Her opportunities of deriving consolation from "The Soul of Anthony Carrington" had been limited by the fact that that book had only been published ten days before: while, as for "Pancakes," to which she had referred in such flattering terms, he feared that another author must have the credit of any refreshment her bereaved spirit might have extracted from that volume, for he had written no work of such a name. His own "Pan Wakes" would, he hoped, administer an equal quantity of balm.

Mr. Secretary Morrison had slept badly on the night before he wrote this letter, and had expended some venom upon its composition.

"Sold again!" said Dunstable.

"You'd better chuck it now. It's no good," said Linton.

"I'll have another shot. Then I'll try and think of something else."

Two days later Mr. Morrison replied to Mr. Edgar Habbesham-Morley, of 3a, Green Street, Park Lane, to the effect that Mr. Montagu Watson was deeply grateful for all the kind things, etc.— 3a, Green Street was Dunstable's home address.

At this juncture the Watson-Dunstable correspondence ceases, and the relations become more personal.

On the afternoon of the twenty-third of the month, Mr. Watson, taking a meditative stroll through the wood which formed part of his property, was infuriated by the sight of a boy.

He was not a man who was fond of boys even in their proper place, and the sight of one in the middle of his wood, prancing lightly about among the nesting pheasants, stirred his never too placid mind to its depths.

He shouted.

The apparition paused.

"Here! Hi! you boy!"

"Sir?" said the stripling, with a winning smile, lifting his cap with the air of a D'Orsay.

"What business have you in my wood?"

"Not business," corrected the visitor, "pleasure."

"Come here!" shrilled the novelist.

The stranger receded coyly.

Mr. Watson advanced at the double.

His quarry dodged behind a tree.

For five minutes the great man devoted his powerful mind solely to the task of catching his visitor.

The latter, however, proved as elusive as the point of a half-formed epigram, and at the end of the five minutes he was no longer within sight.

Mr. Watson went off and addressed his keeper in terms which made that worthy envious for a week.

"It's eddication," he said subsequently to a friend at the "Cowslip Inn." "You and me couldn't talk like that. It wants eddication."

For the next few days the keeper's existence was enlivened by visits from what appeared to be a most enthusiastic bird's-nester.

By no other theory could he account for it. Only a boy with a collection to support would run such risks.

To the keeper's mind the human boy up to the age of twenty or so had no object in life except to collect eggs. After twenty, of course, he took to poaching. This was a boy of about seventeen.

On the fifth day he caught him, and conducted him into the presence of Mr. Montagu Watson.

Mr. Watson was brief and to the point. He recognised his visitor as the boy for whose benefit he had made himself stiff for two days.

The keeper added further damaging facts.

"Bin here every day, he 'as, sir, for the last week. Well, I says to myself, supposition is he'll come once too often. He'll come once too often, I says. And then, I says, I'll cotch him. And I cotched him."

The keeper's narrative style had something of the classic simplicity of Julius Caesar's.

Mr. Watson bit his pen.

"What you boys come for I can't understand," he said irritably. "You're from the school, of course?"

"Yes," said the captive.

"Well, I shall report you to your house-master. What is your name?"

"Dunstable."

"Your house?"

"Day's."

"Very good. That is all."

Dunstable retired.

His next appearance in public life was in Mr. Day's study. Mr. Day had sent for him after preparation. He held a letter in his hand, and he looked annoyed.

"Come in, Dunstable. I have just received a letter complaining of you. It seems that you have been trespassing."

"Yes, sir."

"I am surprised, Dunstable, that a sensible boy like you should have done such a foolish thing. It seems so objectless. You know how greatly the head-master dislikes any sort of friction between the school and the neighbours, and yet you deliberately trespass in Mr. Watson's wood."

"I'm very sorry, sir."

"I have had a most indignant letter from him—you may see what he says. You do not deny it?"

Dunstable ran his eye over the straggling, untidy sentences.

"No, sir. It's quite true."

"In that case I shall have to punish you severely. You will write me out the Greek numerals ten times, and show them up to me on Tuesday."

"Yes, sir."

"That will do."

At the door Dunstable paused.

"Well, Dunstable?" said Mr. Day.

"Er—I'm glad you've got his autograph after all, sir," he said. Then he closed the door.

As he was going to bed that night, Dunstable met the housemaster on the stairs.

"Dunstable," said Mr. Day.

"Yes, sir."

"On second thoughts, it would be better if, instead of the Greek numerals ten times, you wrote me the first ode of the first book of Horace. The numerals would be a little long, perhaps."

TOM, DICK, AND HARRY

This story is reminiscent of "Damon and Pythias" in Part One—an interesting example of how the same idea can be traced in two different literary forms. The note below appeared in Grand.

This story will interest and amuse all cricketers, and while from the male point of view it may serve as a good illustration of the fickleness of woman and the impossibility of forecasting what course she will take, the fair sex will find in it an equally shining proof of the colossal vanity of man.

"It's like this."

Tom Ellison sat down on the bed, and paused.

"Whack it out," said Dick Henley encouragingly.

"We're all friends here, and the password's 'Portland.' What's the matter?"

"I hate talking to a man when he's shaving. I don't want to have you cutting your head off."

"Don't worry about me. This is a safety razor. And, anyhow, what's the excitement? Going to make my flesh creep?"

Tom Ellison kicked uncomfortably at the chair he was trying to balance on one leg.

"It's so hard to explain."

"Have a dash at it."

"Well, look here, Dick, we've always been pals. What?"

"Of course we have."

"We went to the Empire last Boatrace night together—"

"And got chucked out simultaneously."

"In fact, we've always been pals. What?"

"Of course we have."

"Then, whenever there was a rag on, and a bonner in the quad, you always knew you could help yourself to my chairs."

"You had the run of mine."

"We've shared each other's baccy."

"And whisky."

"In short, we've always been pals. What?"

"Of course we have."

"Then, " said Tom Ellison, "what are you trying to cut me out for?"

"Cut you out?"

"You know what I mean. What do you think I came here for? To play cricket? Rot! I'd much rather have gone on tour with the Authentics. I came here to propose to Dolly Burn."

Dick Henley frowned.

"I wish you'd speak of her as Miss Burn," he said austerely.

"There you are, you see," said Tom with sombre triumph; "you

First Appearance: England—*Grand*, July 1905

oughtn't to have noticed a thing like that. It oughtn't to matter to you what I call her. I always think of her as Dolly."

"You've no right to."

"I shall have soon."

"I'll bet you won't."

"How much?"

"Ten to one in anything."

"Done," said Tom. "I mean," he added hastily, "don't be a fool. There are some things one can't bet on. As you ought to have known," he said primly.

"Now, look here," said Dick, "this thing has got to be settled. You say I'm trying to cut you out. I like that! We may fairly describe that as rich. As if my love were the same sort of passing fancy that yours is. You know you fall in love, as you call it, with every girl you meet."

"I don't."

"Very well. If the subject is painful we won't discuss it. Still, how about that girl you used to rave about last summer? Ethel Something?"

Tom blushed.

"A mere platonic friendship. We both collected autographs. And, if it comes to that, how about Dora Thingummy? You had enough to say about her last winter."

Dick reddened.

"We were on good terms. Nothing more. She always sliced with her brassy. So did I. It formed a sort of bond."

There was a pause.

"After all," resumed Dick, "I don't see the point of all this. Why rake up the past? You aren't writing my life."

"You started raking."

"Well, to drop that, what do you propose to do about this? You're a good chap, Tom, when you aren't making an ass of yourself; but I'm hanged if I'm going to have you interfering between me and Dolly."

"Miss Burn."

Another pause.

"Look here," said Dick. "Cards on the table. I've loved her since last Commem."

"So have I."

"We went up the Char together in a Canader. Alone."

"She also did the trip with me. No chaperone."

"Twice with me."

"Same here."

"She gave me a couple of dances at the Oriel ball."

"So she did me. She said my dancing was so much better than the average young man's."

"She told me I must have had a great deal of practice at waltzing."

"In the matter of photographs," said Tom, "she gave me one."

"Me, too."

"Do you mean 'also' or 'a brace'?" inquired Tom anxiously.

" 'Also,' " confessed Dick with reluctance.

"Signed?"

"Rather!"

A third pause.

"I tell you what it is," said Tom; "we must agree on something, or we shall both get left. All we're doing now is to confuse the poor girl. She evidently likes us both the same. What I mean is, we're both so alike that she can't possibly make a choice unless one of us chucks it. You don't feel like chucking it, Dick. What?"

"You needn't be more of an idiot than you can help."

"I only asked. So we are evidently both determined to stick to it. We shall have to toss, then, to settle which is to back out and give the other man a show."

"Toss!" shouted Dick. "For Dolly! Never!"

"But we must do something. You won't back out like a sensible man. We must settle it somehow."

"It's all right," said Dick. "I've got it. We both seem to have come here and let ourselves in for this rotten little village match, on a wicket which will probably be all holes and hillocks, simply for Dolly's sake. So it's only right that we should let the match decide this thing for us. It won't be so cold-blooded as tossing. See?"

"You mean—?"

"Whichever of us makes the bigger score today wins. The loser has to keep absolutely off the grass. Not so much as a look or a remark about the weather. Then, of course, after the winner has had his innings, if he hasn't brought the thing off, and she has chucked him, the loser can have a look in. But not a moment before. Understand?"

"All right."

"It'll give an interest to a rotten match," said Dick.

Tom rose to a point of order.

"There's one objection. You, being a stodgy sort of bat, and having a habit of sitting on the splice, always get put in first. I'm a hitter, so they generally shove me in about fourth wicket. In this sort of match the man who goes in fourth wicket is likely to be not out half a dozen at the end of the innings. Nobody stays in more than three balls. Whereas you, going in first, will have time for a decent knock before the rot starts. Follow?"

"I don't want to take any advantage of you," said Dick condescendingly. "I shan't need it. We'll see Drew after breakfast and get him to put us both in first."

The Rev. Henry Drew, cricketing curate, was the captain of the side.

Consulted on the matter after breakfast, the Rev. Henry looked grave. He was taking this match very seriously, and held decided views on the subject of managing his team.

"The point is, my dear Ellison," he said, "that I want the bowling broken a bit before you go in. Then your free, aggressive style would have a better chance. I was thinking of putting you in fourth wicket. Would not that suit you?"

"I thought so. Tell him, Dick."

"Look here, Drew," said Dick; "you'll regard what I'm going to say as said under seal of the confessional and that sort of thing, won't you?"

"I shall, of course, respect any confidence you impart to me, my dear Henley. What is this dreadful secret?"

Dick explained.

"So you see," he concluded, "it's absolutely necessary that we should start fair."

The Rev. Henry looked as disturbed as if he had suddenly detected symptoms of Pelagianism in a member of his Sunday-school class.

"Is such a contest quite—? Is it not a little—um?" he said.

"Not at all," said Dick, hastening to justify himself and friend. "We must settle the thing somehow, and neither of us will back out. If we didn't do this we should have to toss."

"Heaven forbid!" said the curate, shocked.

"Well, is it a deal? Will you put us in first?"

"Very well."

"Thanks," said Tom.

"Good of you," said Dick.

"Don't mention it," said Harry.

* * *

There are two sorts of country cricket. There is the variety you get at a country-house, where the wicket is prepared with a care as meticulous as that in fashion on any county ground; where red marl and such-like aids to smoothness have been injected into the turf all through the winter; and where the out-fielding is good and the boundaries spacious. And there is the village match, where cows are apt to stroll on to the pitch before the innings and cover-point stands up to his neck in a furze-bush.

The game which was to decide the fate of Tom and Dick belonged to the latter variety. A pitch had been mown in the middle of a meadow (kindly lent by Farmer Rollitt on condition that he should be allowed to umpire, and his eldest son Ted put on to bowl first). The team consisted of certain horny-handed sons of toil, with terrific golf-shots in the direction of square-leg, and the enemy's ranks were composed of the same material. Tom and Dick, in ordinary circumstances, would have gone in to bat in such a match with a feeling of lofty disdain, as befitting experts from the civilised world, come to teach the rustic mind what was what.

But on the present occasion the thought of all that depended on their bats induced a state of nerves which would have done credit to a test match.

"Would you mind taking first b-b-ball, old man?" said Tom.

"All r-right," said Dick. He had been on the point of making the request himself, but it would not do to let Tom see that he was nervous.

He took guard from Farmer Rollitt, and settled himself into position to face the first delivery.

Whether it is due to the pure air of the country or to daily manual toil is not known, but the fact remains that bowlers in village matches, whatever their other shortcomings, seldom fall short in the matter of speed. The present trundler, having swung his arm round like a flail, bounded to the crease and sent down a ball which hummed in the air. It pitched halfway between the wickets in a slight hollow caused by the foot of a cow and shot. Dick reached blindly forward, and the next moment his off-stump was out of the ground.

A howl of approval went up from the supporters of the enemy, lying under the trees.

Tom sat down, limp with joy. Dick out for a duck! What incredible good fortune! He began to frame in his mind epigrammatic sentences for use in the scene which would so shortly take place between Miss Dolly Burn and himself. The next man came in and played flukily but successfully through the rest of the over. "Just a single," said Tom to himself as he faced the bowler at the other end. "Just one solitary single. Miss Burn—may I call you Dolly? Do you remember that moonlight night? On the Char? In my Canadian canoe? We two?"

" 'S THAT?" shrieked bowler and wicket-keeper as one man.

Tom looked blankly at them. He had not gone within a mile and a half of the ball, he was certain. And yet—there was the umpire with his hand raised, as if he were the Pope bestowing a blessing.

He walked quickly back to the trees, flung off his pads, and began to smoke furiously.

"Well?" said a voice.

Dick was standing before him, grinning like a gargoyle.

"Of all the absolutely delirious decisions—" began Tom.

"Oh, yes," said Dick rudely, "I know all about that. Why, I could hear the click from where I was sitting. The point is, what's to be done now? We shall have to settle it on the second innings."

"If there is one."

"Oh, there'll be a second innings all right. There's another man out. On a wicket like this we shall all be out in an hour, and we'll have the other side out in another hour, and then we'll start again on this business. I shall play a big game next innings. It was only that infernal ball shooting that did me."

"And I," said Tom; "if the umpire has got over his fit of delirium tremens, or been removed to Colney Hatch, shall almost certainly make a century."

It was four o'clock by the time Tom and Dick went to the wickets for the second time. Their side had been headed by their opponents by a dozen on the first innings—68 to 56.

A splendid spirit of confidence animated the two batsmen. The umpire who had effected Tom's downfall in the first innings had since received a hard drive in the small of the back as he turned coyly away to avoid the ball, and was now being massaged by strong men in the taproom of the village inn. It was the sort of occurrence, said Tom, which proved once and for all the existence of an all-seeing, benevolent Providence.

As for Dick, he had smoothed out a few of the more important mountain-ranges which marred the smoothness of the wicket, and was feeling that all was right with the world.

The pair started well. The demon bowler of the enemy, having been fêted considerably under the trees by enthusiastic admirers during the innings of his side, was a little incoherent in his deliveries. Four full-pitches did he send down to Dick in his first over, and Dick had placed 16 to his credit before Tom, who had had to look on anxiously, had opened his account. Dick was a slow scorer as a rule, but he knew a full-pitch to leg when he saw one.

From his place at the other crease Tom could see Miss Burn and her mother sitting under the trees, watching the game.

The sight nerved him. By the time he had played through his first over he had reduced Dick's lead by half. An oyster would have hit out in such circumstances, and Tom was always an aggressive batsman. By the end of the third over the scores were level. Each had made 20.

Enthusiasm ran high amongst the spectators, or such of them as were natives of the village. Such a stand for the first wicket had not been seen in all the matches ever played in the neighbourhood. When Tom, with a nice straight drive (which should have been a 4, but was stopped by a cow and turned into a single), brought up the century, small boys burst buttons and octogenarians wept like babes.

The bowling was collared. The demon had long since retired grumbling to the deep field. Weird trundlers, with actions like nothing else on earth, had been tried, had fired their ringing shot, and passed. One individual had gone on with lobs, to the acute delight of everybody except the fieldsmen who had to retrieve the balls and the above-mentioned cow. And still Tom and Dick stayed in and smote, while in the west the sun slowly sank.

The Rev. Henry looked anxious. It was magnificent, but it must not be overdone. A little more and they would not have time to get the foe out for the second time. In which case the latter would win on the first innings. And this thought was as gall to him.

He walked out and addressed the rival captain.

"I think," said he, "we will close our innings."

Tom and Dick made two bee-lines for the scorer and waited palpitatingly for the verdict.

"What's my score?" panted Tom.

"Fifty-fower, sur."

"And mine?" gasped Dick.

"Fifty-fower, too, sur."

* * *

"You see, my dear fellows," said the Rev. Henry when they had finished—and his voice was like unto oil that is poured into a wound—"we had to win this match, and if you had gone on batting we should not have had time to get them out. As it is, we shall have to hurry."

"But, hang it—" said Tom.

"But, look here—" said Dick.

"Yes?"

"What on earth are we to do?" said Tom.

"We're in precisely the same hole as we were before," said Dick.

"We don't know how to manage it."

"We're absolutely bunkered."

"Our competition, you see."

"About Miss Burn, don't you know."

"Which is to propose first?"

"We can't settle it."

The Rev. Henry smiled a faint, saintly smile and raised a protesting hand.

"My advice," he said, "is that both of you should refrain from proposing."

"What?" said Dick.

"*Wha-at?*" said Tom.

"You see," purred the Rev. Henry, "you are both very young fellows. Probably you do not know your own minds. You take these things too seri—"

"Now, look here," said Tom.

"None of that rot," said Dick.

"I shall propose tonight."

"I shall propose this evening."

"I shouldn't," said the Rev. Henry. "The fact is—"

"Well?"

"Well?"

"I didn't tell you before, for fear it should put you off your game; but Miss Burn is engaged already, and has been for three days."

The two rivals started.

"Engaged!" cried Tom.

"Whom to?" hissed Dick.

"Me," murmured Harry.

THE GOOD ANGEL

There is a firm which is noted for its having fifty-seven varieties of food, and there is an ice cream manufacturer who advertises twenty-eight flavors. The Wodehouse trademark is the butler, of whom there are an infinite number. Jeeves became the most celebrated, but the first of the long and illustrious line was Keggs, who made his debut in this story.

Any man under thirty years of age who tells you he is not afraid of an English butler lies. He may not show his fear. Outwardly he may be brave—aggressive even, perhaps to the extent of calling the great man "Here!" or "Hi!" But, in his heart, when he meets that cold, blue, introspective eye, he quakes.

The effect that Keggs, the butler at the Keiths', had on Martin Rossiter was to make him feel as if he had been caught laughing in a cathedral. He fought against the feeling. He asked himself who Keggs was, anyway; and replied defiantly that Keggs was a Menial —and an overfed Menial. But all the while he knew that logic was useless.

When the Keiths had invited him to their country home he had been delighted. They were among his oldest friends. He liked Mr.

First Appearance: England—*Strand*, February 1910

Keith. He liked Mrs. Keith. He loved Elsa Keith, and had done so from boyhood.

But things had gone wrong. As he leaned out of his bedroom window at the end of the first week, preparatory to dressing for dinner, he was more than half inclined to make some excuse and get right out of the place next day. The bland dignity of Keggs had taken all the heart out of him.

Nor was it Keggs alone who had driven his thoughts towards flight. Keggs was merely a passive evil, like toothache or a rainy day. What had begun actively to make the place impossible was a perfectly pestilential young man of the name of Barstowe.

The house-party at the Keiths had originally been, from Martin's view-point, almost ideal. The rest of the men were of the speechless, moustache-tugging breed. They had come to shoot, and they shot. When they were not shooting they congregated in the billiard-room and devoted their powerful intellects exclusively to snooker-pool, leaving Martin free to talk undisturbed to Elsa. He had been doing this for five days with great contentment when Aubrey Barstowe arrived. Mrs. Keith had developed of late leanings towards culture. In her town house a charge of small-shot, fired in any direction on a Thursday afternoon, could not have failed to bring down a poet, a novelist, or a painter. Aubrey Barstowe, author of *The Soul's Eclipse* and other poems, was a constant member of the crowd. A youth of insinuating manners, he had appealed to Mrs. Keith from the start; and unfortunately the virus had extended to Elsa. Many a pleasant, sunshiny Thursday afternoon had been poisoned for Martin by the sight of Aubrey and Elsa together on a distant settee, matching temperaments.

The rest is too painful. It was a rout. The poet did not shoot, so that when Martin returned of an evening his rival was about five hours of soul-to-soul talk up and only two to play. And those two, the after-dinner hours, which had once been the hours for which Martin had lived, were pure torture.

So engrossed was he with his thoughts that the first intimation he had that he was not alone in the room was a genteel cough. Behind him, holding a small can, was Keggs.

"Your 'ot water, sir," said the butler, austerely but not unkindly.

Keggs was a man—one must use that word, though it seems

grossly inadequate—of medium height, pigeon-toed at the base, bulgy half-way up, and bald at the apex. His manner was restrained and dignified, his voice soft and grave.

But it was his eye that quelled Martin. That cold, blue, dukes-have-treated-me-as-an-elder-brother-eye.

He fixed it upon him now, as he added, placing the can on the floor. "It is Frederick's duty, but to-night I hundertook it."

Martin had no answer. He was dazed. Keggs had spoken with the proud humility of an emperor compelled by misfortune to shine shoes.

"Might I have a word with you, sir?"

"Ye-e-ss, yes," stammered Martin. "Won't you take a—I mean, yes, certainly."

"It is perhaps a liberty," began Keggs. He paused, and raked Martin with the eye that had rested on dining dukes.

"Not at all," said Martin, hurriedly.

"I should like," went on Keggs, bowing, "to speak to you on a somewhat intimate subject—Miss Elsa."

Martin's eyes and mouth opened slowly.

"You are going the wrong way to work, if you will allow me to say so, sir."

Martin's jaw dropped another inch.

"Wha-a—"

"Women, sir," proceeded Keggs, "young ladies—are peculiar. I have had, if I may say so, certain hopportunities of observing their ways. Miss Elsa reminds me in some respects of Lady Angelica Fendall, whom I had the honour of knowing when I was butler to her father, Lord Stockleigh. Her ladyship was hinclined to be romantic. She was fond of poetry, like Miss Elsa. She would sit by the hour, sir, listening to young Mr. Knox reading Tennyson, which was no part of his duties, he being employed by his lordship to teach Lord Bertie Latin and Greek and what not. You may have noticed, sir, that young ladies is often took by Tennyson, hespecially in the summer-time. Mr. Barstowe was reading Tennyson to Miss Elsa in the 'all when I passed through just now. *The Princess*, if I am not mistaken."

"I don't know what the thing was," groaned Martin. "She seemed to be enjoying it."

"Lady Angelica was greatly addicted to *The Princess*. Young Mr. Knox was reading portions of that poem to her when his lordship come upon them. Most rashly his lordship made a public hexposé and packed Mr. Knox off next day. It was not my place to volunteer advice, but I could have told him what would happen. Two days later her ladyship slips away to London early in the morning, and they're married at a registry-office. That is why I say that you are going the wrong way to work with Miss Elsa, sir. With certain types of 'igh-spirited young lady hopposition is useless. Now, when Mr. Barstowe was reading to Miss Elsa on the occasion to which I 'ave alluded, you was sitting by, trying to engage her attention. It's not the way, sir. You should leave them alone together. Let her see so much of him, and nobody else but him, that she will grow tired of him. Fondness for poetry, sir, is very much like the whisky 'abit. You can't cure a man what has got that by hopposition. Now, if you will permit me to offer a word of advice, sir, I say, let Miss Elsa 'ave all the poetry she wants."

Martin was conscious of but one coherent feeling at the conclusion of this address, and that was one of amazed gratitude. A lesser man who had entered his room and begun to discuss his private affairs would have had reason to retire with some speed; but that Keggs should descend from his pedestal and interest himself in such lowly matters was a different thing altogether.

"I'm very much obliged—" he was stammering, when the butler raised a deprecatory hand.

"My interest in the matter," he said, smoothly, "is not entirely haltruistic. For some years back, in fact, since Miss Elsa came out, we have had a matrimonial sweepstake in the servants' hall at each house-party. The names of the gentlemen in the party are placed in a hat and drawn in due course. Should Miss Elsa become engaged to any member of the party, the pool goes to the drawer of his name. Should no engagement occur, the money remains in my charge until the following year, when it is added to the new pool. Hitherto I have 'ad the misfortune to draw nothing but married gentlemen, but on this occasion I have secured you, sir. And I may tell you, sir," he added, with stately courtesy, "that, in the opinion of the servants' hall, your chances are 'ighly fancied—very 'ighly. The pool has now reached considerable proportions, and, 'aving had certain losses on the Turf very recent, I am extremely anxious to win it. So I thought, if I might take the liberty, sir, I would place my knowledge of the sex at your disposal. You will find it sound in every respect. That is all. Thank you, sir."

Martin's feelings had undergone a complete revulsion. In the last few minutes the butler had shed his wings and grown horns, cloven feet, and a forked tail. His rage deprived him of words. He could only gurgle.

"Don't thank me, sir," said the butler, indulgently. "I ask no thanks. We are working together for a common hobject, and any little 'elp I can provide is given freely."

"You old scoundrel!" shouted Martin, his wrath prevailing even against that blue eye. "You have the insolence to come to me and—"

He stopped. The thought of these hounds, these demons, coolly gossiping and speculating below stairs about Elsa, making her the subject of little sporting flutters to relieve the monotony of country life, choked him.

"I shall tell Mr. Keith," he said.

The butler shook his bald head gravely.

"I shouldn't, sir. It is a 'ighly fantastic story, and I don't think he would believe it."

"Then I'll— Oh, get out!"

Keggs bowed deferentially.

"If you wish it, sir," he said, "I will withdraw. If I may make the suggestion, sir, I think you should commence to dress. Dinner will be served in a few minutes. Thank you, sir."

He passed softly out of the room.

It was more as a demonstration of defiance against Keggs than because he really hoped that anything would come of it that Martin approached Elsa next morning after breakfast. Elsa was strolling on the terrace in front of the house with the bard, but Martin broke in on the conference with the dogged determination of a steam-drill.

"Coming out with the guns today, Elsa?" he said.

She raised her eyes. There was an absent look in them.

"The guns?" she said. "Oh, no; I hate watching men shoot."

"You used to like it."

"I used to like dolls," she said, impatiently.

Mr. Barstowe gave tongue. He was a slim, tall, sickeningly beautiful young man, with large, dark eyes, full of expression.

"We develop," he said. "The years go by, and we develop. Our souls expand—timidly at first, like little, half-fledged birds stealing out from the—"

"I don't know that I'm so set on shooting to-day, myself," said Martin. "Will you come round the links?"

"I am going out in the motor with Mr. Barstowe," said Elsa.

"The motor!" cried Mr. Barstowe. "Ah, Rossiter, that is the very poetry of motion. I never ride in a motor-car without those words of Shakespeare's ringing in my mind: 'I'll put a girdle round about the earth in forty minutes.' "

"I shouldn't give way to that sort of thing if I were you," said Martin. "The police are pretty down on road-hogging in these parts."

"Mr. Barstowe was speaking figuratively," said Elsa, with disdain.

"Was he?" grunted Martin, whose sorrows were tending to make him every day more like a sulky schoolboy. "I'm afraid I haven't a poetic soul."

"I'm afraid you haven't," said Elsa.

There was a brief silence. A bird made itself heard in a neighbouring tree.

" 'The moan of doves in immemorial elms,' " quoted Mr. Barstowe, softly.

"Only it happens to be a crow in a beech," said Martin, as the bird flew out.

Elsa's chin tilted itself in scorn. Martin turned on his heel and walked away.

"It's the wrong way, sir; it's the wrong way," said a voice. "I was hobserving you from a window, sir. It's Lady Angelica over again. Hopposition is useless, believe me, sir."

Martin faced round, flushed and wrathful. The butler went on, unmoved: "Miss Elsa is going for a ride in the car to-day, sir."

"I know that."

"Uncommonly tricky things, these motor-cars. I was saying so to Robert, the chauffeur, just as soon as I 'eard Miss Elsa was going out with Mr. Barstowe. I said, 'Roberts, these cars is tricky; break down when you're twenty miles from hanywhere as soon as look at you. Roberts,' I said, slipping him a sovereign, ' 'ow awful it would be if the car should break down twenty miles from hanywhere today!' "

Martin stared.

"You bribed Roberts to—"

"Sir! I gave Roberts the sovereign because I am sorry for him. He is a poor man, and has a wife and family to support."

"Very well," said Martin, sternly; "I shall go and warn Miss Keith."

"Warn her, sir!"

"I shall tell her that you have bribed Roberts to make the car break down so that—"

Keggs shook his head.

"I fear she would hardly credit the statement, sir. She might even think that you was trying to keep her from going for your own pussonal ends."

"I believe you're the devil," said Martin.

"I 'ope you will come to look on me, sir," said Keggs, unctuously, "as your good hangel."

Martin shot abominably that day, and, coming home in the evening gloomy and savage, went straight to his room, and did not reappear till dinner-time. Elsa had been taken in by one of the moustache-tuggers. Martin found himself seated on her other side. It was so pleasant to be near her, and to feel that the bard was away at the other end of the table, that for the moment his spirits revived.

"Well, how did you like the ride?" he asked, with a smile. "Did you put that girdle round the world?"

She looked at him—once. The next moment he had an uninterrupted view of her shoulder, and heard the sound of her voice as she prattled gaily to the man on her other side.

His heart gave a sudden bound. He understood now. The demon butler had had his wicked way. Good heavens! She had thought he was taunting her! He must explain at once. He—

"Hock or sherry, sir?"

He looked up into Keggs's expressionless eyes. The butler was wearing his on-duty mask. There was no sign of triumph in his face.

"Oh, sherry. I mean hock. No, sherry. Neither."

This was awful. He must put this right.

"Elsa," he said.

She was engrossed in her conversation with her neighbour·

From down the table in a sudden lull in the talk came the voice of Mr. Barstowe. He seemed to be in the middle of a narrative.

"Fortunately," he was saying, "I had with me a volume of Shelley, and one of my own little efforts. I had read Miss Keith the whole of the latter and much of the former before the chauffeur announced that it was once more possible—"

"Elsa," said the wretched man, "I had no idea—you don't think—"

She turned to him.

"I beg your pardon?" she said, very sweetly.

"I swear I didn't know—I mean, I'd forgotten—I mean—"

She wrinkled her forehead.

"I'm really afraid I don't understand."

"I mean, about the car breaking down."

"The car? Oh, yes. Yes, it broke down. We were delayed quite a little while. Mr. Barstowe read me some of his poems. It was perfectly lovely. I was quite sorry when Roberts told us we could go on again. But do you really mean to tell me, Mr. Lambert, that you—"

And once more the world became all shoulder.

When the men trailed into the presence of the ladies for that brief séance on which etiquette insisted before permitting the stampede to the billiard-room Elsa was not to be seen.

"Elsa?" said Mrs. Keith in answer to Martin's question. "She has gone to bed. The poor child has a headache. I am afraid she had a tiring day."

There was an early start for the guns next morning, and as Elsa did not appear at breakfast Martin had to leave without seeing her. His shooting was even worse than it had been on the previous day.

It was not till late in the evening that the party returned to the house. Martin, on the way to his room, met Mrs. Keith on the stairs. She appeared somewhat agitated.

"Oh, Martin," she said, "I'm so glad you're back. Have you seen anything of Elsa?"

"Elsa?"

"Wasn't she with the guns?"

"With the guns?" said Martin, puzzled. "No."

"I have seen nothing of her all day. I'm getting worried. I can't think what can have happened to her. Are you sure she wasn't with the guns?"

"Absolutely certain. Didn't she come in to lunch?"

"No.

"Tom," she said, as Mr. Keith came up, "I'm so worried about Elsa. I haven't seen her all day. I thought she must be out with the guns."

Mr. Keith was a man who had built up a large fortune mainly by consistently refusing to allow anything to agitate him. He carried this policy into private life.

"Wasn't she in at lunch?" he asked, placidly.

"I tell you I haven't seen her all day. She breakfasted in her room—"

"Late?"

"Yes. She was tired, poor girl."

"If she breakfasted late," said Mr. Keith, "she wouldn't need any lunch. She's gone for a stroll somewhere."

"Would you put back dinner, do you think?" inquired Mrs. Keith, anxiously.

"I am not good at riddles," said Mr. Keith, comfortably, "but I can answer that one. I would not put back dinner. I would not put back dinner for the King."

Elsa did not come back for dinner. Nor was hers the only vacant place. Mr. Barstowe had also vanished. Even Mr. Keith's calm was momentarily ruffled by this discovery. The poet was not a favourite of his—it was only reluctantly that he had consented to his being invited at all; and the presumption being that when two members of a house-party disappear simultaneously they are likely to be spending the time in each other's society, he was annoyed. Elsa was not the girl to make a fool of herself, of course, but—. He was unwontedly silent at dinner.

Mrs. Keith's anxiety displayed itself differently. She was frankly worried, and mentioned it. By the time the fish had been reached conversation at the table had fixed itself definitely on the one topic.

"It isn't the car this time, at any rate," said Mr. Keith. "It hasn't been out to-day."

"I can't understand it," said Mrs. Keith for the twentieth time. And that was the farthest point reached in the investigation of the mystery.

By the time dinner was over a spirit of unrest was abroad. The company sat about in uneasy groups. Snooker-pool was, if not forgotten, at any rate shelved. Somebody suggested search-parties, and one or two of the moustache-tuggers wandered rather aimlessly out into the darkness.

Martin was standing in the porch with Mr. Keith when Keggs approached. As his eyes lit on him, Martin was conscious of a sudden solidifying of the vague suspicion which had been forming in his mind. And yet that suspicion seemed so wild. How could Keggs, with the worst intentions, have had anything to do with this? He could not forcibly have abducted the missing pair and kept them under lock and key. He could not have stunned them and left them in a ditch. Nevertheless, looking at him standing there in his attitude of deferential dignity, with the light from the open door shining on his bald head, Martin felt perfectly certain that he had in some mysterious fashion engineered the whole thing.

"Might I have a word, sir, if you are at leisure?"

"Well, Keggs?"

"Miss Elsa, sir."

"Yes?"

Keggs's voice took on a sympathetic softness.

"It was not my place, sir, to make any remark while in the dining-room, but I could not 'elp but hoverhear the conversation. I gathered from remarks that was passed that you was somewhat hat a loss to account for Miss Elsa's non-appearance, sir."

Mr. Keith laughed shortly.

"You gathered that, eh?"

Keggs bowed.

"I think, sir, that possibly I may be hable to throw light on the matter."

"What!" cried Mr. Keith. "Great Scott, man! Then why didn't you say so at the time? Where is she?"

"It was not my place, sir, to henter into the conversation of the dinner-table," said the butler, with a touch of reproof. "If I might speak now, sir?"

Mr. Keith clutched at his forehead.

"Heavens above! Do you want a signed permit to tell me where my daughter is? Get on, man, get on!"

"I think it 'ighly possible, sir, that Miss Elsa and Mr. Barstowe may be on the hisland in the lake, sir."

About half a mile from the house was a picturesque strip of water, some fifteen hundred yards in width and a little less in length, in the centre of which stood a small and densely wooded island. It was a favourite haunt of visitors at the house when there was nothing else to engage their attention, but during the past week, with shooting to fill up the days, it had been neglected.

"On the island?" said Mr. Keith. "What put that idea into your head?"

"I 'appened to be rowing on the lake this morning, sir. I frequently row of a morning, sir, when there are no duties to detain me in the 'ouse. I find the hexercise hadmirable for the 'ealth. I walk briskly to the boat-'ouse, and—"

"Yes, yes. I don't want a schedule of your daily exercises. Cut out the athletic reminiscences and come to the point."

"As I was rowing on the lake this morning, sir, I 'appened to see a boat 'itched up to a tree on the hisland. I think that possibly Miss Elsa and Mr. Barstowe might 'ave taken a row out there. Mr. Barstowe would wish to see the hisland, sir, bein' romantic."

"But you say you saw the boat there this morning?"

"Yes, sir."

"Well, it doesn't take all day to explore a small island. What's kept them all this while?"

"It is possible, sir, that the rope might not have 'eld. Mr. Barstowe, if I might say so, sir, is one of those himpetuous literary pussons, and possibly he homitted to see that the knot was hadequately tied. Or"—his eye, grave and inscrutable, rested for a moment on Martin's—"some party might 'ave come along and huntied it a-puppus."

"Untied it on purpose?" said Mr. Keith. "What on earth for?"

Keggs shook his head deprecatingly, as one who, realising his limitations, declines to attempt to probe the hidden sources of human actions.

"I thought it right, sir, to let you know," he said.

"Right? I should say so. If Elsa has been kept starving all day on that island by that long-haired—. Here, come along, Martin."

He dashed off excitedly into the night. Martin remained for a moment gazing fixedly at the butler.

"I 'ope, sir," said Keggs, cordially, "that my hinformation will prove of genuine hassistance."

"Do you know what I should like to do to you?" said Martin slowly.

"I think I 'ear Mr. Keith calling you, sir."

"I should like to take you by the scruff of your neck and—"

"There, sir! Didn't you 'ear 'im then? Quite distinct it was."

Martin gave up the struggle with a sense of blank futility. What could you do with a man like this? It was like quarrelling with Westminster Abbey.

"I should 'urry, sir," suggested Keggs, respectfully. "I think Mr. Keith must have met with some haccident."

His surmise proved correct. When Martin came up he found his host seated on the ground in evident pain.

"Twisted my ankle in a hole," he explained, briefly. "Give me an arm back to the house, there's a good fellow, and then run on down to the lake and see if what Keggs said is true."

Martin did as requested—so far, that is to say, as the first half of the commission was concerned. As regarded the second, he took it upon himself to make certain changes. Having seen Mr. Keith to his room, he put the fitting-out of the relief ship into the hands of a group of his fellow-guests whom he discovered in the porch. Elsa's feeling towards her rescuer might be one of unmixed gratitude; but it might, on the other hand, be one of resentment. He did not wish her to connect him in her mind with the episode in any way whatsoever. Martin had once released a dog from a trap, and the dog had bitten him. He had been on an errand of mercy, but the dog had connected him with his sufferings and acted accordingly. It occurred to Martin that Elsa's frame of mind would be uncommonly like that dog's.

The rescue-party set off. Martin lit a cigarette, and waited in the porch.

It seemed a very long time before anything happened, but at last, as he was lighting his fifth cigarette, there came from the darkness the sound of voices. They drew nearer. Someone shouted:

"It's all right. We've found them."

Martin threw away his cigarette and went indoors.

Elsa Keith sat up as her mother came into the room. Two nights and a day had passed since she had taken to her bed.

"How are you feeling to-day, dear?"

"Has he gone, mother?"

"Who?"

"Mr. Barstowe?"

"Yes, dear. He left this morning. He said he had business with his publisher in London."

"Then I can get up," said Elsa, thankfully.

"I think you're a little hard on poor Mr. Barstowe, Elsa. It was just an accident, you know. It was not his fault that the boat slipped away."

"It was, it was, it *was!*" cried Elsa, thumping the pillow malignantly. "I believe he did it on purpose, so that he could read me his horrid poetry without my having a chance to escape. I believe that's the only way he can get people to listen to it."

"But you used to like it, darling. You said he had such a musical voice."

"Musical voice!" The pillow became a shapeless heap. "Mother, it was like a nightmare! If I had seen him again I should have had hysterics. It was *awful!* If he had been even the least bit upset himself I think I could have borne up. But he *enjoyed* it! He *revelled* in it! He said it was like Omar Khayyam in the Wilderness and Shelley's *Epipsychidion*, whatever that is; and he prattled on and on and read and read and read till my head began to split. Mother"— her voice sank to a whisper—"I hit him!"

"Elsa!"

"I did!" she went on, defiantly. "I hit him as hard as I could, and he—he"—she broke off into a little gurgle of laughter—"he tripped over a bush and fell right down; and I wasn't a bit ashamed. I didn't think it unladylike or anything. I was just as proud as I could be. And it stopped him talking."

"But, Elsa, *dear!* Why?"

"The sun had just gone down; and it was a lovely sunset, and the sky looked like a great, beautiful slice of underdone beef; and I said so to him, and he said, sniffily, that he was afraid he didn't see the resemblance. And I asked him if he wasn't starving. And he said no, because as a rule all that he needed was a little ripe fruit. And that was when I hit him."

"Elsa!"

"Oh, I know it was awfully wrong, but I just had to. And now I'll get up. It looks lovely out."

Martin had not gone out with the guns that day. Mrs. Keith had assured him that there was nothing wrong with Elsa, that she was only tired, but he was anxious, and had remained at home, where bulletins could reach him. As he was returning from a stroll in the grounds he heard his name called, and saw Elsa lying in the hammock under the trees near the terrace.

"Why, Martin, why aren't you out with the guns?" she said.

"I wanted to be on the spot so that I could hear how you were."

"How nice of you! Why don't you sit down?"

"May I?"

Elsa fluttered the pages of her magazine.

"You know, you're a very restful person, Martin. You're so big and outdoory. How would you like to read to me for a while? I feel so lazy."

Martin took the magazine.

"What shall I read? Here's a poem by—"

Elsa shuddered.

"Oh, please, no," she cried. "I couldn't bear it. I'll tell you what I should love—the advertisements. There's one about sardines. I started it, and it seemed splendid. It's at the back somewhere."

"Is this it—Langley and Fielding's sardines?"

"That's it."

Martin began to read.

" 'Langley and Fielding's sardines. When you want the daintiest, most delicious sardines, go to your grocer and say, "Langley and Fielding's, please!" You will then be sure of having the finest Norwegian smoked sardines, packed in the purest olive oil.' "

Elsa was sitting with her eyes closed and a soft smile of pleasure curving her mouth.

"Go on," she said, dreamily.

" 'Nothing nicer,' " resumed Martin, with an added touch of eloquence as the theme began to develop, " 'for breakfast, lunch, or supper. Probably your grocer stocks them. Ask him. If he does not, write to us. Price fivepence per tin. The best sardines and the best oil!' "

"Isn't it *lovely?*" she murmured.

Her hand, as it swung, touched his. He held it. She opened her eyes.

"Don't stop reading," she said. "I never heard anything so soothing."

"Elsa!"

He bent towards her. She smiled at him. Her eyes were dancing.

"Elsa, I—"

"Mr. Keith," said a quiet voice, "desired me to say—"

Martin started away. He glared up furiously. Gazing down upon them stood Keggs. The butler's face was shining with a gentle benevolence.

"Mr. Keith desired me to say that he would be glad if Miss Elsa would come and sit with him for a while."

"I'll come at once," said Elsa, stepping from the hammock.

The butler bowed respectfully and turned away. They stood watching him as he moved across the terrace.

"What a saintly old man Keggs looks," said Elsa. "Don't you think so? He looks as if he had never even thought of doing anything he shouldn't. I wonder if he ever has?"

"I wonder!" said Martin.

"He looks like a stout angel. What were you saying, Martin, when he came up?"

THE MAN UPSTAIRS

It was after he quit The Globe *and settled down to write in New York that P. G. Wodehouse started to develop his particular style in the field of humor. But, as the magazines were more interested in the romantic story, he combined the two by writing humorous romances.*

There were three distinct stages in the evolution of Annette Brougham's attitude towards the knocking in the room above. In the beginning it had been merely a vague discomfort. Absorbed in the composition of her waltz, she had heard it almost subconsciously. The second stage set in when it became a physical pain like red-hot pincers wrenching her mind from her music. Finally,

First Appearance: England—*Strand*, March 1910

with a thrill of indignation, she knew it for what it was—an insult.
The unseen brute disliked her playing, and was intimating his
views with a boot-heel.

Defiantly, with her foot on the loud pedal, she struck—almost
slapped—the keys once more.

"Bang!" from the room above. "Bang! Bang!"

Annette rose. Her face was pink, her chin tilted. Her eyes spar-
kled with the light of battle. She left the room and started to mount
the stairs. No spectator, however just, could have helped feeling a
pang of pity for the wretched man who stood unconscious of imminent doom, possibly even triumphant, behind the door at which
she was on the point of tapping.

"Come in!" cried the voice, rather a pleasant voice; but what is
a pleasant voice if the soul be vile?

Annette went in. The room was a typical Chelsea studio, scant-
ily furnished and lacking a carpet. In the centre was an easel,
behind which were visible a pair of trousered legs. A cloud of grey
smoke was curling up over the top of the easel.

"I beg your pardon," began Annette.

"I don't want any models at present," said the Brute. "Leave
your card on the table."

"I am not a model," said Annette, coldly. "I merely came—"

At this the Brute emerged from his fortifications and, removing
his pipe from his mouth, jerked his chair out into the open.

"I beg your pardon," he said. "Won't you sit down?"

How reckless is Nature in the distribution of her gifts! Not only
had this black-hearted knocker on floors a pleasant voice, but, in
addition, a pleasing exterior. He was slightly dishevelled at the
moment, and his hair stood up in a disordered mop; but in spite of
these drawbacks, he was quite passably good-looking. Annette admitted this. Though wrathful, she was fair.

"I thought it was another model," he explained. "They've been
coming in at the rate of ten an hour ever since I settled here. I
didn't object at first, but after about the eightieth child of sunny
Italy had shown up it began to get on my nerves."

Annette waited coldly till he had finished.

"I am sorry," she said, in a this-is-where-you-get-yours voice, "if
my playing disturbed you."

One would have thought nobody but an Eskimo wearing his furs and winter under-clothing could have withstood the iciness of her manner; but the Brute did not freeze.

"I am sorry," repeated Annette, well below zero, "if my playing disturbed you. I live in the room below, and I heard you knocking."

"No, no," protested the young man, affably; "I like it. Really I do."

"Then why knock on the floor?" said Annette, turning to go. "It is so bad for my ceiling," she said over her shoulder. "I thought you would not mind my mentioning it. Good afternoon."

"No; but one moment. Don't go."

She stopped. He was surveying her with a friendly smile. She noticed most reluctantly that he had a nice smile. His composure began to enrage her more and more. Long ere this he should have been writhing at her feet in the dust, crushed and abject.

"You see," he said, "I'm awfully sorry, but it's like this. I love music, but what I mean is, you weren't playing a *tune*. It was just the same bit over and over again."

"I was trying to get a phrase," said Annette, with dignity, but less coldly. In spite of herself she was beginning to thaw. There was something singularly attractive about this shock-headed youth.

"A phrase?"

"Of music. For my waltz. I am composing a waltz."

A look of such unqualified admiration overspread the young man's face that the last remnants of the ice-pack melted. For the first time since they had met Annette found herself positively liking this blackguardly floor-smiter.

"Can you compose music?" he said, impressed.

"I have written one or two songs."

"It must be great to be able to do things—artistic things, I mean, like composing."

"Well, you do, don't you? You paint."

The young man shook his head with a cheerful grin.

"I fancy," he said, "I should make a pretty good housepainter. I want scope. Canvas seems to cramp me."

It seemed to cause him no discomfort. He appeared rather amused than otherwise.

"Let me look."

She crossed over to the easel.

"I shouldn't," he warned her. "You really want to? Is this not mere recklessness? Very well, then."

To the eye of an experienced critic the picture would certainly have seemed crude. It was a study of a dark-eyed child holding a large black cat. Statisticians estimate that there is no moment during the day when one or more young artists somewhere on the face of the globe are not painting pictures of children holding cats.

"I call it 'Child and Cat,' " said the young man. "Rather a neat title, don't you think? Gives you the main idea of the thing right away. That," he explained, pointing obligingly with the stem of his pipe, "is the cat."

Annette belonged to that large section of the public which likes or dislikes a picture according to whether its subject happens to please or displease them. Probably there was not one of the million or so child-and-cat eyesores at present in existence which she would not have liked. Besides, he had been very nice about her music.

"I think it's splendid," she announced.

The young man's face displayed almost more surprise than joy.

"Do you really?" he said. "Then I can die happy—that is, if you'll let me come down and listen to those songs of yours first."

"You would only knock on the floor," objected Annette.

"I'll never knock on another floor as long as I live," said the ex-brute, reassuringly. "I hate knocking on floors. I don't see what people want to knock on floors for, anyway."

Friendships ripen quickly in Chelsea. Within the space of an hour and a quarter Annette had learned that the young man's name was Alan Beverley (for which Family Heraldic affliction she pitied rather than despised him), that he did not depend entirely on his work for a living, having a little money of his own, and that he considered this a fortunate thing. From the very beginning of their talk he pleased her. She found him an absolutely new and original variety of the unsuccessful painter. Unlike Reginald Sellers, who had a studio in the same building, and sometimes dropped in to drink her coffee and pour out his troubles, he did not attribute his non-success to any malice or stupidity on the part of the public. She was so used to hearing Sellers lash the Philistine and hold forth on unappreciated merit that she could hardly believe the miracle when, in answer to a sympathetic bromide on the popular lack of taste in Art, Beverley replied that, as far as he was concerned, the public showed strong good sense. If he had been striving with every nerve to win her esteem, he could not have done it more surely than with that one remark. Though she invariably listened with a sweet patience which encouraged them to continue long after the point at which she had begun in spirit to throw things at them, Annette had no sympathy with men who whined. She herself was a fighter. She hated as much as anyone the sickening blows which Fate hands out to the struggling and ambitious; but she never made them the basis of a monologue act. Often, after a dreary trip round the offices of the music-publishers, she would howl bitterly in secret, and even gnaw her pillow in the watches of the night; but in public her pride kept her unvaryingly bright and cheerful.

Today, for the first time, she revealed something of her woes. There was that about the mop-headed young man which invited confidences. She told him of the stony-heartedness of music-publishers, of the difficulty of getting songs printed unless you paid for them, of their wretched sales.

"But those songs you've been playing," said Beverley, "they've been published?"

"Yes, those three. But they are the only ones."

"And didn't they sell?"

"Hardly at all. You see, a song doesn't sell unless somebody well known sings it. And people promise to sing them, and then don't keep their word. You can't depend on what they say."

"Give me their names," said Beverley, "and I'll go round tomorrow and shoot the whole lot. But can't you do anything?"

"Only keep on keeping on."

"I wish," he said, "that any time you're feeling blue about things you would come up and pour out the poison on me. It's no good bottling it up. Come up and tell me about it, and you'll feel ever so much better. Or let me come down. Any time things aren't going right just knock on the ceiling."

She laughed.

"Don't rub it in," pleaded Beverley. "It isn't fair. There's nobody so sensitive as a reformed floor-knocker. You will come up or let me come down, won't you? Whenever I have that sad, depressed feeling, I go out and kill a policeman. But you wouldn't care for that. So the only thing for you to do is to knock on the ceiling. Then I'll come charging down and see if there's anything I can do to help."

"You'll be sorry you ever said this."

"I won't," he said stoutly.

"If you really mean it, it *would* be a relief," she admitted. "Sometimes I'd give all the money I'm ever likely to make for someone to shriek my grievances at. I always think it must have been so nice for the people in the old novels, when they used to say: 'Sit down and I will tell you the story of my life.' Mustn't it have been heavenly?"

"Well," said Beverley, rising, "you know where I am if I'm wanted. Right up there where the knocking came from."

"Knocking?" said Annette. "I remember no knocking."

"Would you mind shaking hands?" said Beverley.

A particularly maddening hour with one of her pupils drove her up the very next day. Her pupils were at once her salvation and her despair. They gave her the means of supporting life, but they made life hardly worth supporting. Some of them were learning the piano. Others thought they sang. All had solid ivory skulls. There was about a teaspoonful of grey matter distributed among the entire squad, and the pupil Annette had been teaching that afternoon had come in at the tail-end of the division.

In the studio with Beverley she found Reginald Sellers, standing in a critical attitude before the easel. She was not very fond of him. He was a long, offensive, patronising person, with a moustache that looked like a smear of charcoal, and a habit of addressing her as "Ah, little one!"

Beverley looked up.

"Have you brought your hatchet, Miss Brougham? If you have, you're just in time to join in the massacre of the innocents. Sellers has been smiting my child and cat hip and thigh. Look at his eye. There! Did you see it flash then? He's on the warpath again."

"My dear Beverley," said Sellers, rather stiffly, "I am merely endeavouring to give you my idea of the picture's defects. I am sorry if my criticism has to be a little harsh."

"Go right on," said Beverley, cordially. "Don't mind me; it's all for my good."

"Well, in a word, then, it is lifeless. Neither the child nor the cat lives."

He stepped back a pace and made a frame of his hands.

"The cat now," he said. "It is—how shall I put it? It has no—no —er—"

"That kind of cat wouldn't," said Beverley. "It isn't that breed."

"I think it's a dear cat," said Annette. She felt her temper, always quick, getting the better of her. She knew just how incompetent Sellers was, and it irritated her beyond endurance to see Beverley's good-humoured acceptance of his patronage.

"At any rate," said Beverley, with a grin, "you both seem to recognise that it *is* a cat. You're solid on that point, and that's something, seeing I'm only a beginner."

"I know, my dear fellow; I know," said Sellers, graciously. "You mustn't let my criticism discourage you. Don't think that your work lacks promise. Far from it. I am sure that in time you will do very well indeed. Quite well."

A cold glitter might have been observed in Annette's eyes.

"Mr. Sellers," she said, smoothly, "had to work very hard himself before he reached his present position. You know his work, of course?"

For the first time Beverley seemed somewhat confused.

"I—er—why—" he began.

"Oh, but of course you do," she went on, sweetly. "It's in all the magazines."

Beverley looked at the great man with admiration, and saw that he had flushed uncomfortably. He put this down to the modesty of genius.

"In the advertisement pages," said Annette. "Mr. Sellers drew that picture of the Waukeesy Shoe and the Restawhile Settee and the tin of sardines in the Little Gem Sardine advertisement. He is very good at still life."

There was a tense silence. Beverley could almost hear the voice of the referee uttering the count.

"Miss Brougham," said Sellers at last, spitting out the words, "has confined herself to the purely commercial side of my work. There is another."

"Why, of course there is. You sold a landscape for five pounds only eight months ago, didn't you? And another three months before that."

It was enough. Sellers bowed stiffly and stalked from the room. Beverley picked up a duster and began slowly to sweep the floor with it.

"What are you doing?" demanded Annette, in a choking voice.

"The fragments of the wretched man," whispered Beverley. "They must be swept up and decently interred. You certainly have got the punch, Miss Brougham."

He dropped the duster with a startled exclamation, for Annette had suddenly burst into a flood of tears. With her face buried in her hands she sat in her chair and sobbed desperately.

"Good Lord!" said Beverley, blankly.

"I'm a cat! I'm a beast! I hate myself!"

"Good Lord!" said Beverley, blankly.

"I'm a pig! I'm a fiend!"

"Good Lord!" said Beverley, blankly.

"We're all struggling and trying to get on and having hard luck, and instead of doing what I can to help, I go and t-t-taunt him with not being able to sell his pictures! I'm not fit to live! *Oh!*"

"Good Lord!" said Beverley, blankly.

A series of gulping sobs followed, diminishing by degrees into silence. Presently she looked up and smiled, a moist and pathetic smile.

"I'm sorry," she said, "for being so stupid. But he was so horrid and patronising to you, I couldn't help scratching. I believe I'm the worst cat in London."

"No, this is," said Beverley, pointing to the canvas. "At least, according to the late Sellers. But, I say, tell me, isn't the deceased a great artist, then? He came curveting in here with his chest out and started to slate my masterpiece, so I naturally said, 'What-ho! 'Tis a genius!' Isn't he!"

"He can't sell his pictures anywhere. He lives on the little he can get from illustrating advertisements. And I t-taunt—"

"*Please!*" said Beverley, apprehensively.

She recovered herself with a gulp.

"I can't help it," she said, miserably. "I rubbed it in. Oh, it was hateful of me! But I was all on edge from teaching one of my awful pupils, and when he started to patronise you—"

She blinked.

"Poor devil!" said Beverley. "I never guessed. Good Lord!"

Annette rose.

"I must go and tell him I'm sorry," she said. "He'll snub me horribly, but I must."

She went out. Beverley lit a pipe and stood at the window looking thoughtfully down into the street.

It is a good rule in life never to apologise. The right sort of people do not want apologies, and the wrong sort take a mean advantage of them. Sellers belonged to the latter class. When Annette, meek, penitent, with all her claws sheathed, came to him and grovelled he forgave her with a repulsive magnanimity which in a less subdued mood would have stung her to renewed pugnacity. As it was, she allowed herself to be forgiven, and retired with a dismal conviction that from now on he would be more insufferable than ever.

Her surmise proved absolutely correct. His visits to the newcomer's studio began again, and Beverley's picture, now nearing completion, came in for criticism enough to have filled a volume. The good humour with which he received it amazed Annette. She had no proprietary interest in the painting beyond what she acquired from a growing regard for its parent (which disturbed her a good deal when she had time to think of it); but there were moments when only the recollection of her remorse for her previous outbreak kept her from rending the critic. Beverley, however, appeared to have no artistic sensitiveness whatsoever. When Sellers savaged the cat in a manner which should have brought the S.P.C.A. down upon him, Beverley merely beamed. His long-sufferingness was beyond Annette's comprehension.

She began to admire him for it.

To make his position as critic still more impregnable, Sellers was now able to speak as one having authority. After years of floundering, his luck seemed at last to have turned. His pictures, which for months had lain at an agent's, careened like crippled battleships, had at length begun to find a market. Within the past two weeks three landscapes and an allegorical painting had sold for good prices; and under the influence of success he expanded like an opening floweret. When Epstein, the agent, wrote to say that the allegory had been purchased by a Glasgow plutocrat of the name of Bates for one hundred and sixty guineas, Sellers' views on Philistines and their crass materialism and lack of taste underwent a marked modification. He spoke with some friendliness of the man Bates.

"To me," said Beverley, when informed of the event by Annette, "the matter has a deeper significance. It proves that Glasgow has at last produced a sober man. No drinker would have dared face that allegory. The whole business is very gratifying."

Beverley himself was progressing slowly in the field of Art. He had finished the "Child and Cat," and had taken it to Epstein together with a letter of introduction from Sellers. Sellers' habitual attitude now was that of the kindly celebrity who has arrived and wishes to give the youngsters a chance.

Since his departure Beverley had not done much in the way of actual execution. Whenever Annette came to his studio he was either sitting in a chair with his feet on the window-sill, smoking, or in the same attitude listening to Sellers' views on art. Sellers being on the up-grade, a man with many pounds to his credit in the bank, had more leisure now. He had given up his advertisement work, and was planning a great canvas—another allegorical work. This left him free to devote a good deal of time to Beverley, and he did so. Beverley sat and smoked through his harangues. He may have been listening, or he may not. Annette listened once or twice, and the experience had the effect of sending her to Beverley, quivering with indignation.

"Why do you *let* him patronise you like that?" she demanded. "If anybody came and talked to me like that about my music, I'd—I'd —I don't know what I'd do. Yes, even if he were really a great musician."

"Don't you consider Sellers a great artist, then, even now?"

"He seems to be able to sell his pictures, so I suppose they must be good; but nothing could give him the right to patronise you as he does."

" 'My learned friend's manner would be intolerable in an emperor to a black-beetle,' " quoted Beverley. "Well, what are we going to do about it?"

"If only you would sell a picture, too!"

"Ah! Well, I've done my part of the contract. I've delivered the goods. There the thing is at Epstein's. The public can't blame me if it doesn't sell. All they've got to do is to waltz in in their thousands and fight for it. And, by the way, talking of waltzes—"

"Oh, it's finished," said Annette, dispiritedly. "Published too, for that matter."

"Published! What's the matter, then? Why this drooping sadness? Why aren't you running around the square, singing like a bird?"

"Because," said Annette, "unfortunately, I had to pay the expenses of publication. It was only five pounds, but the sales haven't caught up with that yet. If they ever do, perhaps there'll be a new edition."

"And will you have to pay for that?"

"No. The publishers would."

"Who are they?"

"Grusczinsky and Buchterkirch."

"Heavens, then what are you worrying about? The thing's a cert. A man with a name like Grusczinsky could sell a dozen editions by himself. Helped and inspired by Buchterkirch, he will make the waltz the talk of the country. Infants will croon it in their cots."

"He didn't seem to think so when I saw him last."

"Of course not. He doesn't know his own power. Grusczinsky's shrinking diffidence is a by-word in musical circles. He is the genuine Human Violet. You must give him time."

"I'll give him anything if he'll only sell an edition or two," said Annette.

The astounding thing was that he did. There seemed no particular reason why the sale of that waltz should not have been as small and as slow as that of any other waltz by an unknown composer. But almost without warning it expanded from a trickle into a flood. Grusczinsky, beaming paternally whenever Annette entered the shop—which was often—announced two new editions in a week. Beverley, his artistic growth still under a watchful eye of Sellers, said he had never had any doubts as to the success of the thing from the moment when a single phrase in it had so carried him away that he had been compelled to stamp his applause enthusiastically on the floor. Even Sellers forgot his own triumphs long enough to allow him to offer affable congratulations. And money came rolling in, smoothing the path of life.

Those were great days. There was a hat . . .

Life, in short, was very full and splendid. There was, indeed, but one thing which kept it from being perfect. The usual drawback to success is that it annoys one's friends so; but in Annette's case this drawback was absent. Sellers' demeanour towards her was that of an old-established inmate welcoming a novice into the Hall of Fame. Her pupils—worthy souls, though bone-headed—fawned upon her. Beverley seemed more pleased than anyone. Yet it was Beverley who prevented her paradise from being complete. Successful herself, she wanted all her friends to be successful; but Beverley, to her discomfort, remained a cheery failure, and worse, absolutely refused to snub Sellers. It was not as if Sellers' advice and comments were disinterested. Beverley was simply the instrument on which he played his songs of triumph. It distressed Annette to such an extent that now, if she went upstairs and heard Sellers' voice in the studio, she came down again without knocking.

One afternoon, sitting in her room, she heard the telephone-bell ring. The telephone was on the stairs, just outside her door. She went out and took up the receiver.

"Halloa!" said a querulous voice. "Is Mr. Beverley there?"

Annette remembered having heard him go out. She could always tell his footstep.

"He is out," she said. "Is there any message?"

"Yes," said the voice, emphatically. "Tell him that Rupert Morrison rang up to ask what he was to do with all this great stack of music that's arrived. Does he want it forwarded on to him, or what?" The voice was growing high and excited. Evidently Mr. Morrison was in a state of nervous tension when a man does not care particularly who hears his troubles so long as he unburdens himself of them to someone.

"Music?" said Annette.

"Music!" shrilled Mr. Morrison. "Stacks and stacks and stacks of it. Is he playing a practical joke on me, or what?" he demanded, hysterically. Plainly he had now come to regard Annette as a legitimate confidante. She was listening. That was the main point. He wanted someone—he did not care whom—who would listen. "He lends me his rooms," wailed Mr. Morrison, "so that I can be perfectly quiet and undisturbed while I write my novel, and, first thing I know, this music starts to arrive. How can I be quiet and undisturbed when the floor's littered two yards high with great parcels of music, and more coming every day?"

Annette clung weakly to the telephone box. Her mind was in a whirl, but she was beginning to see many things.

"Are you there?" called Mr. Morrison.

"Yes. What—what firm does the music come from?"

"What's that?"

"Who are the publishers who send the music?"

"I can't remember. Some long name. Yes, I've got it. Grusczinsky and someone."

"I'll tell Mr. Beverley," said Annette, quietly. A great weight seemed to have settled on her head.

"Halloa! Halloa! Are you there?" came Mr. Morrison's voice.

"Yes?"

"And tell him there are some pictures, too."

"Pictures?"

"Four great beastly pictures. The size of elephants. I tell you, there isn't room to move. And—"

Annette hung up the receiver.

Mr. Beverley, returned from his walk, was racing up the stairs three at a time in his energetic way, when, as he arrived at Annette's door, it opened.

"Have you a minute to spare?" said Annette.

"Of course. What's the trouble? Have they sold another edition of the waltz?"

"I have not heard, Mr.—Bates."

For once she looked to see the cheerful composure of the man upstairs become ruffled; but he received the blow without agitation.

"You know my name?" he said.

"I know a good deal more than your name. You are a Glasgow millionaire."

"It's true," he admitted, "but it's hereditary. My father was one before me."

"And you use your money," said Annette, bitterly, "creating fools' paradises for your friends, which last, I suppose, until you grow tired of the amusement and destroy them. Doesn't it ever strike you, Mr. Bates, that it's a little cruel? Do you think Mr.

Sellers will settle down again cheerfully to hack-work when you stop buying his pictures, and he finds out that—that——"

"I shan't stop," said the young man. "If a Glasgow millionaire mayn't buy Sellers' allegorical pictures, whose allegorical pictures may he buy? Sellers will never find out. He'll go on painting and I'll go on buying, and all will be joy and peace."

"Indeed! And what future have you arranged for me?"

"You?" he said, reflectively. "I want to marry you."

Annette stiffened from head to foot. He met her blazing eyes with a look of quiet devotion.

"Marry me?"

"I know what you are thinking," he said. "Your mind is dwelling on the prospect of living in a house decorated throughout with Sellers' allegorical pictures. But it won't be. We'll store them in the attic."

She began to speak, but he interrupted her.

"Listen!" he said. "Sit down and I will tell you the story of my life. We'll skip the first twenty-eight years and three months, merely mentioning that for the greater part of that time I was looking for somebody just like you. A month and nine days ago I found you. You were crossing the Embankment. I was also on the Embankment. In a taxi. I stopped the taxi, got out, and observed you just stepping into the Charing Cross Underground. I sprang—"

"This does not interest me," said Annette.

"The plot thickens," he assured her. "We left our hero springing, I think. Just so. Well, you took the West-end train and got off at Sloane Square. So did I. You crossed Sloane Square, turned up King's Road, and finally arrived here. I followed. I saw a notice up, 'Studio to Let.' I reflected that, having done a little painting in an amateur way, I could pose as an artist all right; so I took the studio. Also the name of Alan Beverley. My own is Bill Bates. I had often wondered what it would feel like to be called by some name like Alan Beverley or Cyril Trevelyan. It was simply the spin of the coin which decided me in favour of the former. Once in, the problem was how to get to know you. When I heard you playing I knew it was all right. I had only to keep knocking on the floor long enough—"

"Do—you—mean—to—tell—me"—Annette's voice trembled—"do you mean to tell me that you knocked that time simply to make me come up?"

"That was it. Rather a scheme, don't you think? And now, would you mind telling me how you found out that I had been buying your waltz? Those remarks of yours about fools' paradises were not inspired solely by the affairs of Sellers. But it beats me how you did it. I swore Rozinsky, or whatever his name is, to secrecy."

"A Mr. Morrison," said Annette, indifferently, "rang up on the telephone and asked me to tell you that he was greatly worried by the piles of music which were littering the rooms you lent him."

The young man burst into a roar of laughter.

"Poor old Morrison! I forgot all about him. I lent him my rooms at the Albany. He's writing a novel, and he can't work if the slightest thing goes wrong. It just shows—"

"Mr. Bates!"

"Yes?"

"Perhaps you didn't intend to hurt me. I dare say you meant only to be kind. But—but—oh, can't you see how you have humiliated me? You have treated me like a child, giving me a make-believe success just to—just to keep me quiet, I suppose. You—"

He was fumbling in his pocket.

"May I read you a letter?" he said.

"A letter?"

"Quite a short one. It is from Epstein, the picture-dealer. This is what he says. 'Sir,' meaning me, not 'Dear Bill,' mind you—just 'Sir.' 'I am glad to be able to inform you that I have this morning received an offer of ten guineas for your picture, "Child and Cat." Kindly let me know if I am to dispose of it at this price.' "

"Well?" said Annette, in a small voice.

"I have just been to Epstein's. It seems that the purchaser is a Miss Brown. She gave an address in Bayswater. I called at the address. No Miss Brown lives there, but one of your pupils does. I asked her if she was expecting a parcel from Miss Brown, and she said that she had had your letter and quite understood and would take it in when it arrived."

Annette was hiding her face in her hands.

"Go away!" she said, faintly.

Mr. Bates moved a step nearer.

"Do you remember that story of the people on the island who eked out a precarious livelihood by taking in one another's washing?" he asked, casually.

"Go away!" cried Annette.

"I've always thought," he said, "that it must have drawn them very close together—made them feel rather attached to each other. Don't you?"

"Go away!"

"I don't want to go away. I want to stay and hear you say you'll marry me."

"*Please* go away! I want to think."

She heard him moving towards the door. He stopped, then went on again. The door closed quietly. Presently from the room above came the sound of footsteps—footsteps pacing monotonously to and fro like those of an animal in a cage.

Annette sat listening. There was no break in the footsteps.

Suddenly she got up. In one corner of the room was a long pole used for raising and lowering the window-sash. She took it, and for a moment stood irresolute. Then with a quick movement, she lifted it and stabbed three times at the ceiling.

MISUNDERSTOOD

The streets of London provide a very unusual setting for a Wodehouse story. But he was fond of loveable criminal types, which appear in his later stories.

The profession of Mr. James ("Spider") Buffin was pocket-picking. His hobby was revenge. James had no objection to letting the sun go down on his wrath. Indeed, it was after dark that he corrected his numerous enemies most satisfactorily. It was on a dark night, while he was settling a small score against one Kelly, a mere acquaintance, that he first fell foul of Constable Keating, whose beat took him through the regions which James most frequented.

James, having "laid for" Mr. Kelly, met him in a murky side-street down Clerkenwell way, and attended to his needs with a sand-bag.

First Appearance: England—*Nash's Magazine*, May 1910

It was here that Constable Keating first came prominently into his life. Just as James, with the satisfying feeling that his duty had been done, was preparing to depart, Officer Keating, who had been a distant spectator of the affair, charged up and seized him.

It was intolerable that he should interfere in a purely private falling-out between one gentleman and another, but there was nothing to be done. The policeman weighed close upon fourteen stone, and could have eaten Mr. Buffin. The latter, inwardly seething, went quietly, and in due season was stowed away at the Government's expense for the space of sixty days.

Physically, there is no doubt that his detention did him good. The regular hours and the substitution of bread and water for his wonted diet improved his health thirty per cent. It was mentally that he suffered. His was one of those just-as-good cheap-substitute minds, incapable of harbouring more than one idea at a time, and during those sixty days of quiet seclusion it was filled with an ever-growing resentment against Officer Keating. Every day, as he moved about his appointed tasks, he brooded on his wrongs. Every night was to him but the end of another day that kept him from settling down to the serious business of Revenge. To be haled to prison for correcting a private enemy with a sand-bag—that was what stung. In the privacy of his cell he dwelt unceasingly on the necessity for revenge. The thing began to take on to him the aspect almost of a Holy Mission, a sort of Crusade.

The days slipped by, bringing winter to Clerkenwell, and with it Mr. Buffin. He returned to his old haunts one Friday night, thin but in excellent condition. One of the first acquaintances he met was Officer Keating. The policeman, who had a good memory for faces, recognised him, and stopped.

"So you're out, young feller?" he said genially. When not in the active discharge of his professional duties the policeman was a kindly man. He bore Mr. Buffin no grudge.

"Um," said Mr. Buffin.

"Feeling fine, eh?"

"Um."

"Goin' round to see some of the chaps and pass them the time of day, I shouldn't wonder?"

"Um."

"Well, you keep clear of that lot down in Frith Street, young feller. They're no good. And if you get mixed up with them, first thing you know, you'll be in trouble again. And you want to keep out of that now."

"Um."

"If you never get into trouble," said the policeman sententiously, "you'll never have to get out of it."

"Um," said Mr. Buffin. If he had a fault as a conversationalist, it was a certain tendency to monotony, a certain lack of sparkle and variety in his small-talk.

Constable Keating, with a dignified but friendly wave of the hand, as one should say, "You have our leave to depart," went on his way; while Mr. Buffin, raging, shuffled off in the opposite direction, thinking as hard as his limited mental equipment would allow him.

His thoughts, which were many and confused, finally composed themselves into some order. He arrived at a definite conclusion, which was that if the great settlement was to be carried through successfully it must be done when the policeman was off duty. Till then he had pictured himself catching Officer Keating in an unguarded moment on his beat. This, he now saw, was out of the question. On his beat the policeman had no unguarded moments. There was a quiet alertness in his poise, a danger-signal in itself.

There was only one thing for Mr. Buffin to do. Greatly as it would go against the grain, he must foregather with the man, win his confidence, put himself in a position where he would be able to find out what he did with himself when off duty.

The policeman offered no obstacle to the move. A supreme self-confidence was his leading characteristic. Few London policemen are diffident, and Mr. Keating was no exception. It never occurred to him that there could be an ulterior motive behind Mr. Buffin's advances. He regarded Mr. Buffin much as one regards a dog which one has had to chastise. One does not expect the dog to lie in wait and bite. Officer Keating did not expect Mr. Buffin to lie in wait and bite.

So every day, as he strolled on his beat, there sidled up to him the meagre form of Spider Buffin. Every day there greeted him the Spider's "Good-morning, Mr. Keating," till the sight of Officer Keating walking solidly along the pavement with Spider Buffin shuffling along at his side, listening with rapt interest to his views on Life and his hints on Deportment, became a familiar spectacle in Clerkenwell.

Mr. Buffin played his part well. In fact, too well. It was on the seventh day that, sidling along in the direction of his favourite place of refreshment, he found himself tapped on the shoulder. At the same moment an arm, linking itself in his, brought him gently to a halt. Beside him were standing two of the most eminent of the great Frith Street Gang, Otto the Sausage and Rabbit Butler. It was the finger of the Rabbit that had tapped his shoulder. The arm tucked in his was the arm of Otto the Sausage.

"Hi, Spider," said Mr. Butler, "Sid wants to see you a minute."

The Spider's legs felt boneless. There was nothing in the words to alarm a man, but his practised ear had seemed to detect a certain unpleasant dryness in the speaker's tone. Sid Marks, the all-powerful leader of the Frith Street Gang, was a youth whose company the Spider had always avoided with some care.

The great Sid, seated in state at a neighbouring hostelry, fixed his visitor with a cold and questioning eye. Mr. Buffin looked nervous and interrogative. Mr. Marks spoke.

"Your pal Keating pinched Porky Binns this mornin'," said Sid.

The Spider's heart turned to water.

"You and that slop," observed Sid dreamily, "have been bloomin' thick these days."

Mr. Buffin did not affect to misunderstand. Sid Marks was looking at him in that nasty way. Otto the Sausage was looking at him in that nasty way. Rabbit Butler was looking at him in that nasty way. This was an occasion where manly frankness was the quality most to be aimed at. To be misunderstood in the circles in which Mr. Buffin moved meant something more than the mere risk of being treated with cold displeasure.

He began to explain with feverish eagerness.

"Strike me, Sid," he stammered, "it ain't like that. It's all right. Blimey, you don't fink I'm a nark?"

Mr. Marks chewed a straw in silence.

"I'm layin' for him, Sid," babbled Mr. Buffin. "That's true. Strike me if it ain't. I'm just tryin' to find out where he goes when he's off duty. He pinched me, so I'm layin' for him."

Mr. Marks perpended. Rabbit Butler respectfully gave it as his opinion that it would be well to put Mr. Buffin through it. There was nothing like being on the safe side. By putting Mr. Buffin through it, argued Rabbit Butler, they would stand to win either way. If he *had* "smitched" to Officer Keating about Porky Binns he would deserve it. If he had not—well, it would prevent him doing so on some future occasion. Play for safety, was Mr. Butler's advice, seconded by Otto the Sausage. Mr. Buffin, pale to the lips, thought he had never met two more unpleasant persons.

The Great Sid, having chewed his straw for a while in silence, delivered judgment. The prisoner should have the benefit of the doubt this time. His story, however unplausible, might possibly be true. Officer Keating undoubtedly had pinched him. That was in his favour.

"You can hop it this time," he said, "but if you ever do start smitchin', Spider, yer knows what'll happen."

Mr. Buffin withdrew, quaking.

Matters had now come to a head. Unless he very speedily gave proof of his pure and noble intentions, life would become extremely unsafe for him. He must act at once. The thought of what would happen should another of the Frith Streeters be pinched before he, Mr. Buffin, could prove himself innocent of the crime of friendliness with Officer Keating, turned him cold.

Fate played into his hands. On the very next morning Mr. Keating, all unsuspecting, asked him to go to his home with a message for his wife.

"Tell her," said Mr. Keating, "a newspaper gent has given me seats for the play to-night, and I'll be home at a quarter to seven."

Mr. Buffin felt as Cromwell must have felt at Dunbar when the Scots left their stronghold on the hills and came down to the open plain.

The winter had set in with some severity that year, and Mr. Buffin's toes, as he stood in the shadows close to the entrance of the villa where Officer Keating lived when off duty, were soon thoroughly frozen. He did not dare to stamp his feet, for at any moment now the victim might arrive. And when the victim weighs fourteen stone, against the high priest's eight and a half, it behooves the latter to be circumspect, if the sacrifice is to be anything like a success. So Mr. Buffin waited and froze in silence. It was a painful process, and he added it to the black score which already stood against Officer Keating. Never had his thirst for revenge been more tormenting. It is doubtful if a strictly logical and impartial judge would have held Mr. Keating to blame for the fact that Sid Marks' suspicions (and all that those suspicions entailed) had fallen upon Mr. Buffin; but the Spider did so. He felt fiercely resentful against the policeman for placing him in such an unpleasant and dangerous position. As his thoughts ran on the matter, he twisted his fingers tighter round his stick.

As he did so there came from down the road the brisk tramp of feet and a cheerful whistling of "The Wearing of the Green." It is a lugubrious song as a rule, but, as rendered by Officer Keating returning home with theatre tickets, it had all the joyousness of a march-tune.

Every muscle in Mr. Buffin's body stiffened. He gripped his stick and waited. The road was deserted. In another moment . . .

And then, from nowhere, dark indistinct forms darted out like rats. The whistling stopped in the middle of a bar. A deep-chested oath rang out, and then a confused medley of sound, the rasping of feet, a growling almost canine, a sharp yelp, gasps, and over all the vast voice of Officer Keating threatening slaughter.

For a moment Mr. Buffin stood incapable of motion. The thing had been so sudden, so unexpected. And then, as he realised what was happening, there swept over him in a wave a sense of intolerable injustice. It is not easy to describe his emotions, but they resembled most nearly those of an inventor whose patent has been infringed, or an author whose idea has been stolen. For weeks— and weeks that had seemed like years—he had marked down Officer Keating for his prey. For weeks he had tortured a mind all unused to thinking into providing him with schemes for accomplishing his end. He had outraged his nature by being civil to a policeman. He had risked his life by incurring the suspicions of Sid Marks. He had bought a stick. And he had waited in the cold till his face was blue and his feet blocks of ice. And now . . . *now* . . . after all this . . . a crowd of irresponsible strangers, with no rights in the man whatsoever probably, if the truth were known, filled with mere ignoble desire for his small change, had dared to rush in and jump his claim before his very eyes.

With one passionate cry, Mr. Buffin, forgetting his frozen feet, lifted his stick, and galloped down the road to protect his property . . .

"That's the stuff," said a voice. "Pour some more into him, Jerry."

Mr. Buffin opened his eyes. A familiar taste was in his mouth. Somebody of liberal ideas seemed to be pouring whisky down his throat. Could this be Heaven? He raised his head, and a sharp pain shot through it. And with the pain came recollection. He remembered now, dimly, as if it had all happened in another life, the mad rush down the road, the momentary pause in the conflict, and then its noisy renewal on a more impressive scale. He remembered striking out left and right with his stick. He remembered the cries of the wounded, the pain of his frozen feet, and finally the crash of something hard and heavy on his head.

He sat up, and found himself the centre of a little crowd. There was Officer Keating, dishevelled but intact; three other policemen, one of whom was kneeling by his side with a small bottle in his hand; and, in the grip of the two were standing two youths.

One was Otto the Sausage; the other was Rabbit Butler.

The kneeling policeman was proffering the bottle once more. Mr. Buffin snatched at it. He felt that it was just what at that moment he needed most.

He did what he could. The magistrate asked for his evidence. He said he had none. He said he thought there must be some mistake. With a twisted smile in the direction of the prisoners, he said that he did not remember having seen either of them at the combat. He didn't believe they were there at all. He didn't believe they were capable of such a thing. If there was one man who was less likely to assault a policeman than Otto the Sausage, it was Rabbit Butler. The Bench reminded him that both these innocents had actually been discovered in Officer Keating's grasp. Mr. Buffin smiled a harassed smile, and wiped a drop of perspiration from his brow.

Officer Keating was enthusiastic. He described the affair from start to finish. But for Mr. Buffin he would have been killed. But for Mr. Buffin there would have been no prisoners in court that day. The world was full of men with more or less golden hearts, but there was only one Mr. Buffin. Might he shake hands with Mr. Buffin?

The magistrate ruled that he might. More, he would shake hands with him himself. Summoning Mr. Buffin behind his desk, he proceeded to do so. If there were more men like Mr. Buffin, London would be a better place. It was the occasional discovery in our midst of ethereal natures like that of Mr. Buffin which made one so confident for the future of the race.

The paragon shuffled out. It was bright and sunny in the street, but in Mr. Buffin's heart there was no sunlight. He was not a quick thinker, but he had come quite swiftly to the conclusion that London was no longer the place for him. Sid Marks had been in court chewing a straw and listening with grave attention to the evidence, and for one moment Mr. Buffin had happened to catch his eye. No medical testimony as to the unhealthiness of London could have moved him more.

Once round the corner, he ran. It hurt his head to run, but there were things behind him that could hurt his head more than running.

At the entrance to the Tube he stopped. To leave the locality he must have money. He felt in his pcokets. Slowly, one by one, he pulled forth his little valuables. His knife . . . his revolver . . . the magistrate's gold watch . . . He inspected them sadly. They must all go.

He went into a pawnbroker's shop at the corner of the street. A few moments later, with money in his pockets, he dived into the Tube.

PILLINGSHOT, DETECTIVE

This is typical of the early school stories, and incorporates Wodehouse's life-long enthusiasms for public school life, humor, and detection. It is hardly necessary to explain to the serious Wodehouse collector that fagging is a British public school practice whereby younger pupils are required to serve upperclassmen.

Life at St. Austin's was rendered somewhat hollow and burdensome for Pillingshot by the fact that he fagged for Scott. Not that

First Appearance: England—*The Captain*, September 1910

Scott was the Beetle-Browed Bully in any way. Far from it. He showed a kindly interest in Pillingshot's welfare, and sometimes even did his Latin verses for him. But the noblest natures have flaws, and Scott's was no exception. He was by way of being a humorist, and Pillingshot, with his rather serious outlook on life, was puzzled and inconvenienced by this.

It was through this defect in Scott's character that Pillingshot first became a detective.

He was toasting muffins at the study fire one evening, while Scott, seated on two chairs and five cushions, read "Sherlock Holmes," when the Prefect laid down his book and fixed him with an earnest eye.

"Do you know, Pillingshot," he said, "you've got a bright, intelligent face. I shouldn't wonder if you weren't rather clever. Why do you hide your light under a bushel?"

Pillingshot grunted.

"We must find some way of advertising you. Why don't you go in for a Junior Scholarship?"

"Too old," said Pillingshot with satisfaction.

"Senior, then?"

"Too young."

"I believe by sitting up all night and swotting—"

"Here, I say!" said Pillingshot, alarmed.

"You've got no enterprise," said Scott sadly. "What are those? Muffins? Well, well, I suppose I had better try and peck a bit."

He ate four in rapid succession, and resumed his scrutiny of Pillingshot's countenance.

"The great thing," he said, "is to find out your special line. Till then we are working in the dark. Perhaps it's music? Singing? Sing me a bar or two."

Pillingshot wriggled uncomfortably.

"Left your music at home?" said Scott. "Never mind, then. Perhap's it's all for the best. What are those? Still muffins? Hand me another. After all, one must keep one's strength up. You can have one if you like."

Pillingshot's face brightened. He became more affable. He chatted.

"There's rather a row on downstairs," he said. "In the junior day-room."

"There always is," said Scott. "If it grows too loud, I shall get in amongst them with a swagger-stick. I attribute half my success at bringing off late-cuts to the practice I have had in the junior day-room. It keeps the wrist supple."

"I don't mean that sort of row. It's about Evans."

"What about Evans?"

"He's lost a sovereign."

"Silly young ass."

Pillingshot furtively helped himself to another muffin.

"He thinks some one's taken it," he said.

"What! Stolen it?"

Pillingshot nodded.

"What makes him think that?"

"He doesn't see how else it could have gone."

"Oh, I don't—By Jove!"

Scott sat up with some excitement.

"I've got it," he said. "I knew we should hit on it sooner or later. Here's a field for your genius. You shall be a detective. Pillingshot, I hand this case over to you. I employ you."

Pillingshot gaped.

"I feel certain that's your line. I've often noticed you walking over to school, looking exactly like a blood-hound. Get to work. As a start you'd better fetch Evans up here and question him."

"But, look here—"

"Buck up, man, buck up. Don't you know that every moment is precious?"

Evans, a small, stout youth, was not disposed to be reticent. The gist of his rambling statement was as follows. Rich uncle. Impecunious nephew. Visit of former to latter. Handsome tip, one sovereign. Impecunious nephew pouches sovereign, and it vanishes.

"And I call it beastly rot," concluded Evans volubly. "And if I could find the cad who's pinched it, I'd jolly well—"

"Less of it," said Scott. "Now, then, Pillingshot, I'll begin this thing, just to start you off. What makes you think the quid has been stolen, Evans?"

"Because I jolly well know it has."

"What you jolly well know isn't evidence. We must thresh this thing out. To begin with, where did you last see it?"

"When I put it in my pocket."

"Good. Make a note of that, Pillingshot. Where's your note-book? Not got one? Here you are then. You can tear out the first few pages, the ones I've written on. Ready? Carry on, Evans. When?"

"When what?"

"When did you put it in your pocket?"

"Yesterday afternoon."

"What time?"

"About five."

"Same pair of bags you're wearing now?"

"No, my cricket bags. I was playing at the nets when my uncle came."

"Ah! Cricket bags? Put it down, Pillingshot. That's a clue. Work on it. Where are they?"

"They've gone to the wash."

"About time, too. I noticed them. How do you know the quid didn't go to the wash as well?"

"I turned both the pockets inside out."

"Any hole in the pocket?"

"No."

"Well, when did you take off the bags? Did you sleep in them?"

"I wore 'em till bed-time, and then shoved them on a chair by the side of the bed. It wasn't till next morning that I remembered the quid was in them—"

"But it wasn't," objected Scott.

"I thought it was. It ought to have been."

"He thought it was. That's a clue, young Pillingshot. Work on it. Well?"

"Well, when I went to take the quid out of my cricket bags, it wasn't there."

"What time was that?"

"Half-past seven this morning."

"What time did you go to bed?"

"Ten."

"Then the theft occurred between the hours of ten and seven-thirty. Mind you, I'm giving you a jolly good leg-up, young Pillingshot. But as it's your first case I don't mind. That'll be all from you, Evans. Pop off."

Evans disappeared. Scott turned to the detective.

"Well, young Pillingshot," he said, "what do you make of it?"

"I don't know."

"What steps do you propose to take?"

"I don't know."

"You're a lot of use, aren't you? As a start, you'd better examine the scene of the robbery, I should say."

Pillingshot reluctantly left the room.

"Well?" said Scott, when he returned. "Any clues?"

"No."

"You thoroughly examined the scene of the robbery?"

"I looked under the bed."

"*Under* the bed? What's the good of that? Did you go over every inch of the strip of carpet leading to the chair with a magnifying-glass?"

"Hadn't got a magnifying-glass."

"Then you'd better buck up and get one, if you're going to be a detective. Do you think Sherlock Holmes ever moved a step without his? Not much. Well, anyhow. Did you find any foot-prints or tobacco-ash?"

"There was a jolly lot of dust about."

"Did you preserve a sample?"

"No."

"My word, you've a lot to learn. Now, weighing the evidence, does anything strike you?"

"No."

"You're a bright sort of sleuth-hound, aren't you! It seems to me I'm doing all the work on this case. I'll have to give you another leg-up. Considering the time when the quid disappeared, I should say that somebody in the dormitory must have collared it. How many fellows are there in Evans' dormitory?"

"I don't know."

"Cut along and find out."

The detective reluctantly trudged off once more.

"Well?" said Scott, on his return.

"Seven," said Pillingshot. "Counting Evans."

"We needn't count Evans. If he's ass enough to steal his own quids, he deserves to lose them. Who are the other six?"

"There's Trent. He's prefect."

"The Napoleon of Crime. Watch his every move. Yes?"

"Simms."

"A dangerous man. Sinister to the core."

"And Green, Berkeley, Hanson, and Daubeny."

"Every one of them well known to the police. Why, the place is a perfect Thieves' Kitchen. Look here, we must act swiftly, young Pillingshot. This is a black business. We'll take them in alphabetical order. Run and fetch Berkeley."

Berkeley, interrupted in a game of Halma, came unwillingly.

"Now then, Pillingshot, put your questions," said Scott. "This is a black business, Berkeley. Young Evans has lost a sovereign—"

"If you think I've taken his beastly quid—!" said Berkeley warmly.

"Make a note that, on being questioned, the man Berkeley exhibited suspicious emotion. Go on. Jam it down."

Pillingshot reluctantly entered the statement under Berkeley's indignant gaze.

"Now then, carry on."

"You know, it's all rot," protested Pillingshot. "I never said Berkeley had anything to do with it."

"Never mind. Ask him what his movements were on the night of the—what was yesterday?—on the night of the sixteenth of July."

Pillingshot put the question nervously.

"I was in bed, of course, you silly ass."

"Were you asleep?" inquired Scott.

"Of course I was."

"Then how do you know what you were doing? Pillingshot, make a note of the fact that the man Berkeley's statement was confused and contradictory. It's a clue. Work on it. Who's next? Daubeny. Berkeley, send Daubeny up here."

"All right, Pillingshot, you wait," was Berkeley's exit speech.

Daubeny, when examined, exhibited the same suspicious emotion that Berkeley had shown; and Hanson, Simms, and Green behaved in a precisely similar manner.

"This," said Scott, "somewhat complicates the case. We must have further clues. You'd better pop off now, Pillingshot. I've got a Latin Prose to do. Bring me reports of your progress daily, and don't overlook the importance of trifles. Why, in 'Silver Blaze' it was a burnt match that first put Holmes on the scent."

Entering the junior day-room with some apprehension, the sleuth-hound found an excited gathering of suspects waiting to interview him.

One sentiment animated the meeting. Each of the five wanted to know what Pillingshot meant by it.

"What's the row?" queried interested spectators, rallying round.

"That cad Pillingshot's been accusing us of bagging Evans' quid."

"What's Scott got to do with it?" inquired one of the spectators.

Pillingshot explained his position.

"All the same," said Daubeny, "you needn't have dragged us into it."

"I couldn't help it. He made me."

"Awful ass, Scott," admitted Green.

Pillingshot welcomed this sign that the focus of popular indignation was being shifted.

"Shoving himself into other people's business," grumbled Pillingshot.

"Trying to be funny," Berkeley summed up.

"Rotten at cricket, too."

"Can't play a yorker for nuts."

"See him drop that sitter on Saturday?"

So that was all right. As far as the junior day-room was concerned, Pillingshot felt himself vindicated.

But his employer was less easily satisfied. Pillingshot had hoped that by the next day he would have forgotten the subject. But, when he went into the study to get tea ready, up it came again.

"Any clues yet, Pillingshot?"

Pillingshot had to admit that there were none.

"Hullo, this won't do. You must bustle about. You must get your nose to the trail. Have you cross-examined Trent yet? No? Well, there you are, then. Nip off and do it now."

"But, I say, Scott! He's a prefect!"

"In the dictionary of crime," said Scott sententiously, "there is no such word as prefect. All are alike. Go and take down Trent's statement."

To tax a prefect with having stolen a sovereign was a task at which Pillingshot's imagination boggled. He went to Trent's study in a sort of dream.

A hoarse roar answered his feeble tap. There was no doubt about Trent being in. Inspection revealed the fact that the prefect was working and evidently ill-attuned to conversation. He wore a haggard look and his eye, as it caught that of the collector of statements, was dangerous.

"Well?" said Trent, scowling murderously.

Pillingshot's legs felt perfectly boneless.

"*Well?*" said Trent.

Pillingshot yammered.

"*Well?*"

The roar shook the window, and Pillingshot's presence of mind deserted him altogether.

"Have you bagged a sovereign?" he asked.

There was an awful silence, during which the detective, his limbs suddenly becoming active again, banged the door, and shot off down the passage.

He re-entered Scott's study at the double.

"Well?" said Scott. "What did he say?"

"Nothing."

"Get out your note-book, and put down, under the heading 'Trent': 'Suspicious silence.' A very bad lot, Trent. Keep him under constant espionage. It's a clue. Work on it."

Pillingshot made a note of the silence, but later on, when he and the prefect met in the dormitory, felt inclined to erase it. For silence was the last epithet one would have applied to Trent on that occasion. As he crawled painfully into bed Pillingshot became more than ever convinced that the path of the amateur detective was a thorny one.

This conviction deepened next day.

Scott's help was possibly well meant, but it was certainly inconvenient. His theories were of the brilliant, dashing order, and Pillingshot could never be certain who and in what rank of life the next suspect would be. He spent that afternoon shadowing the Greaser (the combination of boot-boy and butler who did the odd jobs about the school house), and in the evening seemed likely to be about to move in the very highest circles. This was when Scott remarked in a dreamy voice, "You know, I'm told the old man has been spending a good lot of money lately . . ."

To which the burden of Pillingshot's reply was that he would do anything in reason, but he was blowed if he was going to cross-examine the head-master.

"It seems to me," said Scott sadly, "that you don't *want* to find that sovereign. Don't you like Evans, or what is it?"

It was on the following morning, after breakfast, that the close observer might have noticed a change in the detective's demeanour. He no longer looked as if he were weighed down by a secret sorrow. His manner was even jaunty.

Scott noticed it.

"What's up?" he inquired. "Got a clue?"

Pillingshot nodded.

"What is it? Let's have a look."

"Sh—h—h!" said Pillingshot mysteriously.

Scott's interest was aroused. When his fag was making tea in the afternoon, he questioned him again.

"Out with it," he said. "What's the point of all this silent mystery business?"

"Sherlock Holmes never gave anything away."

"Out with it."

"Walls have ears," said Pillingshot.

"So have you," replied Scott crisply, "and I'll smite them in half a second."

Pillingshot sighed resignedly, and produced an envelope. From this he poured some dried mud.

"Here, steady on with my table-cloth," said Scott. "What's this?"

"Mud."

"What about it?"

"Where do you think it came from?"

"How should I know? Road, I suppose."

Pillingshot smiled faintly.

"Eighteen different kinds of mud about here," he said patronisingly. "This is flower-bed mud from the house front-garden."

"Well? What about it?"

"Sh—h—h!" said Pillingshot, and glided out of the room.

"Well?" asked Scott next day. "Clues pouring in all right?"

"Rather."

"What? Got another?"

Pillingshot walked silently to the door and flung it open. He looked up and down the passage. Then he closed the door and returned to the table, where he took from his waistcoat-pocket a used match.

Scott turned it over inquiringly.

"What's the idea of this?"

"A clue," said Pillingshot. "See anything queer about it? See that rummy brown stain on it?"

"Yes."

"Blood!" snorted Pillingshot.

"What's the good of blood? There's been no murder."

Pillingshot looked serious.

"I never thought of that."

"You must think of everything. The worst mistake a detective can make is to get switched off on to another track while he's working on a case. This match is a clue to something else. You can't work on it."

"I suppose not," said Pillingshot.

"Don't be discouraged. You're doing fine."

"I know," said Pillingshot. "I shall find that quid all right."

"Nothing like sticking to it."

Pillingshot shuffled, then rose to a point of order.

"I've been reading those Sherlock Holmes stories," he said, "and Sherlock Holmes always got a fee if he brought a thing off. I think I ought to, too."

"Mercenary young brute."

"It has been a beastly sweat."

"Done you good. Supplied you with a serious interest in life. Well, I expect Evans will give you something—a jewelled snuff-box or something—if you pull the thing off."

"*I* don't."

"Well, he'll buy you a tea or something."

"He won't. He's not going to break the quid. He's saving up for a camera."

"Well, what are you going to do about it?"

Pillingshot kicked the leg of the table.

"*You* put me on to the case," he said casually.

"What! If you think I'm going to squander—"

"I think you ought to let me off fagging for the rest of the term."

Scott reflected.

"There's something in that. All right."

"Thanks."

"Don't mention it. You haven't found the quid yet."

"I know where it is."

"Where?"

"Ah!"

"Fool," said Scott.

After breakfast next day Scott was seated in his study when Pillingshot entered.

"Here you are," said Pillingshot.

He unclasped his right hand and exhibited a sovereign. Scott inspected it.

"Is this the one?" he said.

"Yes," said Pillingshot.

"How do you know?"

"It *is*. I've sifted all the evidence."

"Who had bagged it?"

"I don't want to mention names."

"Oh, all right. As he didn't spend any of it, it doesn't much matter. Not that it's much catch having a thief roaming at large about the house. Anyhow, what put you on to him? How did you get on the track? You're a jolly smart kid, young Pillingshot. How did you work it?"

"I have my methods," said Pillingshot with dignity.

"Buck up. I shall have to be going over to school in a second."

"I hardly like to tell you."

"Tell me! Dash it all, I put you on to the case. I'm your employer."

"You won't touch me up if I tell you?"

"I will if you don't."

"But not if I do?"

"No."

"And how about the fee?"

"That's all right. Go on."

"All right then. Well, I thought the whole thing over, and I couldn't make anything out of it at first, because it didn't seem likely that Trent or any of the other fellows in the dormitory had taken it; and then suddenly something Evans told me the day before yesterday made it all clear."

"What was that?"

"He said that the matron had just given him back his quid, which one of the housemaids had found on the floor by his bed. It had dropped out of his pocket that first night."

Scott eyed him fixedly. Pillingshot coyly evaded his gaze.

"That was it, was it?" said Scott.

Pillingshot nodded.

"It was a clue," he said. "I worked on it."

WHEN DOCTORS DISAGREE

Newspaper advice columns are nothing new, as this story proves. Here is another light tale wherein all ends well—this one set in the working world.

It is possible that, at about the time at which this story opens, you may have gone into the Hotel Belvoir for a hair-cut. Many people did; for the young man behind the scissors, though of a singularly gloomy countenance, was undoubtedly an artist in his line. He clipped judiciously. He left no ridges. He never talked about the weather. And he allowed you to go away unburdened by any bottle of hair-food.

It is possible, too, that, being there, you decided that you might as well go the whole hog and be manicured at the same time.

It is not unlikely, moreover, that when you had got over the first shock of finding your hands so unexpectedly large and red, you felt disposed to chat with the young lady who looked after that branch of the business. In your genial way you may have permitted a note of gay (but gentlemanly) badinage to creep into your end of the dialogue.

In which case, if you had raised your eyes to the mirror, you would certainly have observed a marked increase of gloom in the demeanour of the young man attending to your apex. He took no official notice of the matter. A quick frown. A tightening of the

First Appearance: England—*Strand*, December 1910.

lips. Nothing more. Jealous as Arthur Welsh was of all who in-flicted gay badinage, however gentlemanly, on Maud Peters, he never forgot that he was an artist. Never, even in his blackest mo-ments, had he yielded to the temptation to dig the point of the scissors the merest fraction of an inch into a client's skull.

But Maud, who saw, would understand. And, if the customer was an observant man, he would notice that her replies at that juncture became somewhat absent, her smile a little mechanical.

Jealousy, according to an eminent authority, is the "hydra of calamities, the sevenfold death." Arthur Welsh's was all that and a bit over. It was a constant shadow on Maud's happiness. No fair-minded girl objects to a certain tinge of jealousy. Kept within proper bounds, it is a compliment; it makes for piquancy; it is the gin in the ginger-beer of devotion. But it should be a condiment, not a fluid.

It was the unfairness of the thing which hurt Maud. Her con-science was clear. She knew girls—several girls—who gave the young men with whom they walked out ample excuse for being perfect Othellos. If she had ever flirted on the open beach with the baritone of the troupe of pierrots, like Jane Oddy, she could have excused Arthur's attitude. If, like Pauline Dicey, she had roller-skated for a solid hour with a black-moustached stranger while her fiancé floundered in Mug's Alley she could have understood his frowning disapprovingly. But she was not like Pauline. She scorned the coquetries of Jane. Arthur was the centre of her world, and he knew it. Ever since the rainy evening when he had sheltered her under his umbrella to her Tube station, he had known per-fectly well how things were with her. And yet just because, in a strictly business-like way, she was civil to her customers, he must scowl and bite his lip and behave generally as if it had been brought to his notice that he had been nurturing a serpent in his bosom. It was worse than wicked—it was unprofessional.

She remonstrated with him.

"It isn't fair," she said, one morning when the rush of customers had ceased and they had the shop to themselves.

Matters had been worse than usual that morning. After days of rain and greyness the weather had turned over a new leaf. The sun glinted among the bottles of Unfailing Lotion in the window, and everything in the world seemed to have relaxed and become cheerful. Unfortunately, everything had included the customers. During the last few days they had taken their seats in moist gloom, and, brooding over the prospect of coming colds in the head, had had little that was pleasant to say to the divinity who was shaping their ends. But to-day it had been different. Warm and happy, they had bubbled over with gay small-talk.

"It isn't fair," she repeated.

Arthur, who was stropping a razor and whistling tunelessly, raised his eyebrows. His manner was frosty.

"I fail to understand your meaning," he said.

"You know what I mean. Do you think I didn't see you frowning when I was doing that gentleman's nails?"

The allusion was to the client who had just left—a jovial individual with a red face, who certainly had made Maud giggle a good deal. And why not? If a gentleman tells really funny stories, what harm is there in giggling? You had to be pleasant to people. If you snubbed customers, what happened? Why, sooner or later, it got round to the boss, and then where were you? Besides, it was not as if the red-faced customer had been rude. Write down on paper what he had said to her, and nobody could object to it. Write down on paper what she had said to him, and you couldn't object to that either. It was just Arthur's silliness.

She tossed her head.

"I am gratified," said Arthur, ponderously—in happier moments Maud had admired his gift of language; he read a great deal; encyclopaedias and papers and things—"I am gratified to find that you had time to bestow a glance on me. You appeared absorbed."

Maud sniffed unhappily. She had meant to be cold and dignified throughout the conversation, but the sense of her wrongs was beginning to be too much for her. A large tear splashed on to her tray of orange-sticks. She wiped it away with the chamois leather.

"It isn't fair," she sobbed. "It isn't. You know I can't help it if gentlemen talk and joke with me. You know it's all in the day's work. I'm expected to be civil to gentlemen who come in to have their hands done. Silly I should look sitting as if I'd swallowed a poker. I do think you might understand, Arthur, you being in the profession yourself."

He coughed.

"It isn't so much that you talk to them as that you seem to *like*—"

He stopped. Maud's dignity had melted completely. Her face was buried in her arms. She did not care if a million customers came in, all at the same time.

"Maud!"

She heard him moving towards her, but she did not look up. The next moment his arms were round her, and he was babbling.

And a customer, pushing open the door unnoticed two minutes later, retired hurriedly to get shaved elsewhere, doubting whether Arthur's mind was on his job.

For a time this little thunderstorm undoubtedly cleared the air. For a day or two Maud was happier than she ever remembered to have been. Arthur's behaviour was unexceptionable. He bought her a wrist-watch—light brown leather, very smart. He gave her some chocolates to eat in the Tube. He entertained her with amazing statistics, culled from the weekly paper which he bought on Tuesdays. He was, in short, the perfect lover. On the second day the red-faced man came in again. Arthur joined in the laughter at his stories. Everything seemed ideal.

It could not last. Gradually things slipped back into the old routine. Maud, looking up from her work, would see the frown and the bitten lip. She began again to feel uncomfortable and self-conscious as she worked. Sometimes their conversation on the way to the Tube was almost formal.

It was useless to say anything. She had a wholesome horror of being one of those women who nagged; and she felt that to complain again would amount to nagging. She tried to put the thing out of her mind, but it insisted on staying there. In a way she understood his feelings. He loved her so much, she supposed, that he hated the idea of her exchanging a single word with another man. This, in the abstract, was gratifying; but in practice it distressed her. She wished she were some sort of foreigner, so that nobody could talk to her. But then they would look at her, and that probably would produce much the same results. It was a hard world for a girl.

And then the strange thing happened. Arthur reformed. One might almost say that he reformed with a jerk. It was a parallel case to those sudden conversions at Welsh revival meetings. On Monday evening he had been at his worst. On the following morning he was a changed man. Not even after the original thunderstorm had he been more docile. Maud could not believe it at first. The lip, once bitten, was stretched in a smile. She looked for the frown. It was not there.

Next day it was the same; and the day after that. When a week had gone by, and still the improvement was maintained, Maud felt that she might now look upon it as permanent. A great load seemed to have been taken off her mind. She revised her views on the world. It was a very good world, quite one of the best, with Arthur beaming upon it like a sun.

A number of eminent poets and essayists, in the course of the last few centuries, have recorded, in their several ways, their opinion that one can have too much of a good thing. The truth applies even to such a good thing as absence of jealousy. Little by little Maud began to grow uneasy. It began to come home to her that she preferred the old Arthur, of the scowl and the gnawed lip. Of him she had at least been sure. Whatever discomfort she may have suffered from his spirited imitations of Othello, at any rate they had proved that he loved her. She would have accepted gladly an equal amount of discomfort now in exchange for the same certainty. She could not read this new Arthur. His thoughts were a closed book. Superficially, he was all that she could have wished. He still continued to escort her to the Tube, to buy her occasional presents, to tap, when conversing, the pleasantly sentimental vein. But now these things were not enough. Her heart was troubled. Her thoughts frightened her. The little black imp at the back of her mind kept whispering and whispering, till at last she was forced to listen. "He's tired of you. He doesn't love you any more. He's tired of you."

It is not everybody who, in times of mental stress, can find ready to hand among his or her personal acquaintances an expert counsellor, prepared at a moment's notice to listen with sympathy and advise with tact and skill. Everyone's world is full of friends, relatives and others, who will give advice on any subject that may be presented to them; but there are crises in life which cannot be left to the amateur. It is the aim of a certain widely read class of paper to fill this void.

Of this class *Fireside Chat* was one of the best-known representatives. In exchange for one penny its five hundred thousand readers received every week a serial story about life in the highest circles, a short story packed with heart-interest, articles on the removal of stains and the best method of coping with the cold mutton, anecdotes of Royalty, photographs of peeresses, hints on dress, chats about baby, brief but pointed dialogues between Blogson and Snogson, poems, Great Thoughts from the Dead and Brainy, half-hours in the editor's cosy sanctum, a slab of brown paper, and—the journal's leading feature—Advice on Matters of the Heart. The weekly contribution of the advice specialist of *Fireside Chat*, entitled "In the Consulting Room, by Dr. Cupid," was made up mainly of Answers to Correspondents. He affected the bedside manner of the kind, breezy old physician; and probably gave a good deal of comfort. At any rate, he always seemed to have plenty of cases on his hands.

It was to this expert that Maud took her trouble. She had been a regular reader of the paper for several years; and had, indeed, consulted the great man once before, when he had replied favourably to her query as to whether it would be right for her to accept caramels from Arthur, then almost a stranger. It was only natural that she should go to him now, in an even greater dilemma. The letter was not easy to write, but she finished it at last; and, after an anxious interval, judgement was delivered as follows:—

"Well, well, well! Bless my soul, what is all this? M. P. writes me:—

" 'I am a young lady, and until recently was very, very happy, except that my fiancé, though truly loving me, was of a very jealous disposition, though I am sure I gave him no cause. He would scowl when I spoke to any other man, and this used to make me unhappy. But for some time now he has quite changed, and does not seem to mind at all, and though at first this made me feel happy, to think that he had got over his jealousy, I now feel unhappy because I am beginning to be afraid that he no longer cares for me. Do you think this is so, and what ought I to do?'

"My dear young lady, I should like to be able to reassure you; but it is kindest sometimes, you know, to be candid, however it may hurt. It had been my experience that, when jealousy flies out of the window, indifference comes in at the door. In the old days a knight would joust for the love of a ladye, risking physical injury rather than permit others to rival him in her affections. I think, M.

P., that you should endeavour to discover the true state of your fiancé's feelings. I do not, of course, advocate anything in the shape of unwomanly behaviour, of which I am sure, my dear young lady, you are incapable; but I think that you should certainly try to pique your fiancé, to test him. At your next ball, for instance, refuse him a certain number of dances, on the plea that your programme is full. At garden-parties, at-homes, and so on, exhibit pleasure in the society and conversation of other gentlemen, and mark his demeanour as you do so. These little tests should serve either to relieve your apprehensions, provided they are groundless, or to show you the truth. And, after all, if it is the truth, it must be faced, must it not, M. P.?"

Before the end of the day Maud knew the whole passage by heart. The more her mind dwelt on it, the more clearly did it seem to express what she had felt but could not put into words. The point about jousting struck her as particularly well taken. She had looked up "joust" in the dictionary, and it seemed to her that in these few words was contained the kernel of her trouble. In the old days, if any man had attempted to rival him in her affections (outside business hours), Arthur would undoubtedly have jousted—and jousted with the vigour of one who means to make his presence felt. Now, in similar circumstances, he would probably step aside politely, as who should say, "After you, my dear Alphonse."

There was no time to lose. An hour after her first perusal of Dr. Cupid's advice, Maud had begun to act upon it. By the time the first lull in the morning's work had come, and there was a chance for private conversations, she had invented an imaginary young man, a shadowy Lothario, who, being introduced into her home on the previous Sunday by her brother Horace, had carried on in a way you wouldn't believe, paying all manner of compliments.

"He said I had such white hands," said Maud.

Arthur nodded, stropping a razor the while. He appeared to be bearing the revelations with complete fortitude. Yet, only a few weeks before, a customer's comment on this same whiteness had stirred him to his depths.

"And this morning—what do you think? Why, he meets me as bold as you please, and gives me a cake of toilet soap. Like his impudence!"

She paused, hopefully.

"Always useful, soap," said Arthur, politely sententious.

"Lovely it was," went on Maud, dully conscious of failure, but stippling in like an artist the little touches which give atmosphere and verisimilitude to a story. "All scented. Horace will tease me about it, *I* can tell you."

She paused. Surely he must—Why, a sea-anemone would be torn with jealousy at such a tale.

Arthur did not even wince. He was charming about it. Thought it very kind of the young fellow. Didn't blame him for being struck by the whiteness of her hands. Touched on the history of soap, which he happened to have been reading up in the encyclopaedia at the free library. And behaved altogether in such a thoroughly gentlemanly fashion that Maud stayed awake half the night, crying.

If Maud had waited another twenty-four hours there would have been no need for her to have taxed her powers of invention, for on the following day there entered the shop and her life a young man who was not imaginary—a Lothario of flesh and blood. He made his entry with that air of having bought most of the neighbouring property which belongs exclusively to minor actors, men of weight on the Stock Exchange, and American professional pugilists.

Mr. "Skipper" Shute belonged to the last-named of the three classes. He had arrived in England two months previously for the purpose of holding a conference at eight-stone four with one Joseph Edwardes, to settle a question of superiority at that weight which had been vexing the sporting public of two countries for over a year. Having successfully out-argued Mr. Edwardes, mainly by means of strenuous work in the clinches, he was now on the eve of starting on a lucrative music-hall tour with his celebrated inaudible monologue. As a result of these things he was feeling very, very pleased with the world in general, and with Mr. Skipper Shute in particular. And when Mr. Shute was pleased with himself his manner was apt to be of the breeziest.

He breezed into the shop, took a seat, and, having cast an experienced eye at Maud, and found her pleasing, extended both hands, and observed, "Go the limit, kid."

At any other time Maud might have resented being addressed as "kid" by a customer, but now she welcomed it. With the exception of a slight thickening of the lobe of one ear, Mr. Shute bore no outward signs of his profession. And being, to use his own phrase, a "swell dresser," he was really a most presentable young man.

Just, in fact, what Maud needed. She saw in him her last hope. If any faint spark of his ancient fire still lingered in Arthur, it was through Mr. Shute that it must be fanned.

She smiled upon Mr. Shute. She worked on his robust fingers as if it were an artistic treat to be permitted to handle them. So carefully did she toil that she was still busy when Arthur, taking off his apron and putting on his hat, went out for his twenty-minutes' lunch, leaving them alone together.

The door had scarcely shut when Mr. Shute bent forward.

"Say!"

He sank his voice to a winning whisper.

"You look good to muh," he said, gallantly.

"The idea!" said Maud, tossing her head.

"On the level," Mr. Shute assured her.

Maud laid down her orange-sticks.

"Don't be silly," she said. "There—I've finished."

"I've not," said Mr. Shute. "Not by a mile. Say!"

"Well?"

"What do you do with your evenings?"

"I go home."

"Sure. But when you don't? It's a poor heart that never rejoices. Don't you ever whoop it up?"

"Whoop it up?"

"The mad whirl," explained Mr. Shute. "Ice-cream soda and buck-wheat cakes, and a happy evening at lovely Luna Park."

"I don't know where Luna Park is."

"What did they teach you at school? It's out in that direction," said Mr. Shute, pointing over his shoulder. "You go straight on about three thousand miles till you hit little old New York; then you turn to the right. Say, don't you ever get a little treat? Why not come along to the White City some old evening? This evening?"

"Mr. Welsh is taking me to the White City to-night."

"And who's Mr. Welsh?"

"The gentleman who has just gone out."

"Is that so? Well, he doesn't look a live one, but maybe it's just because he's had bad news to-day. You never can tell." He rose. "Farewell, Evelina, fairest of your sex. We shall meet again; so keep a stout heart."

And, taking up his cane, straw hat, and yellow gloves, Mr. Shute departed, leaving Maud to her thoughts.

She was disappointed. She had expected better results. Mr. Shute had lowered with ease the record for gay badinage, hitherto held by the red-faced customer; yet to all appearances there had been no change in Arthur's manner. But perhaps he had scowled (or bitten his lip), and she had not noticed it. Apparently he had struck Mr. Shute, an unbiased spectator, as gloomy. Perhaps at some moment when her eyes had been on her work—She hoped for the best.

Whatever his feelings may have been during the afternoon, Arthur was undeniably cheerful that evening. He was in excellent spirits. His light-hearted abandon on the Wiggle-Woggle had been noted and commented upon by several lookers-on. Confronted with the Hairy Ainus, he had touched a high level of facetiousness. And now, as he sat with her listening to the band, he was crooning joyously to himself in accompaniment to the music, without, it would appear, a care in the world.

Maud was hurt and anxious. In a mere acquaintance this blithe attitude would have been welcome. It would have helped her to enjoy her evening. But from Arthur at that particular moment she looked for something else. Why was he cheerful? Only a few hours ago she had been—yes, flirting with another man before his very eyes. What right had he to be cheerful? He ought to be heated, full of passionate demands for an explanation—a flushed, throaty thing to be coaxed back into a good temper and then forgiven—all this at great length—for having been in a bad one. Yes, she told herself, she had wanted certainty one way or the other, and here it was. Now she knew. He no longer cared for her.

She trembled.

"Cold?" said Arthur. "Let's walk. Evening's beginning to draw in now. Lum-da-diddley-ah. That's what I call a good tune. Give me something lively and bright. Dumty-umpty-iddley-ah. Dum tum—"

"Funny thing—" said Maud, deliberately.

"What's a funny thing?"

"The gentleman in the brown suit whose hands I did this afternoon—"

"He was," agreed Arthur, brightly. "A very funny thing."

Maud frowned. Wit at the expense of Hairy Ainus was one thing—at her own another.

"I was about to say," she went on precisely, "that it was a funny thing, a coincidence, seeing that I was already engaged, that the gentleman in the brown suit whose hands I did this afternoon should have asked me to come here, to the White City, with him to-night."

For a moment they walked on in silence. To Maud it seemed a hopeful silence. Surely it must be the prelude to an outburst.

"Oh!" he said, and stopped.

Maud's heart gave a leap. Surely that was the old tone?

A couple of paces, and he spoke again.

"I didn't hear him ask you."

His voice was disappointingly level.

"He asked me after you had gone out to lunch."

"It's a nuisance," said Arthur, cheerily, "when things clash like that. But perhaps he'll ask you again. Nothing to prevent you coming here twice. Well repays a second visit, I always say. I think—"

"You shouldn't," said a voice behind him. "It hurts the head. Well, kid, being shown a good time?"

The possibility of meeting Mr. Shute had not occurred to Maud. She had assumed that, being aware that she would be there with another, he would have stayed away. It may, however, be remarked that she did not know Mr. Shute. He was not one of your sensitive plants. He smiled pleasantly upon her, looking very dapper in evening dress and a silk hat that, though a size too small for him, shone like a mirror.

Maud hardly knew whether she was glad or sorry to see him. It did not seem to matter much now either way. Nothing seemed to matter much, in fact. Arthur's cheery acceptance of the news that she received invitations from others had been like a blow, leaving her numb and listless.

She made the introductions. The two men eyed each other.

"Pleased to meet you," said Mr. Shute.

"Weather keeps up," said Arthur.

And from that point onward Mr. Shute took command.

It is to be assumed that this was not the first time that Mr. Shute had made one of a trio in these circumstances, for the swift dexterity with which he lost Arthur was certainly not that of a novice. So smoothly was it done that it was not until she emerged from the

Witching Waves, guided by the pugilist's slim but formidable right arm, that Maud realised that Arthur had gone.

She gave a little cry of dismay. Secretly she was beginning to be somewhat afraid of Mr. Shute. He was showing signs of being about to step out of the *role* she had assigned to him and attempt something on a larger scale. His manner had that extra touch of warmth which makes all the difference.

"Oh! He's gone!" she cried.

"Sure," said Mr. Shute. "He got a hurry-call from the Uji Village. The chief's cousin wants a hair-cut."

"We must find him. We must."

"Surest thing you know," said Mr. Shute. "Plenty of time."

"We must find him."

Mr. Shute regarded her with some displeasure.

"Seems to be ace-high with you, that dub," he said.

"I don't understand you."

"My observation was," explained Mr. Shute, coldly, "that, judging from appearances, that dough-faced lemon was Willie-boy, the first and only love."

Maud turned on him with flaming cheeks.

"Mr. Welsh is nothing to me! Nothing! Nothing!" she cried.

She walked quickly on.

"Then, if there's a vacancy, star-eyes," said the pugilist at her side, holding on a hat which showed a tendency to wobble, "count me in. Directly I saw you—see here, what's the idea of this roadwork? We aren't racing—"

Maud slowed down.

"That's better. As I was saying, directly I saw you, I said to myself, 'That's the one you need. The original candy kid. The—' "

His hat lurched drunkenly as he answered the girl's increase of speed. He cursed it in a brief aside.

"That's what I said. 'The original candy kid.' So—"

He shot out a restraining hand. "Arthur!" cried Maud. "Arthur!"

"It's not my name," breathed Mr. Shute, tenderly. "Call me Clarence."

Considered as an embrace, it was imperfect. At these moments a silk hat a size too small handicaps a man. The necessity of having to be careful about the nap prevented Mr. Shute from doing himself complete justice. But he did enough to induce Arthur Welsh, who, having sighted the missing ones from afar, had been approaching them at a walking pace, to substitute a run for the walk, and arrive just as Maud wrenched herself free.

Mr. Shute took off his hat, smoothed it, replaced it with extreme care, and turned his attention to the new-comer.

"Arthur!" said Maud.

Her heart gave a great leap. There was no mistaking the meaning in the eye that met hers. He cared! He cared!

"Arthur!"

He took no notice. His face was pale and working. He strode up to Mr. Shute.

"Well?" he said between his teeth.

An eight-stone-four champion of the world has many unusual experiences in his life, but he rarely encounters men who say "Well?" to him between their teeth. Mr. Shute eyed this freak with profound wonder.

"I'll teach you to—to kiss young ladies!"

Mr. Shute removed his hat again and gave it another brush. This gave him the necessary time for reflection.

"I don't need it," he said. "I've graduated."

"Put them up!" hissed Arthur.

Almost a shocked look spread itself over the pugilist's face. So might Raphael have looked if requested to draw a pavement-picture.

"You aren't speaking to ME?" he said, incredulously.

"Put them up!"

Maud, trembling from head to foot, was conscious of one overwhelming emotion. She was terrified—yes. But stronger than the terror was the great wave of elation which swept over her. All her doubts had vanished. At last, after weary weeks of uncertainty, Arthur was about to give the supreme proof. He was going to joust for her.

A couple of passers-by had paused, interested, to watch developments. You could never tell, of course. Many an apparently promising row never got any farther than words. But, glancing at Arthur's face, they certainly felt justified in pausing.

Mr. Shute spoke.

"If it wasn't," he said, carefully, "that I don't want trouble with the Society for the Prevention of Cruelty to Animals I'd—"

He broke off, for, to the accompaniment of a shout of approval from the two spectators, Arthur had swung his right fist, and it had taken him smartly on the side of the head.

Compared with the blows Mr. Shute was wont to receive in the exercise of his profession, Arthur's was a gentle tap. But there was one circumstance which gave it a deadliness all its own. Achilles had his heel. Mr. Shute's vulnerable point was at the other extremity. Instead of countering, he uttered a cry of agony, and clutched wildly with both hands at his hat.

He was too late. It fell to the ground and bounded away, with its proprietor in passionate chase. Arthur snorted and gently chafed his knuckles.

There was a calm about Mr. Shute's demeanour as, having given his treasure a final polish and laid it carefully down, he began to advance on his adversary, which was more than ominous. His lips were a thin line of steel. The muscles stood out over his jaw-bones. Crouching in his professional manner, he moved forward softly, like a cat.

And it was at this precise moment, just as the two spectators, reinforced now by eleven other men of sporting tastes, were congratulating themselves on their acumen in having stopped to watch, that Police-Constable Robert Bryce, intruding fourteen stones of bone and muscle between the combatants, addressed to Mr. Shute these memorable words: " 'Ullo, 'ullo! 'Ullo, 'ullo, 'ul-*lo!*"

Mr. Shute appealed to his sense of justice.

"The mutt knocked me hat off."

"And I'd do it again," said Arthur truculently.

"Not while I'm here you wouldn't, young fellow," said Mr. Bryce, with decision. "I'm surprised at you," he went on, pained. "And you look a respectable young chap, too. You pop off."

A shrill voice from the crowd at this point offered the constable all cinematograph rights if he would allow the contest to proceed.

"And you pop off, too, all of you," continued Mr. Bryce. "Blest if I know what kids are coming to nowadays. And as for you," he said, addressing Mr. Shute, "all you've got to do is to keep that face of yours closed. That's what you've got to do. I've got my eye on you, mind, and if I catch you a-follerin' of him"—he jerked his thumb over his shoulder at Arthur's departing figure—"I'll pinch you. Sure as you're alive." He paused. "I'd have done it already," he added, pensively, "if it wasn't me birthday."

Arthur Welsh turned sharply. For some time he had been dimly aware that somebody was calling his name.

"Oh, Arthur!"

She was breathing quickly. He could see the tears in her eyes. "I've been running. You walked so fast."

He stared down at her gloomily.

"Go away," he said. "I've done with you."

She clutched at his coat.

"Arthur, listen—listen! It's all a mistake. I thought you—you didn't care for me any more, and I was miserable, and I wrote to the paper and asked what should I do, and they said I ought to test you and try and make you jealous, and that that would relieve my apprehensions. And I hated it, but I did it, and you didn't seem to care till now. And you know that there's nobody but you."

"You—The paper? What?" he stammered.

"Yes, yes, yes. I wrote to *Fireside Chat*, and Dr. Cupid said that when jealousy flew out of the window indifference came in at the door, and that I must exhibit pleasure in the society of other gentlemen and mark your demeanour. So I—Oh!"

Arthur, luckier than Mr. Shute, was not hampered by a too small silk hat.

It was a few moments later, as they moved slowly towards the Flip-Flap—which had seemed to both of them a fitting climax for the evening's emotions—that Arthur, fumbling in his waistcoat pocket, produced a small slip of paper.

"What's that?" Maud asked.

"Read it," said Arthur. "It's from *Home Moments*, in answer to a letter I sent them. And," he added with heat, "I'd like to have five minutes alone with the chap who wrote it."

And under the electric light Maud read:—

ANSWERS TO CORRESPONDENTS.

By the Heart Specialist.

Arthur W.—Jealousy, Arthur W., is not only the most wicked, but the most foolish of passions. Shakespeare says:—

It is the green-eyed monster, which doth mock
The meat it feeds on.

You admit that you have frequently caused great distress to the young lady of your affections by your exhibition of this weakness. Exactly. There is nothing a girl dislikes or despises more than jealousy. Be a man, Arthur W. Fight against it. You may find it hard at first, but persevere. Keep a smiling face. If she seems to enjoy talking to other men, show no resentment. Be merry and bright. Believe me, it is the only way."

THE BEST SAUCE

Another vintage yarn written in the years just after the school stories and before the series stories. The English country house is the more usual Wodehouse setting, and the typical Wodehouse heroine is always in command of the situation.

Eve Hendrie sat up in bed. For two hours she had been trying to get to sleep, but without success. Never in her life had she felt more wakeful.

There were two reasons for this. Her mind was disturbed, and she was very hungry. Neither sensation was novel to her. Since first she had become paid companion to Mrs. Rastall-Retford there had hardly been a moment when she had not been hungry. Some time before Mrs. Rastall-Retford's doctor had recommended to that lady a Spartan diet, and in this Eve, as companion, had unwillingly to share. It was not pleasant for either of them, but at least Mrs. Rastall-Retford had the knowledge that she had earned it by years of honest self-indulgence. Eve had not that consolation.

Meagre fare, moreover, had the effect of accentuating Mrs. Rastall-Retford's always rather pronounced irritability. She was a massive lady, with a prominent forehead, some half-dozen chins, and a manner towards those in her employment which would have been resented in a second mate by the crew of a Western ocean tramp. Even at her best she was no ray of sunshine about the house. And since the beginning of the self-denying ordinance she had been at her worst.

First Appearance: England—*Strand*, July 1911

But it was not depression induced by her employer that was disturbing Eve. That was a permanent evil. What was agitating her so extremely to-night was the unexpected arrival of Peter Rayner.

It was Eve's practice to tell herself several times a day that she had no sentiment for Peter Rayner but dislike. She did not attempt to defend her attitude logically, but nevertheless she clung to it, and to-night, when he entered the drawing-room, she had endeavoured to convey by her manner that it was only with the greatest difficulty that she remembered him at all, and that, having accomplished that feat, she now intended to forget him again immediately. And he had grinned a cheerful, affectionate grin, and beamed on her without a break till bedtime.

Before coming as companion to Mrs. Rastall-Retford Eve had been governess to Hildebrand, aged six, the son of a Mrs. Elphinstone. It had been, on the whole, a comfortable situation. She had not liked Mrs. Elphinstone, but Hildebrand had been docile, and altogether life was quite smooth and pleasant until Mrs. Elphinstone's brother came for a visit. Peter Rayner was that brother.

There is a type of man who makes love with the secrecy and sheepish reserve of a cowboy shooting up a Wild West saloon. To this class Peter belonged. He fell in love with Eve at sight, and if, at the end of the first day, there was anyone in the house who was not aware of it, it was only Hildebrand, aged six. And even Hildebrand must have had his suspicions.

Mrs. Elphinstone was among the first to become aware of it. For two days, frostily silent and gimlet-like as to the eye, she observed Peter's hurricane wooing from afar; then she acted. Peter she sent to London, pacifying him with an invitation to return to the house in the following week. This done, she proceeded to eliminate Eve. In the course of the parting interview she expressed herself perhaps a little less guardedly than was either just or considerate; and Eve, flushed and at war with the whole race of Rayners, departed that afternoon to seek a situation elsewhere. She had found it at the house of Mrs. Rastall-Retford.

And now this evening, as she sat in the drawing-room playing the piano to her employer, in had walked the latter's son, a tall, nervous young man, perpetually clearing his throat and fiddling with a pair of gold-rimmed glasses, with the announcement that he had brought his friend, Mr. Rayner, to spend a few days in the old home.

Eve could still see the look on Peter's face as, having shaken hands with his hostess, he turned to her. It was the look of the cowboy who, his weary ride over, sees through the dusk the friendly gleam of the saloon windows, and with a happy sigh reaches for his revolver. There could be no two meanings to that look. It said, as clearly as if he had shouted it, that this was no accidental meeting; that he had tracked her down and proposed to resume matters at the point where they had left off.

Eve was indignant. It was abominable that he should pursue her in this way. She sat thinking how abominable it was for five minutes; and then it suddenly struck her that she was hungrier than ever. She had forgotten her material troubles for the moment. It seemed to her now that she was quite faint with hunger.

A cuckoo clock outside the door struck one. And, as it did so, it came to Eve that on the sideboard in the dining-room there were biscuits.

A moment later she was creeping softly down the stairs.

It was dark and ghostly on the stairs. The house was full of noises. She was glad when she reached the dining-room. It would be pleasant to switch on the light. She pushed open the door, and uttered a cry. The light was already switched on, and at the table, his back to her, was a man.

There was no time for flight. He must have heard the door open. In another moment he would turn and spring.

She spoke tremulously.

"Don't—don't move. I'm pointing a pistol at you."

The man did not move.

"Foolish child!" he said, indulgently. "Suppose it went off!"

She uttered an exclamation of surprise.

"You! What are you doing here, Mr. Rayner?"

She moved into the room, and her relief changed swiftly into indignation. On the table were half a chicken, a loaf, some cold potatoes, and a bottle of beer.

"I'm eating, thank goodness!" said Peter, helping himself to a cold potato. "I had begun to think I never should again."

"Eating!"

"Eating. I know a man of sensibility and refinement ought to shrink from raiding his hostess's larder in the small hours, but hunger's death to the finer feelings. It's the solar plexus punch

which puts one's better self down and out for the count of ten. I am
a large and healthy young man, and, believe me, I need this little
snack. I need it badly. May I cut you a slice of chicken?"

She could hardly bear to look at it, but pride gave her strength.

"No," she snapped.

"You're sure? Poor little thing; I know you're half starved."

Eve stamped.

"How dare you speak to me like that, Mr. Rayner?"

He drank bottled beer thoughtfully.

"What made you come down? I suppose you heard a noise and
thought it was burglars?" he said.

"Yes," said Eve, thankfully accepting the idea. At all costs she
must conceal the biscuit motive.

"That was very plucky of you. Won't you sit down?"

"No, I'm going back to bed."

"Not just yet. I've several things to talk to you about. Sit down.
That's right. Now cover up your poor little pink ankles, or you'll
be catching—"

She started up.

"Mr. Rayner!"

"Sit down."

She looked at him defiantly, then, wondering at herself for doing
it, sat down.

"Now," said Peter, "what do you mean by it? What do you
mean by dashing off from my sister's house without leaving a word
for me as to where you were going? You knew I loved you."

"Good night, Mr. Rayner."

"Sit down. You've given me a great deal of trouble. Do you
know it cost me a sovereign in tips to find out your address? I
couldn't get it out of my sister, and I had to apply to the butler.
I've a good mind to knock it off your first week's pin-money."

"I shall not stay here listening—"

"You knew perfectly well I wanted to marry you. But you fly off
without a word and bury yourself in this benighted place with a
gorgon who nags and bullies you—"

"A nice way to speak of your hostess," said Eve, scornfully.

"A very soothing way. I don't think I ever took such a dislike to
a woman at first sight before. And when she started to bullyrag
you, it was all I could do— But it won't last long now. You must

come away at once. We'll be married after Christmas, and in the meantime you can go and live with my sister—"

Eve listened speechlessly. She had so much to say that the difficulty of selection rendered her dumb.

"When can you start? I mean, do you have to give a month's notice or anything?"

Eve got up with a short laugh.

"Good night, Mr. Rayner," she said. "You have been very amusing, but I am getting tired."

"I'm glad it's all settled," said Peter. "Good night."

Eve stopped. She could not go tamely away without saying a single one of the things that crowded in her mind.

"Do you imagine," she said, "that I intend to marry you? Do you suppose, for one moment—"

"Rather!" said Peter. "You shall have a splendid time from now on, to make up for all you've gone through. I'm going to be awfully good to you, Eve. You sha'n't ever have any more worries, poor old thing." He looked at her affectionately. "I wonder why it is that large men always fall in love with little women. There are you, a fragile, fairy-like, ethereal wisp of a little creature; and here am I—"

"A great, big, greedy pig!" burst out Eve, "who thinks about nothing but eating and drinking."

"I wasn't going to have put it quite like that," said Peter, thoughtfully.

"I hate a greedy man," said Eve, between her teeth.

"I have a healthy appetite," protested Peter. "Nothing more. It runs in the family. At the time of the Civil War the Rayner of the period, who was King Charles's right-hand man, would frequently eat despatches to prevent them falling into the hands of the enemy. He was noted for it."

Eve reached the door and turned.

"I despise you," she said.

"Good night," said Peter, tenderly. "To-morrow morning we'll go for a walk."

His prediction proved absolutely correct. He was smoking a cigarette after breakfast when Eve came to him. Her face was pink and mutinous, but there was a gleam in her eye.

"Are you ready to come out, Mr. Rayner?" she said. "Mrs.

Rastall-Retford says I'm to take you to see the view from the golf links."

"You'll like that," said Peter.

"I shall not like it," snapped Eve. "But Mrs. Rastall-Retford is paying me a salary to do what she tells me, and I have to earn it."

Conversation during the walk consisted mainly of a monologue on the part of Peter. It was a crisp and exhilarating morning, and he appeared to be feeling a universal benevolence towards all created things. He even softened slightly on the subject of Mrs. Rastall-Retford, and advanced the theory that her peculiar manner might be due to her having been ill-treated as a child.

Eve listened in silence. It was not till they were nearing home on their return journey that she spoke.

"Mr. Rayner," she said.

"Yes?" said Peter.

"I was talking to Mrs. Rastall-Retford after breakfast," said Eve, "and I told her something about you."

"My conscience is clear."

"Oh, nothing bad. Some people would say it was very much to your credit." She looked away across the fields. "I told her you were a vegetarian," she added, carelessly.

There was a long silence. Then Peter spoke three words, straight from the heart.

"You little devil!"

Eve turned and looked at him, her eyes sparkling wickedly.

"You see!" she said. "Now perhaps you will go."

"Without you?" said Peter, stoutly. "Never!"

"In London you will be able to eat all day—anything you like. You will be able to creep about your club gnawing cold chicken all night. But if you stay here—"

"You have got a wrong idea of the London clubman's life," said Peter. "If I crept about my club gnawing cold chicken I should have the committee after me. No, I shall stay here and look after you. After all, what is food?"

"I'll tell you what yours will be, if you like. Or would you rather wait and let it be a surprise? Well, for lunch you will have some boiled potatoes and cabbage and a sweet—a sort of light *soufflé* thing. And for dinner—"

"Yes, but one moment," said Peter. "If I'm a vegetarian, how did you account for my taking all the chicken I could get at dinner last night, and looking as if I wanted more?"

"Oh, that was your considerateness. You didn't want to give trouble, even if you had to sacrifice your principles. But it's all right now. You are going to have your vegetables."

Peter drew a deep breath—the breath of the man who braces himself up and thanks whatever gods there be for his unconquerable soul.

"I don't care," he said. " 'A book of verses underneath the bough, a jug of wine, and thou—' "

"Oh, and I forgot," interrupted Eve. "I told her you were a teetotaller as well."

There was another silence, longer than the first.

"The best train," said Eve, at last, "is the ten-fifty."

He looked at her inquiringly.

"The best train?"

"For London."

"What makes you think that I am interested in trains to London?"

Eve bit her lip.

"Mr. Rayner," she said, after a pause, "do you remember at lunch one day at Mrs. Elphinstone's refusing parsnips? You said that, so far as you were concerned, parsnips were first by a mile, and that prussic acid and strychnine also ran."

"Well?" said Peter.

"Oh, nothing," said Eve. "Only I made a stupid mistake. I told the cook you were devoted to parsnips. I'm sorry."

Peter looked at her gravely. "I'm putting up with a lot for your sake," he said.

"You needn't. Why don't you go away?"

"And leave you chained to the rock, Andromeda? Not for Perseus! I've only been here one night, but I've seen enough to know that I've got to take you away from this place. Honestly, it's killing you. I was watching you last night. You're scared if that infernal old woman starts to open her mouth. She's crushing the life out of you. I'm going to stay on here till you say you'll marry me, or till they throw me out."

"There are parsnips for dinner to-night," said Eve, softly.

"I shall get to like them. They are an acquired taste, I expect.

Perhaps I am, too. Perhaps I am the human parsnip, and you will have to learn to love me."

"You are the human burr," said Eve, shortly. "I shouldn't have thought it possible for a man to behave as you are doing."

In spite of herself, there were moments during the next few days when Eve felt twinges of remorse. It was only by telling herself that he had no right to have followed her to this house, and that he was at perfect liberty to leave whenever he wished, that she could harden her heart again. And even this reflection was not entirely satisfactory, for it made her feel how fond he must be of her to endure these evils for her sake.

And there was no doubt about there being evils. It was a dreary house in which to spend winter days. There were no books that one could possibly read. The nearest railway station was five miles away. There was not even a dog to talk to. Generally it rained. Though Eve saw little of Peter, except at meals and in the drawing-room after dinner—for Mrs. Rastall-Retford spent most of the day in her own sitting-room and required Eve to be at her side—she could picture his sufferings, and, try as she would, she could not keep herself from softening a little. Her pride was weakening. Constant attendance on her employer was beginning to have a bad effect on her nerves. Association in a subordinate capacity with Mrs. Rastall-Retford did not encourage a proud and spirited outlook on life.

Her imagination had not exaggerated Peter's sufferings. Many people consider that Dante has spoken the last word on the postmortem housing of the criminal classes. Peter, after the first week of his visit, could have given him a few new ideas.

It is unpleasant to be half starved. It is unpleasant to be cooped up in a country-house in winter with nothing to do. It is unpleasant to have to sit at meals and listen to the only girl you have ever really loved being bullyragged by an old lady with six chins. And all these unpleasantnesses were occurring to Peter simultaneously. It is highly creditable to him that the last should completely have outweighed the others.

He was generally alone. Mr. Rastall-Retford, who would have been better than nothing as a companion, was a man who enjoyed solitude. He was a confirmed vanisher. He would be present at one moment, the next he would have glided silently away. And, even on the rare occasions when he decided not to vanish, he seldom did much more than clear his throat nervously and juggle with his pince-nez.

Peter, in his boyhood, had been thrilled once by a narrative of a man who got stuck in the Sargasso Sea. It seemed to him now that the monotony of the Sargasso Sea had been greatly exaggerated.

Nemesis was certainly giving Peter his due. He had wormed his way into the Rastall-Retford home-circle by grossly deceitful means. The moment he heard that Eve had gone to live with Mrs. Rastall-Retford, and had ascertained that the Rastall-Retford with whom he had been at Cambridge and whom he still met occasionally at his club when he did not see him first, was this lady's son, he had set himself to court young Mr. Rastall-Retford. He had cornered him at the club and begun to talk about the dear old 'Varsity days, ignoring the embarrassment of the latter, whose only clear recollection of the dear old 'Varsity days as linking Peter and himself was of a certain bump-supper night, when sundry of the festive, led and inspired by Peter, had completely wrecked his rooms and shaved off half a growing moustache. He conveyed to young Mr. Rastall-Retford the impression that, in the dear old 'Varsity days, they had shared each other's joys and sorrows, and, generally, had made Damon and Pythias look like a pair of cross-talk knockabouts at one of the rowdier music-halls. Not to invite so old a friend to stay at his home, if he ever happened to be down that way, would, he hinted, be grossly churlish. Mr. Rastall-Retford, impressed, issued the invitation. And now Peter was being punished for his deceit. Nemesis may not be an Alfred Shrubb, but give her time and she gets there.

It was towards the middle of the second week of his visit that Eve, coming into the drawing-room before dinner, found Peter standing in front of the fire. They had not been alone together for several days.

"Well?" said he.

Eve went to the fire and warmed her hands.

"Well?" she said, dispiritedly.

She was feeling nervous and ill. Mrs. Rastall-Retford had been in one of her more truculent moods all day, and for the first time Eve had the sensation of being thoroughly beaten. She dreaded the long hours to bedtime. The thought that there might be bridge after dinner made her feel physically ill. She felt she could not struggle through a bridge night.

On the occasions when she was in one of her dangerous moods, Mrs. Rastall-Retford sometimes chose rest as a cure, sometimes relaxation. Rest meant that she retired to her room immediately after dinner, and expended her venom on her maid; relaxation meant bridge, and bridge seemed to bring out all her worst points. They played the game·for counters at her house, and there had been occasions in Eve's experience when the loss of a hundred or so of these useful little adjuncts to Fun in the Home had lashed her almost into a frenzy. She was one of those bridge players who keep up a running quarrel with Fate during the game, and when she was not abusing Fate she was generally reproaching her partner. Eve was always her partner; and to-night she devoutly hoped that her employer would elect to rest. She always played badly with Mrs. Rastall-Retford, through sheer nervousness. Once she had revoked, and there had been a terrible moment and much subsequent recrimination.

Peter looked at her curiously.

"You're pale to-night," he said.

"I have a headache."

"H'm! How is our hostess? Fair? Or stormy?"

"As I was passing her door I heard her bullying her maid, so I suppose stormy."

"That means a bad time for you?" he said, sympathetically.

"I suppose so. If we play bridge. But she may go to bed directly after dinner."

She tried to keep her voice level, but he detected the break.

"Eve," he said, quickly, "won't you let me take you away from here? You've no business in this sort of game. You're not tough enough. You've got to be loved and made a fuss of and—"

She laughed shakily.

"Perhaps you can give me the address of some lady who wants a companion to love and make a fuss of?"

"I can give you the address of a man."

She rested an arm on the mantelpiece and stood looking into the blaze, without replying.

Before he could speak again there was a step outside the door, and Mrs. Rastall-Retford rustled into the room.

Eve had not misread the storm-signals. Her employer's mood was still as it had been earlier in the day. Dinner passed in almost complete silence. Mrs. Rastall-Retford sat brooding dumbly. Her eye was cold and menacing, and Peter, working his way through his vegetables, shuddered for Eve. He had understood her allusion to bridge, having been privileged several times during his stay to see his hostess play that game, and he hoped that there would be no bridge to-night.

And this was unselfish of him, for bridge meant sandwiches. Punctually at nine o'clock on bridge nights the butler would deposit on a side-table a plate of chicken sandwiches and (in deference to Peter's vegetarian views) a smaller plate of cheese sandwiches. At the close of play Mrs. Rastall-Retford would take one sandwich from each plate, drink a thimbleful of weak whisky and water, and retire.

Peter could always do with a sandwich or two these days. But he was prepared to abandon them joyfully if his hostess would waive bridge for this particular evening.

It was not to be. In the drawing-room Mrs. Rastall-Retford came out of her trance and called imperiously for the cards. Peter, when he saw his hand after the first deal, had a presentiment that if all his hands were to be as good as this, the evening was going to be a trying one. On the other occasions when they had played he had found it an extremely difficult task, even with moderate cards, to bring it about that his hostess should always win the odd rubber, for he was an excellent player, and, like most good players, had an artistic conscience which made it painful to him to play a deliberately bad game, even from the best motives. If all his hands were going to be as strong as this first one he saw that there was disaster ahead. He could not help winning.

Mrs. Rastall-Retford, who had dealt the first hand, made a most improper diamond declaration. Her son unfilially doubled, and, Eve having chicane—a tragedy which her partner evidently seemed to consider could have been avoided by the exercise of ordinary common sense—Peter and his partner, despite Peter's best efforts, won the game handsomely.

The son of the house dealt the next hand. Eve sorted her cards listlessly. She was feeling curiously tired. Her brain seemed dulled.

This hand, as the first had done, went all in favour of the two men. Mr. Rastall-Retford won five tricks in succession, and, judging from the glitter in his mild eye, was evidently going to win as many more as he possibly could. Mrs. Rastall-Retford glowered silently. There was electricity in the air.

The son of the house led a club. Eve played a card mechanically.

"Have you no clubs, Miss Hendrie?"

Eve started, and looked at her hand.

"No," she said.

Mrs. Rastall-Retford grunted suspiciously.

Not long ago, in Westport, Connecticut, U.S.A., a young man named Harold Sperry, a telephone worker, was boring a hole in the wall of a house with a view to passing a wire through it. He whistled joyously as he worked. He did not know that he had selected for purposes of perforation the exact spot where there lay, nestling in the brickwork, a large leaden water-pipe. The first intimation he had of that fact was when a jet of water suddenly knocked him fifteen feet into a rosebush.

As Harold felt then, so did Eve now, when, examining her hand once more to make certain that she had no clubs, she discovered the ace of that ilk peeping coyly out from behind the seven of spades.

Her face turned quite white. It is never pleasant to revoke at bridge, but to Eve just then it seemed a disaster beyond words. She looked across at her partner. Her imagination pictured the scene there would be ere long, unless—

It happens every now and then that the human brain shows in a crisis an unwonted flash of speed. Eve's did at this juncture. To her in her trouble there came a sudden idea.

She looked round the table. Mr. Rastall-Retford, having taken the last trick, had gathered it up in the introspective manner of one planning big *coups*, and was brooding tensely, with knit brows. His mother was frowning over her cards. She was unobserved.

She seized the opportunity. She rose from her seat, moved quickly to the side-table, and, turning her back, slipped the fatal card dexterously into the interior of a cheese sandwich.

Mrs. Rastall-Retford, absorbed, did not notice for an instant. Then she gave tongue.

"What are you doing, Miss Hendrie?"

Eve was breathing quickly.

"I—I thought that Mr. Rayner might like a sandwich."

She was at his elbow with the plate. It trembled in her hand.

"A sandwich! Kindly do not be so officious, Miss Hendrie. The idea—in the middle of a hand—" Her voice died away in a resentful mumble.

Peter started. He had been allowing his thoughts to wander. He looked from the sandwich to Eve and then at the sandwich again. He was puzzled. This had the aspect of being an olive-branch—could it be? Could she be meaning—? Or was it a subtle insult? Who could say? At any rate it was a sandwich, and he seized it, without prejudice.

"I hope at least you have had the sense to remember that Mr. Rayner is a vegetarian, Miss Hendrie," said Mrs. Rastall-Retford. "That is not a chicken sandwich?"

"No," said Eve; "it is not a chicken sandwich."

Peter beamed gratefully. He raised the olive-branch, and bit into it with the energy of a starving man. And as he did so he caught Eve's eye.

"Miss Hendrie!" cried Mrs. Rastall-Retford.

Eve started violently.

"Miss Hendrie, will you be good enough to play? The king of clubs to beat. I can't think what's the matter with you to-night."

"I'm very sorry," said Eve, and put down the nine of spades.

Mrs. Rastall-Retford glared.

"This is absurd," she cried. "You *must* have the ace of clubs. If you have not got it, who has? Look through your hand again. Is it there?"

"No."

"Then where can it be?"

"Where can it be?" echoed Peter, taking another bite.

"Why—why," said Eve, crimson, "I—I—have only five cards. I ought to have six."

"Five?" said Mrs. Rastall-Retford "Nonsense! Count again. Have you dropped it on the floor?"

Mr. Rastall-Retford stooped and looked under the table.

"It is not on the floor," he said. "I suppose it must have been missing from the pack before I dealt."

Mrs. Rastall-Retford threw down her cards and rose ponderously. It offended her vaguely that there seemed to be nobody to blame. "I shall go to bed," she said.

Peter stood before the fire and surveyed Eve as she sat on the sofa. They were alone in the room, Mr. Rastall-Retford having drifted silently away in the wake of his mother. Suddenly Eve began to laugh helplessly.

He shook his head at her.

"This is considerably sharper than a serpent's tooth," he said. "You should be fawning gratefully upon me, not laughing. Do you suppose King Charles laughed at my ancestor when he ate the despatches? However, for the first time since I have been in this house I feel as if I had had a square meal."

Eve became suddenly serious. The smile left her face.

"Mr. Rayner, please don't think I'm ungrateful. I couldn't help laughing, but I can't tell you how grateful I am. You don't know what it would have been like if she had found out that I had revoked. I did it once before, and she kept on about it for days and days. It was awful." She shivered. "I think you must be right, and my nerves *are* going."

He nodded.

"So are you—to-morrow, by the first train. I wonder how soon we can get married. Do you know anything about special licenses?"

She looked at him curiously.

"You're very obstinate," she said.

"Firm," he corrected. "Firm. Could you pack to-night, do you think, and be ready for that ten-fifty to-morrow morning?"

She began to trace an intricate pattern on the floor with the point of her shoe.

"I can't imagine why you are fond of me!" she said. "I've been very horrid to you."

"Nonsense. You've been all that's sweet and womanly."

"And I want to tell you why," she went on. "Your—your sister—"

"Ah, I though as much!"

"She—she saw that you seemed to be getting fond of me, and she—"

"She would!"

"Said some rather horrid things that—hurt," said Eve, in a low voice.

Peter crossed over to where she sat and took her hand.

"Don't you worry about her," he said. "She's not a bad sort really, but about once every six months she needs a brotherly talking-to, or she gets above herself. One is about due during the next few days."

He stroke her hand.

"Fasting," he said, thoughtfully, "clears and stimulates the brain. I fancy I shall be able to think out some rather special things to say to her this time."

POTS O' MONEY

Wodehouse's own unhappy and brief career in banking was the inspiration for this story. Happily, the hero is able to escape into the make-believe world of the theater, just as Plum himself had done a few years earlier.

Owen Bentley was feeling embarrassed. He looked at Mr. Sheppherd, and with difficulty restrained himself from standing on one leg and twiddling his fingers. At one period of his career, before the influence of his uncle Henry had placed him in the London and Suburban Bank, Owen had been an actor. On the strength of a batting average of thirty-three point nought seven for Middlesex, he had been engaged by the astute musical-comedy impresario to whom the idea first occurred that, if you have got to have young men to chant "We are merry and gay, tra-la, for this is Bohemia," in the Artists' Ball scene, you might just as well have young men whose names are known to the public. He had not been an actor long, for loss of form had put him out of first-class cricket, and the impresario had given his place in the next piece to a googly bowler who had done well in the last 'Varsity match; but he had been one long enough to experience that sinking sensation which is known as stage-fright. And now, as he began to explain to Mr. Sheppherd that he wished for his consent to marry his daughter Audrey, he found himself suffering exactly the same symptoms.

From the very start, from the moment when he revealed the fact that his income, salary and private means included, amounted to

First Appearance: England—*Strand*, December 1911

less than two hundred pounds, he had realized that this was going to be one of his failures. It was the gruesome Early Victorian-ness of it all that took the heart out of him. Mr. Sheppherd had always reminded him of a heavy father out of a three-volume novel, but, compared with his demeanour as he listened now, his attitude hitherto had been light and whimsical. Until this moment Owen had not imagined that this sort of thing ever happened nowadays outside the comic papers. By the end of the second minute he would not have been surprised to find himself sailing through the air, urged by Mr. Sheppherd's boot, his transit indicated by a dotted line and a few stars.

Mr. Sheppherd's manner was inclined to bleakness.

"This is most unfortunate," he said. "Most unfortunate. I have my daughter's happiness to consider. It is my duty as a father." He paused. "You say you have no prospects? I should have supposed that your uncle—? Surely, with his influence—?"

"My uncle shot his bolt when he got me into the bank. That finished him, as far as I'm concerned. I'm not his only nephew, you know. There are about a hundred others, all trailing him like bloodhounds."

Mr. Sheppherd coughed the small cough of disapproval. He was feeling more than a little aggrieved.

He had met Owen for the first time at dinner at the house of his uncle Henry, a man of unquestioned substance, whose habit it was to invite each of his eleven nephews to dinner once a year. But Mr. Sheppherd did not know this. For all he knew, Owen was in the habit of hobnobbing with the great man every night. He could not say exactly that it was sharp practice on Owen's part to accept his invitation to call, and having called, to continue calling long enough to make the present deplorable situation possible; but he felt that it would have been in better taste for the young man to have effaced himself and behaved more like a bank-clerk and less like an heir.

"I am exceedingly sorry for this, Mr. Bentley," he said, "but you will understand that I cannot— It is, of course, out of the question. It would be best, in the circumstances, I think, if you did not see my daughter again—"

"She's waiting in the passage outside," said Owen, simply.

"—after to-day. Good-bye."

Owen left the room. Audrey was hovering in the neighbourhood of the door. She came quickly up to him, and his spirits rose, as they always did, at the sight of her.

"Well?" she said.

He shook his head.

"No good," he said.

Audrey considered the problem for a moment, and was rewarded with an idea.

"Shall I go in and cry?"

"It wouldn't be any use."

"Tell me what happened."

"He said I mustn't see you again."

"He didn't mean it."

"He thinks he did."

Audrey reflected.

"We shall simply have to keep writing, then. And we can talk on the telephone. That isn't seeing each other. Has your bank a telephone?"

"Yes. But—"

"That's all right, then. I'll ring you up every day."

"I wish I could make some money," said Owen, thoughtfully. "But I seem to be one of those chaps who can't. Nothing I try comes off. I've never drawn anything except a blank in a sweep. I spent about two pounds on sixpenny postal orders when the Limerick craze was on, and didn't win a thing. Once when I was on tour I worked myself to a shadow, dramatizing a novel. Nothing came of that, either."

"What novel?"

"A thing called *White Roses*, by a woman named Edith Butler."

Audrey looked up quickly.

"I suppose you knew her very well? Were you great friends?"

"I didn't know her at all. I'd never met her. I just happened to buy the thing at a bookstall, and thought it would make a good play. I expect it was pretty bad rot. Anyhow, she never took the trouble to send it back or even acknowledge receipt."

"Perhaps she never got it?"

"I registered it."

"She was a cat," said Audrey, decidedly. "I'm glad of it though.

If another woman had helped you make a lot of money, I should have died of jealousy."

Routine is the death of heroism. For the first few days after his parting with Mr. Sheppherd, Owen was in heroic mood, full of vaguely dashing schemes, regarding the world as his oyster, and burning to get at it, sword in hand. But routine, with its ledgers and its copying-ink and its customers, fell like a grey cloud athwart his horizon, blotting out rainbow visions of sudden wealth, dramatically won. Day by day the glow faded and hopelessness grew.

If the glow did not entirely fade it was due to Audrey, who more than fulfilled her promise of ringing him up on the telephone. She rang him up at least once, frequently several times, every day, a fact which was noted and commented upon in a harshly critical spirit by the head of his department, a man with no soul and a strong objection to doing his subordinates' work for them.

As a rule, her conversation, though pleasing, was discursive and lacked central motive, but one morning she had genuine news to impart.

"Owen"—her voice was excited—"have you seen the paper to-day? Then listen. I'll read it out. Are you listening? This is what it says: 'The Piccadilly Theatre will reopen shortly with a dramatized verison of Miss Edith Butler's popular novel, *White Roses*, prepared by the authoress herself. A strong cast is being engaged, including—' And then a lot of names. What are you going to do about it, Owen?"

"What am I going to do?"

"Don't you see what's happened? That awful woman has stolen your play. She has waited all these years, hoping you would forget. What are you laughing at?"

"I wasn't laughing."

"Yes, you were. It tickled my ear. I'll ring off if you do it again. You don't believe me. Well, you wait and see if I'm not—"

"Edith Butler's incapable of such a thing."

There was a slight pause at the other end of the wire.

"I thought you said you didn't know her," said Audrey, jealously.

"I don't—I don't, " said Owen, hastily. "But I've read her books. They're simply chunks of superfatted sentiment. She's a sort of literary onion. She compels tears. A woman like that couldn't steal a play if she tried."

"You can't judge authors from their books. You must go and see the play when it comes on. Then you'll see I'm right. I'm absolutely certain that woman is trying to swindle you. Don't laugh in that horrid way. Very well, I told you I should ring off, and now I'm going to."

At the beginning of the next month Owen's annual holiday arrived. The authorities of the London and Suburban Bank were no niggards. They recognized that a man is not a machine. They gave their employees ten days in the year in which to tone up their systems for another twelve months' work.

Owen had spent his boyhood in the Shropshire village of which his father had been rector, and thither he went when his holiday came round, to the farm of one Dorman. He was glad of the chance to get to Shropshire. There is something about the country there, with its green fields and miniature rivers, that soothes the wounded spirit and forms a pleasant background for sentimental musings.

It was comfortable at the farm. The household consisted of Mr. Dorman, an old acquaintance, his ten-year-old son George, and Mr. Dorman's mother, an aged lady with a considerable local reputation as a wise woman. Rumour had it that the future held no mysteries for her, and it was known that she could cure warts, bruised fingers, and even the botts by means of spells.

Except for these, Owen had fancied that he was alone in the house. It seemed not, however. There was a primeval piano in his sitting-room, and on the second morning it suited his mood to sit down at this and sing "Asthore," the fruity pathos of which ballad appealed to him strongly at this time, accompanying himself by an ingenious arrangement in three chords. He had hardly begun, however, when Mr. Dorman appeared, somewhat agitated.

"If you don't mind, Mr. Owen," he said. "I forgot to tell you. There's a lit'ery gent boarding with me in the room above, and he can't bear to be disturbed."

A muffled stamping from the ceiling bore out his words.

"Writing a book, he is," continued Mr. Dorman. "He caught young George a clip over the ear-'ole yesterday for blowing his trumpet on the stairs. Gave him sixpence afterwards, and said he'd skin him if he ever did it again. So, if you don't mind—"

"Oh, all right," said Owen. "Who is he?"

"Gentleman of the name of Prosser."

Owen could not recollect having come across any work by anyone of that name; but he was not a wide reader; and, whether the man above was a celebrity or not, he was entitled to quiet.

"I never heard of him," he said, "but that's no reason why I should disturb him. Let him rip. I'll cut the musical effects in future."

The days passed smoothly by. The literary man remained invisible, though occasionally audible, tramping the floor in the frenzy of composition. Nor, until the last day of his visit, did Owen see old Mrs. Dorman.

That she was not unaware of his presence in the house, however, was indicated on the last morning. He was smoking an after-breakfast pipe at the open window and waiting for the dog-cart that was to take him to the station, when George, the son of the house, entered.

George stood in the doorway, grinned, and said:

"Farsezjerligranmatellyerforchbythercards?"

"Eh?" said Owen.

The youth repeated the word.

"Once again."

On the second repetition light began to creep in. A boyhood spent in the place, added to this ten days' stay, had made Owen something of a linguist.

"Father says would I like grandma to do what?"

"Tell yer forch'n by ther cards."

"Where is she?"

"Backyarnder."

Owen followed him into the kitchen, where he found Mr. Dorman, the farmer, and, seated at the table, fumbling with a pack of cards, an old woman, whom he remembered well.

"Mother wants to tell your fortune," said Mr. Dorman, in a hoarse aside. "She always will tell visitors' fortunes. She told Mr. Prosser's, and he didn't half like it, because she said he'd be engaged in two months and married inside the year. He said wild horses wouldn't make him do it."

"She can tell me that if she likes. I sha'n't object."

"Mother, here's Mr. Owen."

"I seed him fast enough," said the old woman, briskly. "Shuffle, an' cut three times."

She then performed mysterious manoeuvres with the cards.

"I see pots o' money," announced the sibyl.

"If she says it, it's there right enough," said her son.

"She means my bonus," said Owen. "But that's only ten pounds. And I lose it if I'm late twice more before Christmas."

"It'll come sure enough."

"Pots," said the old woman, and she was still mumbling the encouraging word when Owen left the kitchen and returned to the sitting-room.

He laughed rather ruefully. At that moment he could have found a use for pots o' money.

He walked to the window, and looked out. It was a glorious morning. The heat-mist was dancing over the meadow beyond the brook, and from the farmyard came the liquid charawks of carefree fowls. It seemed wicked to leave these haunts of peace for London on such a day.

An acute melancholy seized him. Absently, he sat down at the piano. The prejudices of literary Mr. Prosser had slipped from his mind. Softly at first, then gathering volume as the spirit of the song gripped him, he began to sing "Asthore." He became absorbed.

He had just, for the sixth time, won through to "Iyam-ah waiting for-er theeee-yass-thorre," and was doing some intricate three-chord work preparatory to starting over again, when a loaf of bread whizzed past his ear. It missed him by an inch, and crashed against a plaster statuette of the Infant Samuel on the top of the piano.

It was a standard loaf, containing eighty per cent of the semolina, and it practically wiped the Infant Samuel out of existence. At the same moment, at his back, there sounded a loud, wrathful snort.

He spun round. The door was open, and at the other side of the table was standing a large, black-bearded, shirt-sleeved man, in an attitude rather reminiscent of Ajax defying the lightning. His hands trembled. His beard bristled. His eyes gleamed ferociously beneath enormous eyebrows. As Owen turned, he gave tongue in a voice like the discharge of a broadside.

"Stop it!"

Owen's mind, wrenched too suddenly from the dreamy future to the vivid present, was not yet completely under control. He gaped.

"Stop—that—infernal—noise!" roared the man.

He shot through the door, banging it after him, and pounded up the stairs.

Owen was annoyed. The artistic temperament was all very well, but there were limits. It was absurd that obscure authors should behave in this way. Prosser! Who on earth was Prosser? Had anyone ever heard of him? No! Yet here he was going about the country clipping small boys over the ear-hole, and flinging loaves of bread at bank-clerks as if he were Henry James or Marie Corelli. Owen reproached himself bitterly for his momentary loss of presence of mind. If he had only kept his head, he could have taken a flying shot at the man with the marmalade-pot. It had been within easy reach. Instead of which, he had merely stood and gaped. Of all sad words of tongue or pen, the saddest are these, "It might have been."

His manly regret was interrupted by the entrance of Mr. Dorman with the information that the dog-cart was at the door.

Audrey was out of town when Owen arrived in London, but she returned a week later. The sound of her voice through the telephone did much to cure the restlessness from which he had been suffering since the conclusion of his holiday. But the thought that she was so near yet so inaccessible produced in him a meditative melancholy which enveloped him like a cloud that would not lift. His manner became distrait. He lost weight.

If customers were not vaguely pained by his sad, pale face, it was only because the fierce rush of modern commercial life leaves your business man little leisure for observing pallor in bank-clerks. What did pain them was the gentle dreaminess with which he performed his duties. He was in the Inward Bills Department, one of the features of which was the sudden inrush towards the end of the afternoon, of hatless, energetic young men with leather bags strapped to their left arms, clamouring for mysterious crackling documents, much fastened with pins. Owen had never quite understood what it was that these young men did want, and now his detached mind refused even more emphatically to grapple with the problem. He distributed the documents at random with the air of a preoccupied monarch scattering largess to the mob, and the subsequent chaos had to be handled by a wrathful head of the department in person.

Man's power of endurance is limited. At the end of the second week the overwrought head appealed passionately for relief, and

Owen was removed to the Postage Department, where, when he had leisure from answering Audrey's telephone calls, he entered the addresses of letters in a large book and took them to the post. He was supposed also to stamp them, but a man in love cannot think of everything, and he was apt at times to overlook this formality.

One morning, receiving from one of the bank messengers the usual intimation that a lady wished to speak to him on the telephone, he went to the box and took up the receiver.

"Is that you, Owen? Owen, I went to *White Roses* last night. Have you been yet?"

"Not yet."

"Then you must go to-night. Owen, I'm *certain* you wrote it. It's perfectly lovely. I cried my eyes out. If you don't go to-night, I'll never speak to you again, even on the telephone. Promise."

"Must I?"

"Yes, you must. Why, suppose it *is* yours! It may mean a fortune. The stalls were simply packed. I'm going to ring up the theatre now and engage a seat for you, and pay for it myself."

"No—I say—" protested Owen.

"Yes, I shall. I can't trust you to go, if I don't. And I'll ring up early to-morrow to hear all about it. Good-bye."

Owen left the box somewhat depressed. Life was quite gloomy enough as it was, without going out of one's way to cry one's eyes out over sentimental plays.

His depression was increased by the receipt, on his return to his department, of a message from the manager, stating that he would like to see Mr. Bentley in his private room for a moment. Owen never enjoyed these little chats with Authority. Out of office hours, in the circle of his friends, he had no doubt the manager was a delightful and entertaining companion; but in his private room his conversation was less enjoyable.

The manager was seated at his table, thoughtfully regarding the ceiling. His resemblance to a stuffed trout, always striking, was subtly accentuated, and Owen, an expert in these matters, felt that his fears had been well founded—there was trouble in the air. Somebody had been complaining of him, and he was now about, as the phrase went, to be "run in."

A large man, seated with his back to the door, turned as he entered, and Owen recognized the well-remembered features of Mr. Prosser, the literary loaf-slinger.

Owen regarded him without resentment. Since returning to London he had taken the trouble of looking up his name in *Who's Who?* and had found that he was not so undistinguished as he had supposed. He was, it appeared, a Regius Professor and the author of some half-dozen works on sociology—a record, Owen felt, that almost justified loaf-flinging and ear-hole clipping in moments of irritation.

The manager started to speak, but the man of letters anticipated him.

"Is this the fool?" he roared. "Young man, I have no wish to be hard on a congenital idiot who is not responsible for his actions, but I must insist on an explanation. I understand that you are in charge of the correspondence in this office. Well, during the last week you have three times sent unstamped letters to my fiancée, Miss Vera Delane, Woodlands, Southbourne, Hants. What's the matter with you? Do you think she likes paying twopence a time, or what is it?"

Owen's mind leaped back at the words. They recalled something to him. Then he remembered.

He was conscious of a not unpleasant thrill. He had not known that he was superstitious, but for some reason he had not been able to get those absurd words of Mr. Dorman's mother out of his mind. And here was another prediction of hers, equally improbable, fulfilled to the letter.

"Great Scott!" he cried. "Are you going to be married?"

Mr. Prosser and the manager started simultaneously.

"Mrs. Dorman said you would be," said Owen. "Don't you remember?"

Mr. Prosser looked keenly at him.

"Why, I've seen you before," he said. "You're the young turnip-head scallywag at the farm."

"That's right," said Owen.

"I've been wanting to meet you again. I thought the whole thing over, and it struck me," said Mr. Prosser, handsomely, "that I may have seemed a little abrupt at our last meeting."

"No, no."

"The fact is, I was in the middle of an infernally difficult passage of my book that morning, and when you began—"

"It was my fault entirely. I quite understand."

Mr. Prosser produced a card-case.

"We must see more of each other," he said. "Come and have a bit of dinner some night. Come to-night."

"I'm very sorry. I have to go to the theatre to-night."

"Then come and have a bit of supper afterwards. Excellent. Meet me at the Savoy at eleven-fifteen. I'm glad I didn't hit you with that loaf. Abruptness has been my failing through life. My father was just the same. Eleven-fifteen at the Savoy, then."

The manager, who had been listening with some restlessness to the conversation, now intervened. He was a man with a sense of fitness of things, and he objected to having his private room made the scene of what appeared to be a reunion of old college chums. He hinted as much.

"Ha! Prrumph!" he observed, disapprovingly. "Er—Mr. Bentley, that is all. You may return to your work—ah h'mmm! Kindly be more careful another time in stamping the letters."

"Yes, by Jove," said Mr. Prosser, suddenly reminded of his wrongs, "that's right. Exercise a little ordinary care, you ivory-skulled young son of a gun. Do you think Miss Delane is *made* of twopences? Keep an eye on him," he urged the manager. "These young fellows nowadays want someone standing over them with a knout all the time. Be more careful another time, young man. Eleven-fifteen, remember. Make a note of it, or you'll go forgetting *that*."

The seat which Audrey had bought for him at the Piccadilly Theatre proved to be in the centre of the sixth row of stalls— practically a death-trap. Whatever his sufferings might be, escape was impossible. He was securely wedged in.

The cheaper parts of the house were sparsely occupied, but the stalls were full. Owen, disapproving of the whole business, refused to buy a programme, and settled himself in his seat prepared for the worst. He had a vivid recollection of *White Roses*, the novel, and he did not anticipate any keen enjoyment from it in its dramatized form. He had long ceased to be a member of that large public for which Miss Edith Butler catered. The sentimental adventures of governesses in ducal houses—the heroine of *White Roses* was a governess—no longer contented his soul.

There is always a curiously dream-like atmosphere about a play founded on a book. One seems to have seen it all before. During the whole of the first act Owen attributed to this his feeling of familiarity with what was going on on the stage. At the beginning of the second act he found himself anticipating events. But it was not till the third act that the truth sank in.

The third was the only act in which, in his dramatization, he had taken any real liberties with the text of the novel. But in this act he had introduced a character who did not appear in the novel—a creature of his own imagination. And now, with bulging eyes, he observed this creature emerge from the wings, and heard him utter lines which he now clearly remembered having written.

Audrey had been right! Serpent Edith Butler had stolen his play.

His mind, during the remainder of the play, was active. By the time the final curtain fell and he passed out into the open air he had perceived some of the difficulties of the case. To prove oneself the author of an original play is hard, but not impossible. Friends to whom one had sketched the plot may come forward as witnesses. One may have preserved rough notes. But a dramatization of a novel is another matter. All dramatizations of any given novel must necessarily be very much alike.

He started to walk along Piccadilly, and had reached Hyde Park Corner before he recollected that he had an engagement to take supper with Mr. Prosser at the Savoy Hotel. He hailed a cab.

"You're late," boomed the author of sociological treatises, as he appeared. "You're infernally late. I suppose, in your woollen-headed way, you forgot all about it. Come along. We'll just have time for an olive and a glass of something before they turn the lights out."

Owen was still thinking deeply as he began his supper. Surely there was some way by which he could prove his claims. What had he done with the original manuscript? He remembered now. He had burnt it. It had seemed mere useless litter then. Probably, he felt bitterly, the woman Butler had counted on this.

Mr. Prosser concluded an animated conversation with a waiter on the subject of the wines of France, leaned forward and, having helped himself briskly to anchovies, began to talk. He talked loudly and rapidly. Owen, his thoughts far away, hardly listened.

Presently the waiter returned with the selected brand. He filled

Owen's glass, and Owen drank, and felt better. Finding his glass magically full once more, he emptied it again. And then suddenly he found himself looking across the table at his host, and feeling a sense of absolute conviction that this was the one man of all others whom he would have selected as a confidant. How kindly, though somewhat misty, his face was! How soothing, if a little indistinct, his voice!

"Prosser," he said, "you are a man of the world, and I should like your advice. What would you do in a case like this? I go to a theatre to see a play, and what do I find?"

He paused, and eyed his host impressively.

"What's that tune they're playing?" said Mr. Prosser. "You hear it everywhere. One of those Viennese things, I suppose."

Owen was annoyed. He began to doubt whether, after all, Mr. Prosser's virtues as a confidant were not more apparent than real.

"I find, by Jove," he continued, "that I wrote the thing myself."

"It's not a patch on 'The Merry Widow,' " said Mr. Prosser.

Owen thumped the table.

"I tell you I find I wrote the thing myself."

"What thing?"

"This play I'm telling you about. This *White Roses* thing."

He found that he had at last got his host's ear. Mr. Prosser seemed genuinely interested.

"What do you mean?"

Owen plunged into his story. He started from its dim beginning, from the days when he had bought the novel on his journey from Bath to Cheltenham. He described his methods of work, his registering of the package, his suspense, his growing resignation. He sketched the progress of his life. He spoke of Audrey and gave a crisp character-sketch of Mr. Sheppherd. He took his hearer right up to when the truth had come home to him.

Towards the end of his narrative the lights went, and he finished his story in the hotel courtyard. In the cool air he felt revived. The outlines of Mr. Prosser became sharp and distinct again.

The sociologist listened admirably. He appeared absorbed, and did not interrupt once.

"What makes you so certain that this was your version?" he asked, as they passed into the Strand.

Owen told him of the creature of his imagination in Act III.

"But you have lost your manuscript?"

"Yes; I burnt it."

"Just what one might have expected you to do," said Mr. Prosser, unkindly. "Young man, I begin to believe that there may be something in this. You haven't got a ghost of a proof that would hold water in a court of law, of course; but still, I'm inclined to believe you. For one thing, you haven't the intelligence to invent such a story."

Owen thanked him.

"In fact, if you can answer me one question I shall be satisfied."

It seemed to Owen that Mr. Prosser was tending to get a little above himself. As an intelligent listener he had been of service, but that appeared to be no reason why he should constitute himself a sort of judge and master of the ceremonies.

"That's very good of you," he said; "but will Edith Butler be satisfied? That's more to the point."

"I *am* Edith Butler," said Mr. Prosser.

Owen stopped. "You?"

"You need not babble it from the house-tops. You are the only person besides my agent who knows it, and I wouldn't have told you if I could have helped it. It isn't a thing I want known. Great Scott, man, don't goggle at me like a fish! Haven't you heard of pseudonyms before?"

"Yes, but—"

"Well, never mind. Take it from me that I *am* Edith Butler. Now listen to me. That manuscript reached me when I was in the country. There was no name on it. That in itself points strongly to the fact that you were its author. It was precisely the chuckle-headed sort of thing you would have done, to put no name on the thing."

"I enclosed a letter, anyhow."

"There was a letter enclosed. I opened the parcel out of doors. There was a fresh breeze blowing at the time. It caught the letter, and that was the last I saw of it. I had read as far as 'Dear Madam.' But one thing I do remember about it, and that was that it was sent to me from some hotel in Cheltenham, and I could remember it if I heard it. Now, then?"

"I can tell it you. It was Wilbraham's. I was stopping there."

"You pass," said Mr. Prosser. "It was Wilbraham's."

Owen's heart gave a jump. For a moment he walked on air.

"Then do you mean to say that it's all right—that you believe—"

"I do," said Mr. Prosser. "By the way," he said, "the notice of *White Roses* went up last night."

Owen's heart turned to lead.

"But—but—" he stammered. "But to-night the house was packed."

"It was. Packed with paper. All the merry dead-heads in London were there. It has been the worst failure this season. And, by George," he cried, with sudden vehemence, "serve 'em right. If I told them once it would fail in England, I told them a hundred times. The London public won't stand that sort of blithering twaddle."

Owen stopped and looked round. A cab was standing across the road. He signalled to it. He felt incapable of walking home. No physical blow could have unmanned him more completely than this hideous disappointment just when, by a miracle, everything seemed to be running his way.

"Sooner ride than walk," said Mr. Prosser, pushing his head through the open window. "Laziness—slackness—that's the curse of the modern young man. Where shall I tell him to drive to?"

Owen mentioned his address. It struck him that he had not thanked his host for his hospitality.

"It was awfully good of you to give me supper, Mr. Prosser," he said. "I've enjoyed it tremendously."

"Come again," said Mr. Prosser. "I'm afraid you're disappointed about the play?"

Owen forced a smile.

"Oh, no, that's all right," he said. "It can't be helped."

Mr. Prosser half turned, then thrust his head through the window again.

"I knew there was something I had forgotten to say," he said. "I ought to have told you that the play was produced in America before it came to London. It ran two seasons in New York and one in Chicago, and there are three companies playing it still on the road. Here's my card. Come round and see me to-morrow. I can't tell you the actual figures off-hand, but you'll be all right. You'll have pots o' money."

RUTH IN EXILE

This story is another delightful example of the humorous romance so popular before World War I. The Wodehouse world of "All's well that ends well" was never better.

The clock struck five—briskly, as if time were money. Ruth Warden got up from her desk and, having put on her hat, emerged into the outer office where M. Gandinot received visitors. M. Gandinot, the ugliest man in Roville-sur-Mer, presided over the local *mont-de-piété*, and Ruth served him, from ten to five, as a sort of secretary-clerk. Her duties, if monotonous, were simple. They consisted of sitting, detached and invisible, behind a ground-glass screen, and entering details of loans in a fat book. She was kept busy as a rule, for Roville possesses two casinos, each offering the attraction of *petits chevaux*, and just round the corner is Monte Carlo. Very brisk was the business done by M. Gandinot, the pawnbroker, and very frequent were the pitying shakes of the head and clicks of the tongue of M. Gandinot, the man; for in his unofficial capacity Ruth's employer had a gentle soul, and winced at the evidences of tragedy which presented themselves before his official eyes.

He blinked up at Ruth as she appeared, and Ruth, as she looked at him, was conscious, as usual, of a lightening of the depression which, nowadays, seemed to have settled permanently upon her. The peculiar quality of M. Gandinot's extraordinary countenance was that it induced mirth—not mocking laughter, but a kind of smiling happiness. It possessed that indefinable quality which characterises the Billiken, due, perhaps, to the unquenchable optimism which shone through the irregular features; for M. Gandinot, despite his calling, believed in his fellow-man.

"You are going, mademoiselle?"

As Ruth was wearing her hat and making for the door, and as she always left at this hour, a purist might have considered the question superfluous; but M. Gandinot was a man who seized every opportunity of practising his English.

First Appearance: England—*Strand*, July 1912

"You will not wait for the good papa who calls so regularly for you?"

"I think I won't to-day, M. Gandinot. I want to get out into the air. I have rather a headache. Will you tell my father I have gone to the Promenade?"

M. Gandinot sighed as the door closed behind her. Ruth's depression had not escaped his notice. He was sorry for her. And not without cause, for Fate had not dealt too kindly with Ruth.

It would have amazed Mr. Eugene Warden, that genial old gentleman, if, on one of those occasions of manly emotion when he was in the habit of observing that he had been nobody's enemy but his own, somebody had hinted that he had spoiled his daughter's life. Such a thought had never entered his head. He was one of those delightful, irresponsible, erratic persons into whose heads thoughts of this kind do not enter, and who are about as deadly to those whose lives are bound up with theirs as a Upas tree.

In the memory of his oldest acquaintance, Ruth's father had never done anything but drift amiably through life. There had been a time when he had done his drifting in London, feeding cheerfully from the hand of a longsuffering brother-in-law. But though blood, as he was wont to remark while negotiating his periodical loans, is thicker than water, a brother-in-law's affection has its limits. A day came when Mr. Warden observed with pain that his relative responded less nimbly to the touch. And a little while later the other delivered his ultimatum. Mr. Warden was to leave England, and stay away from England, to behave as if England no longer existed on the map, and a small but sufficient allowance would be made to him. If he declined to do this, not another penny of the speaker's money would he receive. He could choose.

He chose. He left England, Ruth with him. They settled in Roville, that haven of the exile who lives upon remittances.

Ruth's connection with the *mont-de-piété* had come about almost automatically. Very soon after their arrival it became evident that, to a man of Mr. Warden's nature, resident a stone's-throw distant from two casinos, the small allowance was not likely to go very far. Even if Ruth had not wished to work, circumstances would have compelled her. As it was, she longed for something to occupy her, and, the vacancy at the *mont-de-piété* occurring, she had snatched at it. There was a certain fitness in her working there. Business transactions with that useful institution had always been conducted by her, it being Mr. Warden's theory that Woman can extract in these crises just that extra franc or two which is denied to the mere male. Through constantly going round, running across, stepping over, and popping down to the *mont-de-piété* she had established almost a legal claim on any post that might be vacant there.

And under M. Gandinot's banner she had served ever since.

Five minutes' walk took her to the Promenade des Anglais, that apparently endless thoroughfare which is Roville's pride. The evening was fine and warm. The sun shone gaily on the white-walled houses, the bright Gardens, and the two gleaming casinos. But Ruth walked listlessly, blind to the glitter of it all.

Visitors who go to Roville for a few weeks in the winter are apt to speak of the place, on their return, in a manner that conveys the impression that it is a Paradise on earth, with gambling facilities thrown in. But, then, they are visitors. Their sojourn comes to an end. Ruth's did not.

A voice spoke her name. She turned, and saw her father, dapper as ever, standing beside her.

"What an evening, my dear!" said Mr. Warden. "What an evening! Smell the sea!"

Mr. Warden appeared to be in high spirits. He hummed a tune and twirled his cane. He chirruped frequently to Bill, the companion of his walks abroad, a wiry fox-terrier of a demeanour, like his master's, both jaunty and slightly disreputable. An air of gaiety pervaded his bearing.

"I called in at the *mont-de-piété* but you had gone. Gandinot told me you had come here. What an ugly fellow that Gandinot is! But a good sort. I like him. I had a chat with him."

The high spirits were explained. Ruth knew her father. She guessed, correctly, that M. Gandinot, kindest of pawnbrokers, had obliged, in his unofficial capacity, with a trifling loan.

"Gandinot ought to go on the stage," went on Mr. Warden, pursuing his theme. "With that face he would make his fortune. You can't help laughing when you see it. One of these days—"

He broke off. Stirring things had begun to occur in the neighbourhood of his ankles, where Bill, the fox-terrier, had encountered an acquaintance, and, to the accompaniment of a loud, gargling noise, was endeavouring to bite his head off. The acquaintance, a gentleman of uncertain breed, equally willing, was chewing

Bill's paw with the gusto of a gourmet. An Irish terrier, with no personal bias towards either side, was dancing round and attacking each in turn as he came uppermost. And two poodles leaped madly in and out of the melée, barking encouragement.

It takes a better man than Mr. Warden to break up a gathering of this kind. The old gentleman was bewildered. He added his voice to the babel, and twice smote Bill grievously with his cane with blows intended for the acquaintance, but beyond that he effected nothing. It seemed probable that the engagement would last till the combatants had consumed each other, after the fashion of the Kilkenny cats, when there suddenly appeared from nowhere a young man in grey.

The world is divided into those who can stop dog-fights and those who cannot. The young man in grey belonged to the former class. Within a minute from his entrance on the scene the poodles and the Irish terrier had vanished; the dog of doubtful breed was moving off up the hill, yelping, with the dispatch of one who remembered an important appointment, and Bill, miraculously calmed, was seated in the centre of the Promenade, licking honourable wounds.

Mr. Warden was disposed to effervesce with gratitude. The scene had shaken him, and there had been moments when he had given his ankles up for lost.

"Don't mention it," said the young man. "I enjoy arbitrating in these little disputes. Dogs seem to like me and trust my judgment. I consider myself a sort of honorary dog."

"Well, I am bound to say, Mr.—?"

"Vince—George Vince."

"My name is Warden. My daughter."

Ruth inclined her head, and was conscious of a pair of very penetrating brown eyes looking eagerly into hers in a manner which she thoroughly resented. She was not used to the other sex meeting her gaze and holding it as if confident of a friendly welcome. She made up her mind in that instant that this was a young man who required suppression.

"I've seen you several times out here since I arrived, Miss Warden," said Mr. Vince. "Four in all," he added, precisely.

"Really?" said Ruth.

She looked away. Her attitude seemed to suggest that she had finished with him, and would be obliged if somebody would come and sweep him up.

As they approached the casino restlessness crept into Mr. Warden's manner. At the door he stopped and looked at Ruth.

"I think, my dear—" he said.

"Going to have a dash at the *petits chevaux?*" inquired Mr. Vince.
"I was there just now. I have an infallible system."

Mr. Warden started like a war-horse at the sound of the trumpet.

"Only it's infallible the wrong way," went on the young man.
"Well, I wish you luck. I'll see Miss Warden home."

"Please don't trouble," said Ruth, in the haughty manner which had frequently withered unfortunate fellow-exiles in their tracks.

It had no such effect on Mr. Vince.

"I shall like it," he said.

Ruth set her teeth. She would see whether he would like it.

They left Mr. Warden, who shot in at the casino door like a homing rabbit, and walked on in silence, which lasted till Ruth, suddenly becoming aware that her companion's eyes were fixed on her face, turned her head, to meet a gaze of complete, not to say loving, admiration. She flushed. She was accustomed to being looked at admiringly, but about this particular look there was a subtle quality that distinguished it from the ordinary—something proprietorial.

Mr. Vince appeared to be a young man who wasted no time on conventional conversation-openings.

"Do you believe in affinities, Miss Warden?" he said.

"No," said Ruth.

"You will before we've done," said Mr. Vince, confidently.
"Why did you try to snub me just now?"

"Did I?"

"You mustn't again. It hurts me. I'm a sensitive man. Diffident. Shy. Miss Warden, will you marry me?"

Ruth had determined that nothing should shake her from the icy detachment, but this did. She stopped with a gasp, and stared at him.

Mr. Vince reassured her.

"I don't expect you to say 'Yes.' That was just a beginning—the shot fired across the bows by way of warning. In you, Miss Warden, I have found my affinity. Have you ever considered this matter of affinities? Affinities are the—the—. Wait a moment."

He paused, reflecting.

"I—" began Ruth.

" 'Sh!" said the young man, holding up his hand.

Ruth's eyes flashed. She was not used to having " 'Sh!" said to her by young men, and she resented it.

"I've got it," he declared, with relief. "I knew I should, but these good things take time. Affinities are the zero on the roulette-board of life. Just as we select a number on which to stake our money, so do we select a type of girl whom we think we should like to marry. And just as zero pops up instead of the number, so does our affinity come along and upset all our preconceived notions on the type of girl we should like to marry."

"I—" began Ruth again.

"The analogy is in the rough at present. I haven't had time to condense and polish it. But you see the idea. Take my case, for instance. When I saw you a couple of days ago I knew in an instant that you were my affinity. But for years I had been looking for a woman almost your exact opposite. You are dark. Three days ago I couldn't have imagined myself marrying anyone who was not fair. Your eyes are grey. Three days ago my preference for blue eyes was a byword. You have a shocking temper. Three days ago—"

"Mr. Vince!"

"There!" said that philosopher, complacently. "You stamped. The gentle, blue-eyed blonde whom I was looking for three days ago would have drooped timidly. Three days ago my passion for timid droopers amounted to an obsession."

Ruth did not reply. It was useless to bandy words with one who gave such clear evidence of being something out of the common run of word-bandiers. No verbal attack could crush this extraordinary young man. She walked on, all silence and stony profile, uncomfortably conscious that her companion was in no way abashed by the former and was regarding the latter with that frank admiration which had made itself so obnoxious to her before, until they reached their destination. Mr. Vince, meanwhile, chatted cheerfully, and pointed out objects of interest by the wayside.

At the door Ruth permitted herself a word of farewell.

"Good-bye," she said.

"Till to-morrow evening," said Mr. Vince. "I shall be coming to dinner."

Mr. Warden ambled home, very happy and contented, two hours later, with half a franc in his pocket, this comparative wealth being due to the fact that the minimum stake permitted by the Roville casino is just double that sum. He was sorry not to have

won, but his mind was too full of rosy dreams to permit of remorse. It was the estimable old gentleman's dearest wish that his
daughter should marry some rich, open-handed man who would
keep him in affluence for the remainder of his days, and to that end
he was in the habit of introducing to her notice any such that came
his way. There was no question of coercing Ruth. He was too
tender-hearted for that. Besides, he couldn't. Ruth was not the sort
of girl who is readily coerced. He contented himself with giving
her the opportunity to inspect his exhibits. Roville is a sociable
place, and it was not unusual for him to make friends at the casino
and to bring them home, when made, for a cigar. Up to the
present, he was bound to admit, his efforts had not been particularly successful. Ruth, he reflected sadly, was a curious girl. She
did not show her best side to these visitors. There was no encouragement in her manner. She was apt to frighten the unfortunate
exhibits. But of this young man Vince he had brighter hopes. He
was rich. That was proved by the very handsome way in which he
had behaved in the matter of a small loan when, looking in at the
casino after parting from Ruth, he had found Mr. Warden in sore
straits for want of a little capital to back a brand-new system which
he had conceived through closely observing the run of the play. He
was also obviously attracted by Ruth. And, as he was remarkably
presentable—indeed, quite an unusually good-looking young man
—there seemed no reason why Ruth should not be equally attracted
by him. The world looked good to Mr. Warden as he fell asleep
that night.

Ruth did not fall asleep so easily. The episode had disturbed her.
A new element had entered her life, and one that gave promise of
producing strange by-products.

When, on the following evening, Ruth returned from the stroll
on the Promenade which she always took after leaving the *mont-de-
piété*, with a feeling of irritation towards things in general, this
feeling was not diminished by the sight of Mr. Vince, very much
at his ease, standing against the mantel-piece of the tiny parlour.

"How do you do?" he said. "By an extraordinary coincidence I
happened to be hanging about outside this house just now, when
your father came along and invited me in to dinner. Have you ever
thought much about coincidences, Miss Warden? To my mind,
they may be described as the zero on the roulette-board of life."

He regarded her fondly.

"For a shy man, conscious that the girl he loves is inspecting him closely and making up her mind about him," he proceeded, "these unexpected meetings are very trying ordeals. You must not form your judgment of me too hastily. You see me now, nervous, embarrassed, tongue-tied. But I am not always like this. Beneath this crust of diffidence there is sterling stuff, Miss Warden. People who know me have spoken of me as a little ray of sun—But here is your father."

Mr. Warden was more than usually disappointed with Ruth during dinner. It was the same old story. So far from making herself pleasant to this attractive stranger, she seemed positively to dislike him. She was barely civil to him. With a sigh Mr. Warden told himself that he did not understand Ruth, and the rosy dreams he had formed began to fade.

Ruth's ideas on the subject of Mr. Vince as the days went by were chaotic. Though she told herself that she thoroughly objected to him, he had nevertheless begun to have an undeniable attraction for her. In what this attraction consisted she could not say. When she tried to analyse it, she came to the conclusion that it was due to the fact that he was the only element in her life that made for excitement. Since his advent the days had certainly passed more swiftly for her. The dead-level of monotony had been broken. There was a certain fascination in exerting herself to suppress him, which increased daily as each attempt failed.

Mr. Vince put this feeling into words for her. He had a maddening habit of discussing the progress of his courtship in the manner of an impartial lecturer.

"I am making headway," he observed. "The fact that we cannot meet without your endeavouring to plant a temperamental left jab on my spiritual solar plexus encourages me to think that you are beginning at last to understand that we are affinities. To persons of spirit like ourselves the only happy marriage is that which is based on a firm foundation of almost incessant quarrelling. The most beautiful line in English poetry, to my mind is, 'We fell out, my wife and I.' You would be wretched with a husband who didn't like you to quarrel with him. The position of affairs now is that I have become necessary to you. If I went out of your life now I should leave an aching void. You would still have that beautiful punch of yours, and there would be nobody to exercise it on. You would pine away. From now on matters should, I think, move rapidly. During the course of the next week I shall endeavour to propitiate you with gifts. Here is the first of them."

He took a piece of paper from his pocket and handed it to her. It was a pencil-sketch, rough and unfinished, but wonderfully clever. Even Ruth could appreciate that—and she was a prejudiced observer, for the sketch was a caricature of herself. It represented her, drawn up to her full height, with enormous, scornful eyes and curling lips, and the artist had managed to combine an excellent likeness while accentuating everything that was marked in what she knew had come to be her normal expression of scorn and discontent.

"I didn't know you were an artist, Mr. Vince," she said, handing it back.

"A poor amateur. Nothing more. You may keep it."

"I have not the slightest wish to keep it."

"You haven't?"

"It is not in the least clever, and it is very impertinent of you to show it to me. The drawing is not funny. It is simply rude."

"A little more," said Mr. Vince, "and I shall begin to think you don't like it. Are you fond of chocolates?"

Ruth did not answer.

"I am sending you some to-morrow."

"I shall return them."

"Then I shall send some more, and some fruit. Gifts!" soliloquized Mr. Vince. "Gifts! That is the secret. Keep sending gifts. If men would only stick to gifts and quarelling, there would be fewer bachelors."

On the morrow, as promised, the chocolates arrived, many pounds of them in a lordly box. The bludgeoning of fate had not wholly scotched in Ruth a human weakness for sweets, and it was with a distinct effort that she wrapped the box up again and returned it to the sender. She went off to her work at the *mont-de-piété* with the glow of satisfaction which comes to those who exhibit an iron will in trying circumstances.

And at the *mont-de-piété* there occurred a surprising incident.

Surprising incidents, as Mr. Vince would have said, are the zero on the roulette-board of life. They pop up disturbingly when least expected, confusing the mind and altering preconceived opinions. And this was a very surprising incident indeed.

Ruth, as has been stated, sat during her hours of work behind a ground-glass screen, unseen and unseeing. To her the patrons of the establishment were mere disembodied voices—wheedling voices, pathetic voices, voices that protested, voices that hectored, voices that whined, moaned, broke, appealed to the saints, and in various other ways endeavoured to instil into M. Gandinot more spacious and princely views on the subject of advancing money on property pledged. She was sitting behind her screen this morning, scribbling idly on the blotting-pad, for there had been a lull in the business, when the door opened, and the polite "Bon jour, monsieur," of M. Gandinot announced the arrival of another unfortunate.

And then, shaking her like an electric shock, came a voice that she knew—the pleasant voice of Mr. Vince.

The dialogues that took place on the other side of the screen were often protracted and always sordid, but none had seemed to Ruth so interminable, so hideously sordid, as this one.

Round and round its miserable centre—a silver cigarette-case—the dreary argument circled. The young man pleaded; M. Gandinot, adamant in his official role, was immovable.

Ruth could bear it no longer. She pressed her hands over her burning ears, and the voices ceased to trouble her.

And with the silence came thought, and a blaze of understanding that flashed upon her and made all things clear. She understood now why she had closed her ears.

Poverty is an acid which reacts differently on differing natures. It had reduced Mr. Eugene Warden's self-respect to a minimum. Ruth's it had reared up to an abnormal growth. Her pride had become a weed that ran riot in her soul, darkening it and choking finer emotions. Perhaps it was her father's naive stratagems for the enmeshing of a wealthy husband that had produced in her at last a morbid antipathy to the idea of playing beggar-maid to any man's King Cophetua. The state of mind is intelligible. The Cophetua legend has never been told from the beggar-maid's point of view, and there must have been moments when, if a woman of spirit, she resented that monarch's somewhat condescending attitude, and felt that, secure in his wealth and magnificence, he had taken her grateful acquiescence very much for granted.

This, she saw now, was what had prejudiced her against George Vince. She had assumed that he was rich. He had conveyed the impression of being rich. And she had been on the defensive against him accordingly. Now, for the first time, she seemed to know him. A barrier had been broken down. The royal robes had proved tinsel, and no longer disguised the man she loved.

A touch on her arm aroused her. M. Gandinot was standing by her side. Terms, apparently, had been agreed upon and the interview concluded, for in his hand was a silver cigarette-case.

"Dreaming, mademoiselle? I could not make you hear. The more I call to you, the more you did not answer. It is necessary to enter this loan."

He recited the details and Ruth entered them in her ledger. This done, M. Gandinot, doffing his official self, sighed.

"It is a place of much sorrow, mademoiselle, this office. How he would not take no for answer, that young man, recently departed. A fellow-countryman of yours, mademoiselle. You would say, 'What does this young man, so well-dressed, in a *mont-de-piété?*' But I know better, I, Gandinot. You have an expression, you English— I heard it in Paris in a café, and inquired its meaning—when you say of a man that he swanks. How many young men have I seen here, admirably dressed—rich, you would say. No, no. The *mont-de-piété* permits no secrets. To swank, mademoiselle, what is it? To deceive the world, yes. But not the *mont-de-piété*. Yesterday also, when you had departed, was he here, that young man. Yet here he is once more today. He spends his money quickly, alas! that poor young swanker."

When Ruth returned home that evening she found her father in the sitting-room, smoking a cigarette. He greeted her with effusion, but with some uneasiness—for the old gentleman had nerved himself to a delicate task. He had made up his mind tonight to speak seriously to Ruth on the subject of her unsatisfactory behaviour to Mr. Vince. The more he saw of that young man the more positive was he that this was the human gold-mine for which he had been searching all these weary years. Accordingly, he threw away his cigarette, kissed Ruth on the forehead, and began to speak.

It had long been Mr. Warden's opinion that, if his daughter had a fault, it was a tendency towards a quite unnecessary and highly inconvenient frankness. She had not that easy tact which he would have liked a daughter of his to possess. She would not evade, ignore, agree not to see. She was at times painfully blunt.

This happened now. He was warming to his subject when she interrupted him with a question.

"What makes you think Mr. Vince is rich, father?" she asked.

Mr. Warden was embarrassed. The subject of Mr. Vince's opulence had not entered into his discourse. He had carefully avoided it. The fact that he was thinking of it and that Ruth knew that he was thinking of it, and that he knew that Ruth knew, had nothing to do with the case. The question was not in order, and it embarrassed him.

"I—why—I don't—I never said he was rich, my dear. I have no doubt that he has ample—"

"He is quite poor."

Mr. Warden's jaw fell slightly.

"Poor? But, my dear, that's absurd!" he cried. "Why, only this evening—"

He broke off abruptly, but it was too late.

"Father, you've been borrowing money from him!"

Mr. Warden drew in his breath, preparatory to an indignant denial, but he altered his mind and remained silent. As a borrower of money he had every quality but one. He could not conceal his operations from his daughter. He had come to look on her perspicacity in this matter as a sort of second sight. It had frequently gone far to spoiling for him the triumph of success.

"And he has to pawn things to live!" Her voice trembled. "He was at the *mont-de-piété* to-day. And yesterday too I heard him. He was arguing with M. Gandinot—haggling—"

Her voice broke. She was sobbing helplessly. The memory of it was too raw and vivid.

Mr. Warden stood motionless. Many emotions raced through his mind, but chief among them the thought that this revelation had come at a very fortunate time. An exceedingly lucky escape, he felt. He was aware, also, of a certain measure of indignation against this deceitful young man who had fraudulently imitated a goldmine with what might have been disastrous results.

The door opened and Jeanne, the maid-of-all-work, announced Mr. Vince.

He entered the room briskly.

"Good evening!" he said. "I have brought you some more chocolates, Miss Warden, and some fruit. Great Scott! What's the matter?"

He stopped, but only for an instant. The next he had darted across the room, and, before the horrified eyes of Mr. Warden, was holding Ruth in his arms. She clung to him.

Bill, the fox-terrier, over whom Mr. Vince had happened to stumble, was the first to speak. Almost simultaneously Mr. Warden joined in, and there was a striking similarity between the two voices, for Mr. Warden, searching for words, emitted as a preliminary to them a sort of passionate yelp.

Mr. Vince removed the hand that was patting Ruth's shoulder and waved it reassuringly at him.

"It's all right," he said.

"All right! All *right!*"

"Affinities," explained Mr. Vince over his shoulder. "Two hearts that beat as one. We're going to be married. What's the matter, dear? Don't you worry; you're all right."

"I refuse!" shouted Mr. Warden. "I absolutely refuse."

Mr. Vince lowered Ruth gently into a chair and, holding her hand, inspected the fermenting old gentleman gravely.

"You refuse?" he said. "Why, I thought you liked me."

Mr. Warden's frenzy had cooled. It had been something foreign to his nature. He regretted it. These things had to be managed with restraint.

"My personal likes and dislikes," he said, "have nothing to do with the matter, Mr. Vince. They are beside the point. I have my daughter to consider. I cannot allow her to marry a man without a penny."

"Quite right," said Mr. Vince, approvingly. "Don't have anything to do with the fellow. If he tries to butt in, send for the police."

Mr. Warden hesitated. He had always been a little ashamed of Ruth's occupation. But necessity compelled. "Mr. Vince, my daughter is employed at the *mont-de-piété*, and was a witness to all that took place this afternoon.

Mr. Vince was genuinely agitated. He looked at Ruth, his face full of concern.

"You don't mean to say that you have been slaving away in that stuffy—. Great Scott! I'll have you out of that quick. You mustn't go there again."

He stooped and kissed her.

"Perhaps you had better let me explain," he said. "Explanations, I always think, are the zero on the roulette-board of life. They're always somewhere about, waiting to pop up. Have you ever heard of Vince's stores, Mr. Warden? Perhaps they are since your time. Well, my father is the proprietor. One of our specialities is children's toys, but we haven't picked a real winner for years, and my father when I last saw him seemed so distressed about it that I said I'd see if I couldn't whack out an idea for something. Something on the lines of the Billiken, only better, was what he felt he needed. I'm not used to brain work, and after a spell of it I felt I wanted a rest. I came here to recuperate, and the very first morning I got the inspiration. You may have noticed that the manager of the *mont-de-piété* here isn't strong on conventional good looks. I saw him at the casino, and the thing flashed on me. He thinks his name's Gandinot, but it isn't. It's Uncle Zip, the Hump-Curer, the Man Who Makes You Smile."

He pressed Ruth's hand affectionately.

"I lost track of him, and it was only the day before yesterday that I discovered who he was and where he was to be found. Well, you can't go to a man and ask him to pose as a model for Uncle Zip, the Hump-Curer. The only way to get sittings was to approach him in the way of business. So I collected what property I had and waded in. That's the whole story. Do I pass?"

Mr. Warden's frosty demeanour had gradually thawed during this recital, and now the sun of his smile shone out warmly. He gripped Mr. Vince's hand with every evidence of esteem, and after that he did not seem to know what to do. Eventually he did what was certainly the best thing, by passing gently from the room. On his face, as he went, was a look such as Moses might have worn on the summit of Pisgah.

It was some twenty minutes later that Ruth made a remark.

"I want you to promise me something," she said. "Promise that you won't go on with that Uncle Zip drawing. I know it means ever so much money, but it might hurt poor M. Gandinot's feelings, and he has been very kind to me."

"That settles it," said Mr. Vince. "It's hard on the children of Great Britain, but say no more. No Uncle Zip for them."

Ruth looked at him, almost with awe.

"You really won't go on with it? In spite of all the money you would make? Are you always going to do just what I ask you, no matter what it costs you?"

He nodded sadly.

"You have sketched out in a few words the whole policy of my married life. I feel an awful fraud. And I had encouraged you to look forward to years of incessant quarrelling. Do you think you can manage without it? I'm afraid it's going to be shockingly dull for you," said Mr. Vince, regretfully.

DEATH AT THE EXCELSIOR

This is a real find for the collector—an honest-to-goodness mystery story. The story was originally entitled "The Education of Detective Oakes"; the title was changed because of major editing alterations in the text.

Some time ago, Mr. Wodehouse wrote an article commenting upon various devices on which writers of mysteries depended. Here is a shortened version of that article, which is appropriate to introduce his only mystery story.

I have always been a great reader of mystery stories or, as they now prefer to call themselves, novels of suspense, and I hold strong views on them, one of which is that the insertion into them of a love interest is a serious mistake.

Whoever first got the idea that anyone wants a girl messing about and getting in the way when the automatics are popping I am at a loss to imagine. Apart from anything else, Woman seems to me to lose her queenly dignity when she is being shoved into cupboards with a bag over her head. And if there is one thing certain, it is that sooner or later some-

First Appearance: England—*Pearson's*, December 1914

thing of that sort will be happening to the heroine of a novel of suspense.

For, though beautiful, with large grey eyes and hair the color of ripe corn, the heroine of a novel of suspense is almost never a very intelligent girl. Indeed, it would scarcely be overstating it to say that her mentality is that of a retarded child of six. She may have escaped death a dozen times. She may know perfectly well that the Blackbird Gang is after her to secure the papers. The police may have warned her on no account to stir outside the house. But when a messenger calls at half-past two in the morning with an unsigned note that says "Come at once," she just reaches for her hat and goes.

The obvious person, of course, to rid us of these pests is the villain or heavy, and in fairness to a willing worker it cannot be denied that he does his best. And yet for one reason or another he always fails, even when he has got the girl chained up in the cellar under the wharf with the water pouring through the grating.

The trouble with the heavy in a novel of suspense is that he suffers from a fatal excess of ingenuity. When he was a boy, his parents must thoughtlessly have told him he was clever, and it has absolutely spoiled him for effective work.

The ordinary man, when circumstances compel him to murder a female acquaintance, borrows a revolver and a few cartridges and does the job in some odd five minutes of the day when he is not at the office. He does not bother about art or technique or scientific methods. He just goes and does it.

But the heavy cannot understand simplicity. It never occurs to him just to point a pistol at the heroine and fire it. If you told him the thing could be done that way, he would suspect you of pulling his leg. The only method he can imagine is to tie her to a chair, erect a tripod, place the revolver on it, tie a string to the trigger, pass the string along the wall till it rests on a hook, attach another string to it, pass this over a hook, tie a brick to the end of the second string and light a candle under it. He has got the thing reasoned out. The candle will burn the second string, the brick will fall, the weight will tighten the first string, thus pulling the trigger,

and there you are. And then of course somebody comes along
and blows the candle out, and all the weary work to do over
again.

If I were writing a mystery story, I would go boldly out
for the big sensation. I would not have the crime committed
by anybody in the book at all. Here are the last few para-
graphs of a little thing I have been turning over in my mind
against the time when I myself fall a victim to the epidemic.

"You say, Jerningham," I gasped, "that you have solved this
inscrutable problem? You really know who it was that put the
puncture in Sir Ralph?"

Travers Jerningham nodded curtly. I was astonished to see
that he displayed none of the satisfaction which one would
naturally have expected. There was a cloud on his forehead
and his thin mouth had drawn itself into a tight line.

"I do," he said.

"But you seem gloomy, Jerningham—moody, why is this?"

"Because it is impossible to bring the criminals to justice."

"Criminals? Was there, then, more than one?"

"There were two. Two of the blackest-hearted menaces to
Society that ever clutched a knife-handle. One held Sir Ralph
down, the other did the stabbing."

"But if you are so sure of this, how is it that you cannot
give the scoundrels their just deserts?"

Travers Jerningham laughed a bitter laugh.

"Because, my dear fellow, they aren't in the book at all.
The fiends were too cunning to let themselves get beyond the
title page. The murderers of Sir Ralph Rackstraw were
Messrs. Hodder and Stoughton."

THE END

That would be something like a punch. But the next thing
that would happen would be the usual flood of imitations.
Somebody would write a thriller in which the crime was
traced to Otis and Googe, Bespoke Printers, London, Harrin-
gay and Glasgow; and then somebody else would hit on the
author's best friend, J. B. Stokes, without whose never-failing
sympathy and encouragement this book would not have been

written; and so on and so on. You cannot copyright an idea, and times have become so hard for thriller-writers that they are after any possible new murderer like a pack of wolves.

Mr. Wodehouse never did write his model mystery novel; in "Death at the Excelsior," his fulminations above notwithstanding, he did create a heroine—not the flashy type, but a heroine nonetheless.

I

The room was the typical bedroom of the typical boarding-house, furnished, insofar as it could be said to be furnished at all, with a severe simplicity. It contained two beds, a pine chest of drawers, a strip of faded carpet, and a wash basin. But there was that on the floor which set this room apart from a thousand rooms of the same kind. Flat on his back, with his hands tightly clenched and one leg twisted oddly under him and with his teeth gleaming through his grey beard in a horrible grin, Captain John Gunner stared up at the ceiling with eyes that saw nothing.

Until a moment before, he had had the little room all to himself. But now two people were standing just inside the door, looking down at him. One was a large policeman, who twisted his helmet nervously in his hands. The other was a tall, gaunt old woman in a rusty black dress, who gazed with pale eyes at the dead man. Her face was quite expressionless.

The woman was Mrs. Pickett, owner of the Excelsior Boarding-House. The policeman's name was Grogan. He was a genial giant, a terror to the riotous element of the waterfront, but obviously ill at ease in the presence of death. He drew in his breath, wiped his forehead, and whispered: "Look at his eyes, ma'am!"

Mrs. Pickett had not spoken a word since she had brought the policeman into the room, and she did not do so now. Constable Grogan looked at her quickly. He was afraid of Mother Pickett, as was everybody else along the waterfront. Her silence, her pale eyes, and the quiet decisiveness of her personality cowed even the tough old salts who patronized the Excelsior. She was a formidable influence in that little community of sailormen.

"That's just how I found him," said Mrs. Pickett. She did not speak loudly, but her voice made the policeman start.

He wiped his forehead again. "It might have been apoplexy," he hazarded.

Mrs. Pickett said nothing. There was a sound of footsteps outside, and a young man entered, carrying a black bag.

"Good morning, Mrs. Pickett. I was told that—Good Lord!" The young doctor dropped to his knees beside the body and raised one of the arms. After a moment he lowered it gently to the floor, and shook his head in grim resignation.

"He's been dead for hours," he announced. "When did you find him?"

"Twenty minutes back," replied the old woman. "I guess he died last night. He never would be called in the morning. Said he liked to sleep on. Well, he's got his wish."

"What did he die of, sir?" asked the policeman.

"It's impossible to say without an examination," the doctor answered. "It looks like a stroke, but I'm pretty sure it isn't. It might be a coronary attack, but I happen to know his blood pressure was normal, and his heart sound. He called in to see me only a week ago, and I examined him thoroughly. But sometimes you can be deceived. The inquest will tell us." He eyed the body almost resentfully. "I can't understand it. The man had no right to drop dead like this. He was a tough old sailor who ought to have been good for another twenty years. If you want my honest opinion—though I can't possibly be certain until after the inquest—I should say he had been poisoned."

"How would he be poisoned?" asked Mrs. Pickett quietly.

"That's more than I can tell you. There's no glass about that he could have drunk it from. He might have got it in capsule form. But why should he have done it? He was always a pretty cheerful sort of old man, wasn't he?"

"Yes, sir," said the Constable. "He had the name of being a joker in these parts. Kind of sarcastic, they tell me, though he never tried it on me."

"He must have died quite early last night," said the doctor. He turned to Mrs. Pickett. "What's become of Captain Muller? If he shares this room he ought to be able to tell us something about it."

"Captain Muller spent the night with some friends at Portsmouth," said Mrs. Pickett. "He left right after supper, and hasn't returned."

The doctor stared thoughtfully about the room, frowning.

"I don't like it. I can't understand it. If this had happened in India I should have said the man had died from some form of snakebite. I was out there two years, and I've seen a hundred cases of it. The poor devils all looked just like this. But the thing's ridiculous. How could a man be bitten by a snake in a Southampton waterfront boarding-house? Was the door locked when you found him, Mrs. Pickett?"

Mrs. Pickett nodded. "I opened it with my own key. I had been calling to him and he didn't answer, so I guessed something was wrong."

The Constable spoke: "You ain't touched anything, ma'am? They're always very particular about that. If the doctor's right, and there's been anything up, that's the first thing they'll ask."

"Everything's just as I found it."

"What's that on the floor beside him?" the doctor asked.

"Only his harmonica. He liked to play it of an evening in his room. I've had some complaints about it from some of the gentlemen, but I never saw any harm, so long as he didn't play it too late."

"Seems as if he was playing it when—it happened," Constable Grogan said. "That don't look much like suicide, sir."

"I didn't say it was suicide."

Grogan whistled. "You don't think—"

"I'm not thinking anything—until after the inquest. All I say is that it's queer."

Another aspect of the matter seemed to strike the policeman. "I guess this ain't going to do the Excelsior any good, ma'am," he said sympathetically.

Mrs. Pickett shrugged her shoulders.

"I suppose I had better go and notify the coroner," said the doctor.

He went out, and after a momentary pause the policeman followed him. Constable Grogan was not greatly troubled with nerves, but he felt a decided desire to be somewhere where he could not see the dead man's staring eyes.

Mrs. Pickett remained where she was, looking down at the still form on the floor. Her face was expressionless, but inwardly she was tormented and alarmed. It was the first time such a thing as this had happened at the Excelsior, and, as Constable Grogan had hinted, it was not likely to increase the attractiveness of the house in the eyes of possible boarders. It was not the threatened pecuniary loss which was troubling her. As far as money was concerned, she could have lived comfortably on her savings, for she was richer than most of her friends supposed. It was the blot on the escutcheon of the Excelsior—the stain on its reputation—which was tormenting her.

The Excelsior was her life. Starting many years before, beyond the memory of the oldest boarder, she had built up the model establishment, the fame of which had been carried to every corner of the world. Men spoke of it as a place where you were fed well, cleanly housed, and where petty robbery was unknown.

Such was the chorus of praise that it is not likely that much harm could come to the Excelsior from a single mysterious death, but Mother Pickett was not consoling herself with such reflections.

She looked at the dead man with pale, grim eyes. Out in the hallway the doctor's voice further increased her despair. He was talking to the police on the telephone, and she could distinctly hear his every word.

II

The offices of Mr. Paul Snyder's Detective Agency in New Oxford Street had grown in the course of a dozen years from a single room to an impressive suite bright with polished wood, clicking typewriters, and other evidences of success. Where once Mr. Snyder had sat and waited for clients and attended to them himself, he now sat in his private office and directed eight assistants.

He had just accepted a case—a case that might be nothing at all or something exceedingly big. It was on the latter possibility that he had gambled. The fee offered was, judged by his present standards of prosperity, small. But the bizarre facts, coupled with something in the personality of the client, had won him over. He briskly touched the bell and requested that Mr. Oakes should be sent in to him.

Elliot Oakes was a young man who both amused and interested Mr. Snyder, for though he had only recently joined the staff, he made no secret of his intention of revolutionizing the methods of the agency. Mr. Snyder himself, in common with most of his assistants, relied for results on hard work and plenty of common sense. He had never been a detective of the showy type. Results had justified his methods, but he was perfectly aware that young Mr. Oakes looked on him as a dull old man who had been miraculously favored by luck.

Mr. Snyder had selected Oakes for the case in hand principally because it was one where inexperience could do no harm, and where the brilliant guesswork which Oakes preferred to call his inductive reasoning might achieve an unexpected success.

Another motive actuated Mr. Snyder in his choice. He had a strong suspicion that the conduct of this case was going to have the beneficial result of lowering Oakes' self-esteem. If failure achieved this end, Mr. Snyder felt that failure, though it would not help the Agency, would not be an unmixed ill.

The door opened and Oakes entered tensely. He did everything tensely, partly from a natural nervous energy, and partly as a pose. He was a lean young man, with dark eyes and a thin-lipped mouth, and he looked quite as much like a typical detective as Mr. Snyder looked like a comfortable and prosperous stock broker.

"Sit down, Oakes," said Mr. Snyder. "I've got a job for you."

Oakes sank into a chair like a crouching leopard, and placed the tips of his fingers together. He nodded curtly. It was part of his pose to be keen and silent.

"I want you to go to this address"—Mr. Snyder handed him an envelope—"and look around. The address on that envelope is of a sailors' boarding-house down in Southampton. You know the sort of place—retired sea captains and so on live there. All most respectable. In all its history nothing more sensational has ever happened than a case of suspected cheating at halfpenny nap. Well, a man had died there."

"Murdered?" Oakes asked.

"I don't know. That's for you to find out. The coroner left it open. 'Death by Misadventure' was the verdict, and I don't blame him. I don't see how it could have been murder. The door was locked on the inside, so nobody could have got in."

"The window?"

"The window was open, granted. But the room is on the second floor. Anyway, you may dismiss the window. I remember the old lady saying there was a bar across it, and that nobody could have squeezed through."

Oakes' eyes glistened. He was interested. "What was the cause of death?" he asked.

Mr. Snyder coughed. "Snake bite," he said.

Oakes' careful calm deserted him. He uttered a cry of astonishment. "Why, that's incredible!"

"It's the literal truth. The medical examination proved that the fellow had been killed by snake poison—cobra, to be exact, which is found principally in India."

"Cobra!"

"Just so. In a Southampton boarding-house, in a room with a locked door, this man was stung by a cobra. To add a little mystification to the limpid simplicity of the affair, when the door was opened there was no sign of any cobra. It couldn't have got out through the door, because the door was locked. It couldn't have got out of the window, because the window was too high up, and snakes can't jump. And it couldn't have gotten up the chimney, because there was no chimney. So there you have it."

He looked at Oakes with a certain quiet satisfaction. It had come to his ears that Oakes had been heard to complain of the infantile nature and unworthiness of the last two cases to which he had been assigned. He had even said that he hoped some day to be given a problem which should be beyond the reasoning powers of a child of six. It seemed to Mr. Snyder that Oakes was about to get his wish.

"I should like further details," said Oakes, a little breathlessly.

"You had better apply to Mrs. Pickett, who owns the boarding-house," Mr. Snyder said. "It was she who put the case in my hands. She is convinced that it is murder. But, if we exclude ghosts, I don't see how any third party could have taken a hand in the thing at all. However, she wanted a man from this agency, and was prepared to pay for him, so I promised her I would send one. It is not our policy to turn business away."

He smiled wryly. "In pursuance of that policy I want you to go and put up at Mrs. Pickett's boarding house and do your best to enhance the reputation of our agency. I would suggest that you pose as a ship's chandler or something of that sort. You will have to be something maritime or they'll be suspicious of you. And if your visit produces no other results, it will, at least, enable you to make the acquaintance of a very remarkable woman. I commend Mrs. Pickett to your notice. By the way, she says she will help you in your investigations."

Oakes laughed shortly. The idea amused him.

"It's a mistake to scoff at amateur assistance, my boy," said Mr. Snyder in the benevolently paternal manner which had made a score of criminals refuse to believe him a detective until the moment when the handcuffs snapped on their wrists. "Crime investigation isn't an exact science. Success or failure depends in a large measure on applied common sense, and the possession of a great deal of special information. Mrs. Pickett knows certain things which neither you nor I know, and it's just possible that she may have some stray piece of information which will provide the key to the entire mystery."

Oakes laughed again. "It is very kind of Mrs. Pickett," he said, "but I prefer to trust to my own methods." Oakes rose, his face purposeful. "I'd better be starting at once," he said. "I'll send you reports from time to time."

"Good. The more detailed the better," said Mr. Snyder genially. "I hope your visit to the Excelsior will be pleasant. And cultivate Mrs. Pickett. She's worth while."

The door closed, and Mr. Snyder lighted a fresh cigar. "Dashed young fool," he murmured, as he turned his mind to other matters.

III

A day later Mr. Snyder sat in his office reading a typewritten report. It appeared to be of a humorous nature, for, as he read, chuckles escaped him. Finishing the last sheet he threw his head back and laughed heartily. The manuscript had not been intended by its author for a humorous effort. What Mr. Snyder had been reading was the first of Elliott Oakes' reports from the Excelsior. It read as follows:

I am sorry to be unable to report any real progress. I have formed several theories which I will put forward later, but at present I cannot say that I am hopeful.

Directly I arrived here I sought out Mrs. Pickett, explained who I was, and requested her to furnish me with any further information which might be of service to me. She is a strange, silent woman, who impressed me as having very little intelligence. Your suggestion that I should avail myself of her assistance seems more curious than ever, now that I have seen her.

The whole affair seems to me at the moment of writing quite inexplicable. Assuming that this Captain Gunner was murdered, there appears to have been no motive for the crime whatsoever. I have made careful inquiries about him, and find that he was a man of fifty-five; had spent nearly forty years of his life at sea, the last dozen in command of his own ship; was of a somewhat overbearing disposition, though with a fund of rough humour; had travelled all over the world, and had been an inmate of the Excelsior for about ten months. He had a small annuity, and no other money at all, which disposes of money as the motive for the crime.

In my character of James Burton, a retired ship's chandler, I have mixed with the other boarders, and have heard all they have to say about the affair. I gather that the deceased was by no means popular. He appears to have had a bitter tongue, and I have not met one man who seems to regret his death. On the other hand, I have heard nothing which would suggest that he had any active and violent enemies. He was simply the unpopular boarder—there is always one in every boarding house—but nothing more.

I have seen a good deal of the man who shared his room—another sea captain, named Muller. He is a big, silent person, and it is not easy to get him to talk. As regards the death of Captain Gunner he can tell me nothing. It seems that on the night of the tragedy he was away at Portsmouth with some friends. All I have got from him is some information as to Captain Gunner's habits, which leads nowhere. The dead man seldom drank, except at night when he would take some whisky. His head was not strong, and a little of the spirit was enough to make him semi-intoxicated, when he would be hilarious and often insulting. I gather that Muller found him a difficult roommate, but he is one of those placid persons who can put up with anything. He and Gunner were in the habit of playing draughts together every night in their room, and Gunner had a harmonica which he played frequently. Apparently, he was playing it very soon before he died, which is significant, as seeming to dispose of the idea of suicide.

As I say, I have one or two theories, but they are in a very nebulous state. The most plausible is that on one of his visits to India—I have ascertained that he made several voyages there—Captain Gunner may in some way have fallen foul of the natives. The fact that he certainly died of the poison of an Indian snake supports this theory. I am making inquiries as to the movements of several Indian sailors who were here in their ships at the time of the tragedy.

I have another theory. Does Mrs. Pickett know more about this affair than she appears to? I may be wrong in my estimate of her mental qualities. Her apparent stupidity may be cunning. But here again, the absence of motive brings me up against a dead wall. I must confess that at present I do not see my way clearly. However, I will write again shortly.

Mr. Snyder derived the utmost enjoyment from the report. He liked the substance of it, and above all, he was tickled by the bitter tone of frustration which characterized it. Oakes was baffled, and his knowledge of Oakes told him that the sensation of being baffled was gall and wormwood to that high-spirited young man. Whatever might be the result of this investigation, it would teach him the virtue of patience.

He wrote his assistant a short note:

Dear Oakes,

Your report received. You certainly seem to have got the hard case which, I hear, you were pining for. Don't build too much on plausible motives in a case of this sort. Fauntleroy, the London murderer, killed a woman for no other reason than that she had thick ankles. Many years ago, I myself was on a case where a man murdered an intimate friend because of a dispute about a bet. My experience is that five murderers out of ten act on the whim of the moment, without anything which, properly speaking, you could call a motive at all.

Yours very cordially,
Paul Snyder

P. S. I don't think much of your Pickett theory However, you're in charge. I wish you luck.

IV

Young Mr. Oakes was not enjoying himself. For the first time in his life, the self-confidence which characterized all his actions seemed to be failing him. The change had taken place almost overnight. The fact that the case had the appearance of presenting the unusual had merely stimulated him at first. But then doubts had crept in and the problem had begun to appear insoluble.

True, he had only just taken it up, but something told him that, for all the progress he was likely to make, he might just as well have been working on it steadily for a month. He was completely baffled. And every moment which he spent in the Excelsior Boarding-House made it clearer to him that that infernal old woman with the pale eyes thought him an incompetent fool. It was that, more than anything, which made him acutely conscious of his lack of success. His nerves were being sorely troubled by the quiet scorn of Mrs. Pickett's gaze. He began to think that perhaps he had been a shade too self-confident and abrupt in the short interview which he had had with her on his arrival.

As might have been expected, his first act, after his brief interview with Mrs. Pickett, was to examine the room where the tragedy had taken place. The body was gone, but otherwise nothing had been moved.

Oakes belonged to the magnifying-glass school of detection. The first thing he did on entering the room was to make a careful examination of the floor, the walls, the furniture, and the window-sill. He would have hotly denied the assertion that he did this because it looked well, but he would have been hard put to it to advance any other reason.

If he discovered anything, his discoveries were entirely negative, and served only to deepen the mystery of the case. As Mr. Snyder had said, there was no chimney, and nobody could have entered through the locked door.

There remained the window. It was small, and apprehensiveness, perhaps, of the possibility of burglars, had caused the proprietress to make it doubly secure with an iron bar. No human being could have squeezed his way through it.

It was late that night that he wrote and dispatched to headquarters the report which had amused Mr. Snyder.

Two days later Mr. Snyder sat at his desk, staring with wide, unbelieving eyes at a telegram he had just received. It read as follows:

HAVE SOLVED GUNNER MYSTERY. RETURNING . . . . OAKES.

Mr. Snyder narrowed his eyes and rang the bell.

"Send Mr. Oakes to me directly he arrives," he said.

He was pained to find that his chief emotion was one of bitter annoyance. The swift solution of such an apparently insoluble problem would reflect the highest credit on the Agency, and there were picturesque circumstances connected with the case which would make it popular with the newspapers and lead to its being given a great deal of publicity.

Yet, in spite of all this, Mr. Snyder was annoyed. He realized now how large a part the desire to reduce Oakes' self-esteem had played with him. He further realized, looking at the thing honestly, that he had been firmly convinced that the young man would not come within a mile of a reasonable solution of the mystery. He had desired only that his failure would prove a valuable educational experience for him. For he believed that failure at this particular point in his career would make Oakes a more valuable asset to the Agency. But now here Oakes was, within a ridiculously short space of time, returning to the fold, not humble and defeated, but triumphant. Mr. Snyder looked forward with apprehension to the young man's probable demeanor under the intoxicating influence of victory.

His apprehensions were well grounded. He had barely finished the third of the series of cigars, which, like milestones, marked the progress of his afternoon, when the door opened and young Oakes entered. Mr. Snyder could not repress a faint moan at the sight of him. One glance was enough to tell him that his worst fears were realised.

"I got your telegram," said Mr. Snyder.

Oakes nodded. "It surprised you, eh?" he asked.

Mr. Snyder resented the patronizing tone of the question, but he had resigned himself to be patronized, and keep his anger in check.

"Yes," he replied, "I must say it did surprise me. I didn't gather from your report that you had even found a clue. Was it the Indian theory that turned the trick?"

Oakes laughed tolerantly. "Oh, I never really believed that preposterous theory for one moment. I just put it in to round out my report. I hadn't begun to think about the case then—not really think."

Mr. Snyder, nearly exploding with wrath, extended his cigar-case. "Light up, and tell me all about it," he said, controlling his anger.

"Well, I won't say I haven't earned this," said Oakes, puffing away. He let the ash of his cigar fall delicately to the floor—another action which seemed significant to his employer. As a rule, his assistants, unless particularly pleased with themselves, used the ashtray.

"My first act on arriving," Oakes said, "was to have a talk with Mrs. Pickett. A very dull old woman."

"Curious. She struck me as rather intelligent."

"Not on your life. She gave me no assistance whatever. I then examined the room where the death had taken place. It was exactly as you described it. There was no chimney, the door had been locked on the inside, and the one window was very high up. At first sight, it looked extremely unpromising. Then I had a chat with some of the other boarders. They had nothing of any importance to contribute. Most of them simply gibbered. I then gave up trying to get help from the outside, and resolved to rely on my own intelligence."

He smiled triumphantly. "It is a theory of mine, Mr. Snyder, which I have found valuable that, in nine cases out of ten, remarkable things don't happen."

"I don't quite follow you there," Mr. Snyder interrupted.

"I will put it another way, if you like. What I mean is that the simplest explanation is nearly always the right one. Consider this case. It seemed impossible that there should have been any reasonable explanation of the man's death. Most men would have worn themselves out guessing at wild theories. If I had started to do that, I should have been guessing now. As it is—here I am. I trusted to my belief that nothing remarkable ever happens, and I won out."

Mr. Snyder sighed softly. Oakes was entitled to a certain amount of gloating, but there could be no doubt that his way of telling a story was downright infuriating.

"I believe in the logical sequence of events. I refuse to accept effects unless they are preceded by causes. In other words, with all due respect to your possibly contrary opinions, Mr. Snyder, I simply decline to believe in a murder unless there was a motive for it. The first thing I set myself to ascertain was—what was the motive for the murder of Captain Gunner? And, after thinking it over and making every possible inquiry, I decided that there was no motive. Therefore, there was no murder."

Mr. Snyder's mouth opened, and he obviously was about to protest. But he appeared to think better of it and Oakes proceeded: "I then tested the suicide theory. What motive was there for suicide? There was no motive. Therefore, there was no suicide."

This time Mr. Snyder spoke. "You haven't been spending the last few days in the wrong house by any chance, have you? You will be telling me next that there wasn't any dead man."

Oakes smiled. "Not at all. Captain John Gunner was dead, all right. As the medical evidence proved, he died of the bite of a cobra. It was a small cobra which came from Java."

Mr. Snyder stared at him. "How do you know?"

"I do know, beyond any possibility of doubt."

"Did you see the snake?"

Oakes shook his head.

"Then, how in heaven's name—"

"I have enough evidence to make a jury convict Mr. Snake without leaving the box."

"Then suppose you tell me this. How did your cobra from Java get out of the room?"

"By the window," replied Oakes, impassively.

"How can you possibly explain that? You say yourself that the window was high up."

"Nevertheless, it got out by the window. The logical sequence of events is proof enough that it was in the room. It killed Captain Gunner there, and left traces of its presence outside. Therefore, as the window was the only exit, it must have escaped by that route. It may have climbed or it may have jumped, but somehow it got out of that window."

"What do you mean—it left traces of its presence outside?"

"It killed a dog in the backyard behind the house," Oakes said. "The window of Captain Gunner's room projects out over it. It is full of boxes and litter and there are a few stunted shrubs scattered about. In fact, there is enough cover to hide any small object like the body of a dog. That's why it was not discovered at first. The maid at the Excelsior came on it the morning after I sent you my report while she was emptying a box of ashes in the yard. It was just an ordinary stray dog without collar or license. The analyst examined the body, and found that the dog had died of the bite of a cobra."

"But you didn't find the snake?"

"No. We cleaned out that yard till you could have eaten your breakfast there, but the snake had gone. It must have escaped through the door of the yard, which was standing ajar. That was a couple of days ago, and there has been no further tragedy. In all likelihood it is dead. The nights are pretty cold now, and it would probably have died of exposure."

"But, I just don't understand how a cobra got to Southampton," said the amazed Mr. Snyder.

"Can't you guess it? I told you it came from Java."

"How did you know it did?"

"Captain Muller told me. Not directly, but I pieced it together from what he said. It seems that an old shipmate of Captain Gunner's was living in Java. They corresponded, and occasionally this man would send the captain a present as a mark of his esteem. The last present he sent was a crate of bananas. Unfortunately, the snake must have got in unnoticed. That's why I told you the cobra was a small one. Well, that's my case against Mr. Snake, and short of catching him with the goods, I don't see how I could have made out a stronger one. Don't you agree?"

It went against the grain for Mr. Snyder to acknowledge defeat, but he was a fair-minded man, and he was forced to admit that Oakes did certainly seem to have solved the impossible.

"I congratulate you, my boy," he said as heartily as he could. "To be completely frank, when you started out, I didn't think you could do it. By the way, I suppose Mrs. Pickett was pleased?"

"If she was, she didn't show it. I'm pretty well convinced she hasn't enough sense to be pleased at anything. However, she has invited me to dinner with her tonight. I imagine she'll be as boring as usual, but she made such a point of it, I had to accept."

VI

For some time after Oakes had gone, Mr. Snyder sat smoking and thinking, in embittered meditation. Suddenly there was brought the card of Mrs. Pickett, who would be grateful if he could spare her a few moments. Mr. Snyder was glad to see Mrs. Pickett. He was a student of character, and she had interested him at their first meeting. There was something about her which had seemed to him unique, and he welcomed this second chance of studying her at close range.

She came in and sat down stiffly, balancing herself on the extreme edge of the chair in which a short while before young Oakes had lounged so luxuriously.

"How are you, Mrs. Pickett?" said Mr. Snyder genially. "I'm

very glad that you could find time to pay me a visit. Well, so it wasn't murder after all."

"Sir?"

"I've just been talking to Mr. Oakes, whom you met as James Burton," said the detective. "He has told me all about it."

"He told *me* all about it," said Mrs. Pickett dryly.

Mr. Snyder looked at her inquiringly. Her manner seemed more suggestive than her words.

"A conceited, headstrong young fool," said Mrs. Pickett.

It was no new picture of his assistant that she had drawn. Mr. Snyder had often drawn it himself, but at the present juncture it surprised him. Oakes, in his hour of triumph, surely did not deserve this sweeping condemnation.

"Did not Mr. Oakes' solution of the mystery satisfy you, Mrs. Pickett?"

"No!"

"It struck me as logical and convincing," Mr. Snyder said.

"You may call it all the fancy names you please, Mr. Snyder. But Mr. Oakes' solution was not the right one."

"Have you an alternative to offer?"

Mrs. Pickett tightened her lips.

"If you have, I should like to hear it."

"You will—at the proper time."

"What makes you so certain that Mr. Oakes is wrong?"

"He starts out with an impossible explanation, and rests his whole case on it. There couldn't have been a snake in that room because it couldn't have gotten out. The window was too high."

"But surely the evidence of the dead dog?"

Mrs. Pickett looked at him as if he had disappointed her. "I had always heard *you* spoken of as a man with common sense, Mr. Snyder."

"I have always tried to use common sense."

"Then why are you trying now to make yourself believe that something happened which could not possibly have happened just because it fits in with something which isn't easy to explain?"

"You mean that there is another explanation of the dead dog?" Mr. Snyder asked.

"Not *another*. What Mr. Oakes takes for granted is not an explanation. But there is a common sense explanation, and if he had not been so headstrong and conceited he might have found it."

"You speak as if you had found it," chided Mr. Snyder.

"I have." Mrs. Pickett leaned forward as she spoke, and stared at him defiantly.

Mr. Snyder started. "*You* have?"

"Yes."

"What is it?"

"You will know before tomorrow. In the meantime try and think it out for yourself. A successful and prosperous detective agency like yours, Mr. Snyder, ought to do something in return for a fee."

There was something in her manner so reminiscent of the school teacher reprimanding a recalcitrant pupil that Mr. Snyder's sense of humor came to his rescue. "We do our best, Mrs. Pickett," he said. "But you mustn't forget that we are only human and cannot guarantee results."

Mrs. Pickett did not pursue the subject. Instead, she proceeded to astonish Mr. Snyder by asking him to swear out a warrant for the arrest of a man known to them both on a charge of murder.

Mr. Snyder's breath was not often taken away in his own office. As a rule, he received his clients' communications calmly, strange as they often were. But at her words he gasped. The thought crossed his mind that Mrs. Pickett might well be mentally unbalanced. The details of the case were fresh in his memory, and he distinctly recollected that the person she mentioned had been away from the boarding house on the night of Captain Gunner's death, and could, he imagined, produce witnesses to prove it.

Mrs. Pickett was regarding him with an unfaltering stare. To all outward appearances, she was the opposite of unbalanced.

"But you can't swear out a warrant without evidence," he told her.

"I have evidence," she replied firmly.

"Precisely what kind of evidence?" he demanded.

"If I told you now you would think that I was out of my mind."

"But, Mrs. Pickett, do you realize what you are asking me to do? I cannot make this agency responsible for the arbitrary arrest of a man on the strength of a single individual's suspicions. It might ruin me. At the least it would make me a laughing stock."

"Mr. Snyder, you may use your own judgment whether or not to make the arrest on that warrant. You will listen to what I have to say, and you will see for yourself how the crime was committed. If after that you feel that you cannot make the arrest I will accept your decision. I know who killed Captain Gunner," she said. "I knew it from the beginning. It was like a vision. But I had no proof. Now things have come to light and everything is clear."

Against his judgment, Mr. Snyder was impressed. This woman had the magnetism which makes for persuasiveness.

"It—it sounds incredible." Even as he spoke, he remembered that it had long been a professional maxim of his that nothing was incredible, and he weakened still further.

"Mr. Snyder, I ask you to swear out that warrant."

The detective gave in. "Very well," he said.

Mrs. Pickett rose. "If you will come and dine at my house tonight I think I can prove to you that it will be needed. Will you come?"

"I'll come," promised Mr. Snyder.

VII

When Mr. Snyder arrived at the Excelsior and shortly after he was shown into the little private sitting room where he found Oakes, the third guest of the evening unexpectedly arrived.

Mr. Snyder looked curiously at the newcomer. Captain Muller had a peculiar fascination for him. It was not Mr. Snyder's habit to trust overmuch to appearances. But he could not help admitting that there was something about this man's aspect which brought Mrs. Pickett's charges out of the realm of the fantastic into that of the possible. There was something odd—an unnatural aspect of gloom—about the man. He bore himself like one carrying a heavy burden. His eyes were dull, his face haggard. The next moment the detective was reproaching himself with allowing his imagination to run away with his calmer judgment.

The door opened, and Mrs. Pickett came in. She made no apology for her lateness.

To Mr. Snyder one of the most remarkable points about the dinner was the peculiar metamorphosis of Mrs. Pickett from the brooding silent woman he had known to the gracious and considerate hostess.

Oakes appeared also to be overcome with surprise, so much so that he was unable to keep his astonishment to himself. He had come prepared to endure a dull evening absorbed in grim silence, and he found himself instead opposite a bottle of champagne of a brand and year which commanded his utmost respect. What was even more incredible, his hostess had transformed herself into a pleasant old lady whose only aim seemed to be to make him feel at home.

Beside each of the guests' plates was a neat paper parcel. Oakes picked his up, and stared at it in wonderment. "Why, this is more than a party souvenir, Mrs. Pickett," he said. "It's the kind of mechanical marvel I've always wanted to have on my desk."

"I'm glad you like it, Mr. Oakes," Mrs. Pickett said, smiling. "You must not think of me simply as a tired old woman whom age has completely defeated. I am an ambitious hostess. When I give these little parties, I like to make them a success. I want each of you to remember this dinner."

"I'm sure I will."

Mrs. Pickett smiled again. "I think you all will. You, Mr. Snyder." She paused. "And you, Captain Muller."

To Mr. Snyder there was so much meaning in her voice as she said this that he was amazed that it conveyed no warning to Muller. Captain Muller, however, was already drinking heavily. He looked up when addressed and uttered a sound which might have been taken for an expression of polite acquiescence. Then he filled his glass again.

Mr. Snyder's parcel revealed a watch-charm fashioned in the shape of a tiny, candid-eye camera. "That," said Mrs. Pickett, "is a compliment to your profession." She leaned toward the captain. "Mr. Snyder is a detective, Captain Muller."

He looked up. It seemed to Mr. Snyder that a look of fear lit up his heavy eyes for an instant. It came and went, if indeed it came at all, so swiftly that he could not be certain.

"So?" said Captain Muller. He spoke quite evenly, with just the amount of interest which such an announcement would naturally produce.

"Now for yours, Captain," said Oakes. "I guess it's something special. It's twice the size of mine, anyway."

It may have been something in the old woman's expression as she watched Captain Muller slowly tearing the paper that sent a thrill of excitement through Mr. Snyder. Something seemed to warn him of the approach of a psychological moment. He bent forward eagerly.

There was a strangled gasp, a thump, and onto the table from the captain's hands there fell a little harmonica. There was no mistaking the look on Muller's face now. His cheeks were like wax, and his eyes, so dull till then, blazed with a panic and horror which he could not repress. The glasses on the table rocked as he clutched at the cloth.

Mrs. Pickett spoke. "Why, Captain Muller, has it upset you? I thought that, as his best friend, the man who shared his room, you would value a memento of Captain Gunner. How fond you must have been of him for the sight of his harmonica to be such a shock."

The captain did not speak. He was staring fascinated at the thing on the table. Mrs. Pickett turned to Mr. Snyder. Her eyes, as they met his, held him entranced.

"Mr. Snyder, as a detective, you will be interested in a curious and very tragic affair which happened in this house a few days ago. One of my boarders, Captain Gunner, was found dead in his room. It was the room which he shared with Captain Muller. I am very proud of the reputation of my house, Mr. Snyder, and it was a blow to me that this should have happened. I applied to an agency for a detective, and they sent me a stupid boy, with nothing to recommend him except his belief in himself. He said that Captain Gunner had died by accident, killed by a snake which had come out of a crate of bananas. I knew better. I knew that Captain Gunner had been murdered. Are you listening, Captain Muller? This will interest you, as you were such a friend of his."

The captain did not answer. He was staring straight before him, as if he saw something invisible in eyes forever closed in death.

"Yesterday we found the body of a dog. It had been killed, as Captain Gunner had been, by the poison of a snake. The boy from the agency said that this was conclusive. He said that the snake had escaped from the room after killing Captain Gunner and had in turn killed the dog. I knew that to be impossible, for, if there had been a snake in that room it could not have made its escape."

Her eyes flashed, and became remorselessly accusing. "It was not a snake that killed Captain Gunner. It was a cat. Captain Gunner had a friend who hated him. One day, in opening a crate of bananas, this friend found a snake. He killed it, and extracted the poison. He knew Captain Gunner's habits. He knew that he played a harmonica. This man also had a cat. He knew that cats hated the sound of a harmonica. He had often seen this particular cat fly at Captain Gunner and scratch him when he played. He took the cat and covered its claws with the poison. And then he left it in the room with Captain Gunner. He knew what would happen."

Oakes and Mr. Snyder were on their feet. Captain Muller had not moved. He sat there, his fingers gripping the cloth. Mrs. Pickett rose and went to a closet. She unlocked the door. "Kitty!" she called. "Kitty! Kitty!"

A black cat ran swiftly out into the room. With a clatter and a crash of crockery and a ringing of glass the table heaved, rocked and overturned as Muller staggered to his feet. He threw up his hands as if to ward something off. A choking cry came from his lips. "Gott! Gott!"

Mrs. Pickett's voice rang through the room, cold and biting: "Captain Muller, you murdered Captain Gunner!"

The captain shuddered. Then mechanically he replied: "Gott! Yes, I killed him."

"You heard, Mr. Snyder," said Mrs. Pickett. "He has confessed before witnesses. Take him away."

Muller allowed himself to be moved toward the door. His arm in Mr. Snyder's grip felt limp. Mrs. Pickett stopped and took something from the debris on the floor. She rose, holding the harmonica.

"You are forgetting your souvenir, Captain Muller," she said.

THE TEST CASE

The route of a Wodehouse short story usually followed this procedure: First, it was published in an English magazine. Then it would be published in an American magazine. Next, it would be collected to form a volume of short stories to be published in England, and then in America. For this reason, "The Test Case" is a rarity; for it appeared only once. It is most curious that it was never published in an English magazine, since the characters and locale are English. Reggie Pepper, the prototype of the Drones Club character, a social but not too bright, idle young-man-about-town, is Mr. Wodehouse's first character around whom he established a series of stories.

First Appearance: United States—*Illustrated Sunday Magazine*, December 12, 1915

But shortly after the appearance in 1915 of Bertie Wooster, he over-shadowed Reggie and took over where Reggie left off. Here is the last of the seven Reggie Pepper stories.

Well-meaning chappies at the club sometimes amble up to me and tap me on the wishbone, and say "Reggie, old top,"—my name's Reggie Pepper—"you ought to get married, old man." Well, what I mean to say is, it's all very well, and I see their point and all that sort of thing; but it takes two to make a marriage, and to date I haven't met a girl who didn't seem to think the contract was too big to be taken on.

Looking back, it seems to me that I came nearer to getting over the home-plate with Ann Selby than with most of the others. In fact, but for circumstances over which I had no dashed control, I am inclined to think that we should have brought it off. I'm bound to say that, now that what the poet chappie calls the first fine frenzy has been on the ice for awhile and I am able to consider the thing calmly, I am deuced glad we didn't. She was one of those strong-minded girls, and I hate to think of what she would have done to me.

At the time, though, I was frightfully in love, and, for quite a while after she definitely gave me the mitten, I lost my stroke at golf so completely that a child could have given me a stroke a hole and got away with it. I was all broken up, and I contend to this day that I was dashed badly treated.

Let me give you what they call the data.

One day I was lunching with Ann, and was just proposing to her as usual, when, instead of simply refusing me, as she generally did, she fixed me with a thoughtful eye and kind of opened her heart.

"Do you know, Reggie, I am in doubt."

"Give me the benefit of it," I said. Which I maintain was pretty good on the spur of the moment, but didn't get a hand. She simply ignored it, and went on.

"Sometimes," she said, "you seem to me entirely vapid and brainless; at other times you say or do things which suggest that there are possibilities in you; that, properly stimulated and encouraged, you might overcome the handicap of large private means and do something worthwhile. I wonder if that is simply my imagination?" She watched me very closely as she spoke.

"Rather not. You've absolutely summed me up. With you beside me, stimulating and all that sort of rot, don't you know, I should show a flash of speed which would astonish you."

"I wish I could be certain."

"Take a chance on it."

She shook her head.

"I must be certain. Marriage is such a gamble. I have just been staying with my sister Hilda and her husband—"

"Dear old Harold Bodkin. I know him well. In fact, I've a standing invitation to go down there and stay as long as I like. Harold is one of my best pals. Harold is a corker. Good old Harold is—"

"I would rather you didn't eulogize him, Reggie. I am extremely angry with Harold. He is making Hilda perfectly miserable."

"What on earth do you mean? Harold wouldn't dream of hurting a fly. He's one of those dreamy, sentimental chumps who—"

"It is precisely his sentimentality which is at the bottom of the whole trouble. You know, of course, that Hilda is not his first wife?"

"That's right. His first wife died about five years ago."

"He still cherishes her memory."

"Very sporting of him."

"Is it! If you were a girl, how would you like to be married to a man who was always making you bear in mind that you were only number two in his affections; a man whose idea of a pleasant conversation was a string of anecdotes illustrating what a dear woman his first wife was. A man who expected you to upset all your plans if they clashed with some anniversary connected with his other marriage?"

"That does sound pretty rotten. Does Harold do all that?"

"That's only a small part of what he does. Why, if you will believe me, every evening at seven o'clock he goes and shuts himself up in a little room at the top of the house, and meditates."

"What on earth does he do that for?"

"Apparently his first wife died at seven in the evening. There is a portrait of her in the room. I believe he lays flowers in front of it. And Hilda is expected to greet him on his return with a happy smile."

"Why doesn't she kick?"

"I have been trying to persuade her to, but she won't. She just pretends she doesn't mind. She has a nervous, sensitive temperament, and the thing is slowly crushing her. Don't talk to me of Harold."

Considering that she had started him as a topic, I thought this pretty unjust. I didn't want to talk of Harold. I wanted to talk about myself.

"Well, what has all this got to do with your not wanting to marry me?" I said.

"Nothing, except that it is an illustration of the risks a woman runs when she marries a man of a certain type."

"Great Scott! You surely don't class me with Harold?"

"Yes, in a way you are very much alike. You have both always had large private means, and have never had the wholesome discipline of work."

"But, dash it, Harold, on your showing, is an absolute nut. Why should you think that I would be anything like that?"

"There's always the risk."

A hot idea came to me.

"Look here, Ann," I said, "Suppose I pull off some stunt which only a deuced brainy chappie could get away with? Would you marry me then?"

"Certainly. What do you propose to do?"

"Do! What do I propose to do! Well, er, to be absolutely frank, at the moment I don't quite know."

"You never will know, Reggie. You're one of the idle rich, and your brain, if you ever had one, has atrophied."

Well, that seemed to me to put the lid on it. I didn't mind a heart-to-heart talk, but this was mere abuse. I changed the subject.

"What would you like after that fish?" I said coldly.

You know how it is when you get an idea. For awhile it sort of simmers inside you, and then suddenly it sizzles up like a rocket, and there you are, right up against it. That's what happened now. I went away from that luncheon, vaguely determined to pull off some stunt which would prove that I was right there with the gray matter, but without any clear notion of what I was going to do. Side by side with this in my mind was the case of dear old Harold. When I wasn't brooding on the stunt, I was brooding on Harold. I was fond of the good old lad, and I hated the idea of his slowly wrecking the home purely by being a chump. And all of a sudden the two things clicked together like a couple of chemicals, and there I was with a corking plan for killing two birds with one stone—putting one across that would startle and impress Ann, and at the same time healing the breach between Harold and Hilda.

My idea was that, in a case like this, it's no good trying opposition. What you want is to work it so that the chappie quits of his own accord. You want to egg him on to overdoing the thing till he gets so that he says to himself, "Enough! Never again!" That was what was going to happen to Harold.

When you're going to do a thing, there's nothing like making a quick start. I wrote to Harold straight away, proposing myself for a visit. And Harold wrote back telling me to come right along.

Harold and Hilda lived alone in a large house. I believe they did a good deal of entertaining at times, but on this occasion I was the only guest. The only other person of note in the place was Ponsonby, the butler.

Of course, if Harold had been an ordinary sort of chappie, what I had come to do would have been a pretty big order. I don't mind many things, but I do hesitate to dig into my host's intimate private affairs. But Harold was such a simple-minded Johnnie, so grateful for a little sympathy and advice, that my job wasn't so very difficult.

It wasn't as if he minded talking about Amelia, which was his first wife's name. The difficulty was to get him to talk of anything else. I began to understand what Ann meant by saying it was tough on Hilda.

I'm bound to say the old boy was clay in my hands. People call me a chump, but Harold was a super-chump, and I did what I liked with him. The second morning of my visit, after breakfast, he grabbed me by the arm.

"This way, Reggie. I'm just going to show old Reggie Amelia's portrait, dear."

There was a little room all by itself on the top floor. He explained to me that it had been his studio. At one time Harold used to do a bit of painting in an amateur way.

"There!" he said, pointing at the portrait. "I did that myself, Reggie. It was away being cleaned when you were here last. It's like dear Amelia, isn't it?"

I suppose it was, in a way. At any rate, you could recognize the likeness when you were told who it was supposed to be.

He sat down in front of it, and gave it the thoughtful once-over.

"Do you know, Reggie, old top, sometimes when I sit here, I feel as if Amelia were back again."

"It would be a bit awkward for you if she was."

"How do you mean?"

"Well, old lad, you happen to be married to someone else."

A look of childlike enthusiasm came over his face.

"Reggie, I want to tell you how splendid Hilda is. Lots of other women might object to my still cherishing Amelia's memory, but Hilda has been so nice about it from the beginning. She understands so thoroughly."

I hadn't much breath left after that, but I used what I had to say: "She doesn't object?"

"Not a bit," said Harold. "It makes everything so pleasant."

When I had recovered a bit, I said, "What do you mean by everything?"

"Well," he said, "for instance, I come up here every evening at seven and—er—think for a few minutes."

"A few minutes?!"

"What do you mean?"

"Well, a few minutes isn't long."

"But I always have my cocktail at a quarter past."

"You could postpone it."

"And Ponsonby likes us to start dinner at seven-thirty."

"What on earth has Ponsonby to do with it?"

"Well, he likes to get off by nine, you know. I think he goes off and plays bowls at the roadhouse. You see, Reggie, old man, we have to study Ponsonby a little. He's always on the verge of giving notice—in fact, it was only by coaxing him on one or two occasions that we got him to stay on—and he's such a treasure that I don't know what we should do if we lost him. But, if you think that I ought to stay longer—?"

"Certainly I do. You ought to do a thing like this properly, or not at all."

He sighed.

"It's a frightful risk, but in future we'll dine at eight."

It seemed to me that there was a suspicion of a cloud on Ponsonby's shining morning face, when the news was broken to him that for the future he couldn't unleash himself on the local bowling talent as early as usual, but he made no kick, and the new order of things began.

My next offensive movement I attribute to a flash of absolute genius. I was glancing through a photograph album in the drawing-room before lunch, when I came upon a face which I vaguely remembered. It was one of those wide, flabby faces, with bulging eyes, and something about it struck me as familiar. I consulted Harold, who came in at that moment.

"That?" said Harold. "That's Percy." He gave a slight shudder. "Amelia's brother, you know. An awful fellow. I haven't seen him for years."

Then I placed Percy. I had met him once or twice in the old days, and I had a brainwave. Percy was everything that poor old Harold disliked most. He was hearty at breakfast, a confirmed back-slapper, and a man who prodded you in the chest when he spoke to you.

"You haven't seen him for years!" I said in a shocked voice.

"Thank heaven!" said Harold devoutly.

I put down the photograph album, and looked at him in a deuced serious way. "Then it's high time you asked him to come here."

Harold blanched. "Reggie, old man, you don't know what you are saying. You can't remember Percy. I wish you wouldn't say these things, even in fun."

"I'm not saying it in fun. Of course, it's none of my business, but you have paid me the compliment of confiding in me about Amelia, and I feel justified in speaking. All I can say is that, if you cherish her memory as you say you do, you show it in a very strange way. How you can square your neglect of Percy with your alleged devotion to Amelia's memory, beats me. It seems to me that you have no choice. You must either drop the whole thing and admit that your love for her is dead, or else you must stop this infernal treatment of her favorite brother. You can't have it both ways."

He looked at me like a hunted stag. "But, Reggie, old man! Percy! He asks riddles at breakfast."

"I don't care."

"Hilda can't stand him."

"It doesn't matter. You must invite him. It's not a case of what you like or don't like. It's your duty."

He struggled with his feelings for a bit. "Very well," he said in a crushed sort of voice.

At dinner that night he said to Hilda: "I'm going to ask Amelia's brother down to spend a few days. It is so long since we have seen him."

Hilda didn't answer at once. She looked at him in rather a curious sort of way, I thought. "Very well, dear," she said.

I was deuced sorry for the poor girl, but I felt like a surgeon. She would be glad later on, for I was convinced that in a very short while poor old Harold must crack under the strain, especially after I had put across the coup which I was meditating for the very next evening.

It was quite simple. Simple, that is to say, in its working, but a devilish brainy thing for a chappie to have thought out. If Ann had really meant what she had said at lunch that day, and was prepared to stick to her bargain and marry me as soon as I showed a burst of intelligence, she was mine.

What it came to was that, if dear old Harold enjoyed meditating in front of Amelia's portrait, he was jolly well going to have all the meditating he wanted, and a bit over, for my simple scheme was to lurk outside till he had gone into the little room on the top floor, and then, with the aid of one of those jolly little wedges which you use to keep windows from rattling, see to it that the old boy remained there till they sent out search parties.

There wasn't a flaw in my reasoning. When Harold didn't roll in at the sound of the dinner gong, Hilda would take it for granted that he was doing an extra bit of meditating that night, and her pride would stop her sending out a hurry call for him. As for Harold, when he found that all was not well with the door, he would probably yell with considerable vim. But it was odds against anyone hearing him. As for me, you might think that I was going to suffer owing to the probable postponement of dinner. Not so, but far otherwise, for on the night I had selected for the coup I was dining out at the neighboring inn with my old college chum Freddie Meadowes. It is true that Freddie wasn't going to be within fifty miles of the place on that particular night, but they weren't to know that.

Did I describe the peculiar isolation of that room on the top floor, where the portrait was? I don't think I did. It was, as a matter of fact, the only room in those parts, for, in the days when he did his amateur painting, old Harold was strong on the artistic seclusion business and hated noise, and his studio was the only room in use on that floor.

In short, to sum up, the thing was a cinch.

Punctually at ten minutes to seven, I was in readiness on the scene. There was a recess with a curtain in front of it a few yards from the door, and there I waited, fondling my little wedge, for Harold to walk up and allow the proceedings to start. It was almost pitch-dark, and that made the time of waiting seem longer. Presently—I seemed to have been there longer than ten minutes—I heard steps approaching. They came past where I stood, and went on into the room. The door closed, and I hopped out and sprinted up to it, and the next moment I had the good old wedge under the wood—as neat a job as you could imagine. And then I strolled downstairs, and toddled off to the inn.

I didn't hurry over my dinner, partly because the browsing and sluicing at the inn was really astonishingly good for a roadhouse and partly because I wanted to give Harold plenty of time for meditation. I suppose it must have been a couple of hours or more when I finally turned in at the front door. Somebody was playing the piano in the drawing room. It could only be Hilda who was playing, and I had doubts as to whether she wanted company just then—mine, at any rate.

Eventually I decided to risk it, for I wanted to hear the latest about dear old Harold, so in I went, and it wasn't Hilda at all; it was Ann Selby.

"Hello," I said. "I didn't know you were coming down here." It seemed so odd, don't you know, as it hadn't been more than ten days or so since her last visit.

"Good evening, Reggie," she said.

"What's been happening?" I asked.

"How do you know anything has been happening?"

"I guessed it."

"Well, you're quite right, as it happens, Reggie. A good deal has been happening." She went to the door, and looked out, listening. Then she shut it, and came back. "Hilda has revolted!"

"Revolted?"

"Yes, put her foot down—made a stand—refused to go on meekly putting up with Harold's insane behavior."

"I don't understand."

She gave me a look of pity. "You always were so dense, Reggie. I will tell you the whole thing from the beginning. You remember what I spoke to you about, one day when we were lunching together? Well, I don't suppose you have noticed it—I know what you are—but things have been getting steadily worse. For one thing, Harold insisted on lengthening his visits to the top room, and naturally Ponsonby complained. Hilda tells me that she had to plead with him to induce him to stay on. Then the climax came. I don't know if you recollect Amelia's brother Percy? You must have met him when she was alive—a perfectly unspeakable person with a loud voice and overpowering manners. Suddenly, out of a blue sky, Harold announced his intention of inviting him to stay. It was the last straw. This afternoon I received a telegram from poor Hilda, saying that she was leaving Harold and coming to stay with me, and a few hours later the poor child arrived at my apartment."

You mustn't suppose that I stood listening silently to this speech. Every time she seemed to be going to stop for breath I tried to horn in and tell her all these things which had been happening were not mere flukes, as she seemed to think, but parts of a deuced carefully planned scheme of my own. Everytime I'd try to interrupt, Ann would wave me down, and carry on without so much as a semicolon.

But at this point I did manage a word in. "I know, I know, I know! I did it all. It was I who suggested to Harold that he should lengthen the meditations, and insisted on his inviting Percy to stay."

I had hardly got the words out, when I saw that they were not making the hit I had anticipated. She looked at me with an expression of absolute scorn, don't you know.

"Well, really, Reggie," she said at last, "I never have had a very high opinion of your intelligence, as you know, but this is a revelation to me. What motive you can have had, unless you did it in a spirit of pure mischief—" She stopped, and there was a glare of undiluted repulsion in her eyes. "Reggie! I can't believe it! Of all the things I loathe most, a practical joker is the worst. Do you mean to tell me you did all this as a practical joke?"

"Great Scott, no! It was like this—"

I paused for a bare second to collect my thoughts, so as to put the thing clearly to her. I might have known what would happen. She dashed right in and collared the conversation.

"Well, never mind. As it happens, there is no harm done. Quite the reverse, in fact. Hilda left a note for Harold telling him what she had done and where she had gone and why she had gone, and Harold found it. The result was that, after Hilda had been with me for some time, in he came in a panic and absolutely grovelled before the dear child. It seems incredible but he had apparently had no notion that his absurd behavior had met with anything but approval from Hilda. He went on as if he were mad. He was beside himself. He clutched his hair and stamped about the room, and then he jumped at the telephone and called this house and got Ponsonby and told him to go straight to the little room on the top floor and take Amelia's portrait down. I thought that a little unnecessary myself, but he was in such a whirl of remorse that it was useless to try and get him to be rational. So Hilda was consoled, and he calmed down, and we all came down here in the automobile. So you see—"

At this moment the door opened, and in came Harold.

"I say—hello, Reggie, old man—I say, it's a funny thing, but we can't find Ponsonby anywhere."

There are moments in a chappie's life, don't you know, when Reason, so to speak, totters, as it were, on its bally throne. This was one of them. The situation seemed somehow to have got out of my grip. I suppose, strictly speaking, I ought, at this juncture, to have cleared my throat and said in an audible tone, "Harold, old top, *I* know where Ponsonby is." But somehow I couldn't. Something seemed to keep the words back. I just stood there and said nothing.

"Nobody seems to have seen anything of him," said Harold. "I wonder where he can have got to."

Hilda came in, looking so happy I hardly recognized her. I remember feeling how strange it was that anybody could be happy just then.

"*I* know," she said. "Of course! Doesn't he always go off to the inn and play bowls at this time?"

"Why, of course," said Harold. "So he does."

And he asked Ann to play something on the piano. And pretty

soon we had settled down to a regular jolly musical evening. Ann must have played a matter of two or three thousand tunes, when Harold got up.

"By the way," he said. "I suppose he did what I told him about the picture before he went out. Let's go and see."

"Oh, Harold, what does it matter?" asked Hilda.

"Don't be silly, Harold," said Ann.

I would have said the same thing, only I couldn't say anything.

Harold wasn't to be stopped. He led the way out of the room and upstairs, and we all trailed after him. We had just reached the top floor, when Hilda stopped, and said "Hark!"

It was a voice.

"Hi!" it said. "Hi!"

Harold legged it to the door of the studio. "Ponsonby?"

From within came the voice again, and I have never heard anything to touch the combined pathos, dignity and indignation it managed to condense into two words.

"Yes, sir?"

"What on earth are you doing in there?"

"I came here, sir, in accordance with your instructions on the telephone, and—"

Harold rattled the door. "The darned thing's stuck."

"Yes, sir."

"How on earth did that happen?"

"I could not say, sir."

"How *can* the door have stuck like this?" said Ann.

Somebody—I suppose it was me, though the voice didn't sound familiar—spoke. "Perhaps there's a wedge under it," said this chappie.

"A wedge? What do you mean?"

"One of those little wedges you use to keep windows from rattling, don't you know."

"But why—? You're absolutely right, Reggie, old man, there is!"

He yanked it out, and flung the door open, and out came Ponsonby, looking like Lady Macbeth.

"I wish to give notice, sir," he said, "and I should esteem it a favor if I might go to the pantry and procure some food, as I am extremely hungry."

And he passed from our midst, with Hilda after him, saying: "But, Ponsonby! Be reasonable, Ponsonby!"

Ann Selby turned on me with a swish. "Reggie," she said, "did *you* shut Ponsonby in there?"

"Well, yes, as a matter of fact, I did."

"But why?" asked Harold.

"Well, to be absolutely frank, old top, I thought it was you."

"You thought it was me? But why—what did you want to lock me in for?"

I hesitated. It was a delicate business telling him the idea. And while I was hesitating, Ann jumped in.

"I can tell you why, Harold. It was because Reggie belongs to that sub-species of humanity known as practical jokers. This sort of thing is his idea of humor."

"Humor! Losing us a priceless butler," said Harold. "If that's your idea of—"

Hilda came back, pale and anxious. "Harold, dear, do come and help me reason with Ponsonby. He is in the pantry gnawing a cold chicken, and he only stops to say 'I give notice.'"

"Yes," said Ann. "Go, both of you. I wish to speak to Reggie alone."

That's how I came to lose Ann. At intervals during her remarks I tried to put my side of the case, but it was no good. She wouldn't listen. And presently something seemed to tell me that now was the time to go to my room and pack. Half an hour later I slid silently into the night.

Wasn't it Shakespeare or somebody who said that the road to Hell—or words to that effect—was paved with good intentions? If it was Shakespeare, it just goes to prove what they are always saying about him—that he knew a bit. Take it from one who knows, the old boy was absolutely right.